# THE DICTIONARY OF
# DREAMS
## AND THEIR
# MEANINGS

THE DICTIONARY OF
# DREAMS
AND THEIR
## MEANINGS

RICHARD CRAZE

HERMES
HOUSE

This edition is published by Hermes House
an imprint of Anness Publishing Ltd
Hermes House, 88–89 Blackfriars Road, London SE1 8HA
tel. 020 7401 2077; fax 020 7633 9499
www.hermeshouse.com; www.annesspublishing.com

Anness Publishing has a new picture agency outlet
for images for publishing, promotions or advertising. Please visit
our website www.practicalpictures.com for more information.

ETHICAL TRADING POLICY
Because of our ongoing ecological investment programme,
you, as our customer, can have the pleasure and reassurance of
knowing that a tree is being cultivated on your behalf to
naturally replace the materials used to make the book you are
holding For further information about this scheme, go to
www.annesspublishing.com/trees

PUBLISHER: Joanna Lorenz
EDITORIAL DIRECTOR: Helen Sudell
SENIOR EDITOR: Joanne Rippin
ADDITIONAL TEXT: Raje Airey and Jenny Barrett
PICTURE RESEARCHER: Frances Vargo
For picture acknowledgements see p252
DESIGNER: Adelle Morris
EDITORIAL READER: Kate Humby
PRODUCTION MANAGER: Steve Lang

A CIP catalogue record for this book is available
from the British Library

PUBLISHER'S NOTE
Although the advice and information in this book are believed to
be accurate and true at the time of going to press, neither the
authors nor the publisher can accept any legal responsibility or
liability for any errors or omissions that may be made.

# CONTENTS

# INTRODUCTION

In practically every age and culture, dreams have fascinated and puzzled us and we have searched for countless ways to understand their significance and to interpret their meaning. There is a famous story told by the Taoist philosopher Chuang-tzu (399-295 BC). While sleeping he had a dream in which he dreamt he was a butterfly. He could fly and land on flowers, drawing up nectar and feeling the warmth of the sun on his wings. The dream was so vivid that when he woke he couldn't decide who he was: was he a man dreaming he was a butterfly, or could he be a butterfly dreaming he was a man?

When we sleep we drift into another dimension, a dimension that is not bound by space or time. In this magical land the impossible becomes possible, and the nonsensical appears perfectly plausible. This is the land of dreams, a mysterious shape-shifting world where boundaries dissolve and merge, so that when we wake it can take a moment to distinguish between what is a dream and what is not. As Chuang-tzu's story illustrates, our dreams can cause us to question how we see the world and ourselves and how we define what is "real". This is not to say that there is genuine confusion between the outer world in which we live our lives and the world of dreams. Where confusion exists, it is usually labelled insanity. Rather it is an acknowledgement of a different dimension and of a different experience. For dreams are from the inner world, having their own internal logic and subjective meaning and are as valid in their own way as what is happening in the world "out there".

## VALUING DREAMS

Among many cultures the dream experience is valued and the mysteries of sleep and dreaming are taken seriously. Whenever this is the case, dream interpretation is also valued. In early cultures for instance, shamans, priests or sages were consulted and their position in society was revered. For a long time in Western society, an interest in dreams went underground. Dreams were variously associated with insanity or were the work of the devil, or were simply written off as meaningless nonsense. These attitudes were revolutionized in the 20th century with fresh insights from science and psychotherapy. Since then our interest in dreams has been growing at a remarkable rate, as more and more of us search for ways to make sense of our lives and to fulfil our potential. We are recognizing that our dreams, far from being nonsense or a sign of mental illness, often contain intriguing and valuable information, which, once decoded, can help us understand our subconscious. We are also learning how to become our own dream interpreters.

## ABOUT THIS BOOK

This book is a guide to making sense of dreams. It recognizes that no two people are exactly alike and therefore no two dreams are the same. When interpreting dreams the book takes the view that it is experience rather than theory that counts: you can become your own dream expert. This approach is very different to many dream dictionaries where it is possible to "look up" the meaning of a particular dream symbol or theme and "apply" it to your dream. For instance, you may dream of a tree. Some dream books may say that a tree signifies growth, and if it is bearing fruit, that it prophesies abundance and wealth. What they fail to do is encourage you to look at the tree itself and find out what it means for you. To do this is to approach your dream and yourself with a spirit of enquiry, asking questions about the dream content in order to arrive at your own understanding.

The book is divided into two main sections. The first contains chapters on the history, nature and sense of dreams as well as one on working with dreams. This section is intended to give an overview of dream theories, past and present, and to provide information that can help you recognize different types of dream and dream symbols. It also offers practical suggestions for how to program your dreams and to improve dream recall, as well as techniques to help you unravel the mystery of your dreams.

The second section is the Dream Lexicon. Divided thematically, it begins with an exploration of the world we live in – its abstract qualities and the natural environment. It then looks at our own development through the cycles of life, and aspects of mind, body and spirit. Other people and how we engage with them and with the world at large are discussed in the following chapters, along with a section on motion and mechanics. Lastly we see how magic and fantasy figure in our dreams.

It is hoped that you will find what is here both illuminating and stimulating and can use it as a springboard for further discovery. Remember, dreams come from the dark, the time of the moon, madness and mystery. To understand them, you need to feel your way around, using intuition and instinct rather than reason and logic, and so begin to unlock the secrets of the night.

Trust in dreams, for in them is the hidden gate to eternity.                    KAHLIL GIBRAN

**ABOVE** Artists for centuries have tried to portray their dreams in pictorial representation. What they paint and what we dream may not seem the same but we share the same need to purge the internal demons of dream.

**LEFT** Images of dreams are but an instant, frozen in time forever, whereas in reality our dreams are flexible, ongoing, and changing rapidly and continuously.

**BELOW** Surrealist art for most people seems to come closest to how we sense our dreams and may help us to convey the feel of a dream, if not its reality.

**ABOVE** Sometimes an artist does seem to crystallize a moment in a dream that can haunt us all of our lives.

# PART ONE

# ALL ABOUT DREAMING

Theories of dreaming have varied widely over time and across cultures. To the ancients, dreams were regarded as messages from the gods or as oracles to predict the future. It was widely believed that dreams had the power to solve problems, heal sickness and bring spiritual revelation. In more recent times, dreams became the subject of psychological and scientific investigation. Widely recognized as the product of the unconscious mind, dream activity is now measured in sleep laboratories.

This section combines the wisdom of the past with contemporary understanding to provide a detailed picture, which tells us all about dreaming. It begins with a historical and cultural overview to the role of dreams. This is followed by an exploration of the nature of dreams, looking at influential ideas from modern times and describing different types of dreams. We then examine the sense and substance of dreams, and finally look at how to work with, and become more aware of, your dream world.

# WHY WE DREAM

THERE ARE FEW THINGS WE DO WITH SUCH REGULARITY AND INTENSITY AS SLEEP AND DREAM. WE SPEND ALMOST ONE THIRD OF OUR LIVES SLEEPING AND WE DREAM — ON AVERAGE FOR A TOTAL OF TWO HOURS OR SO — EVERY NIGHT. YET PRECISELY WHY WE DREAM IS STILL UNCERTAIN. MANY THEORIES HAVE BEEN PUT FORWARD: FOR THE SCIENTIST, DREAMS ARE A PRODUCT OF A CERTAIN KIND OF SLEEP AND A WAY FOR THE BRAIN TO PROCESS IMPORTANT DATA; FOR THE MYSTIC, THEY ARE AN OPPORTUNITY FOR THE SOUL TO LEAVE THE BODY AND EXPERIENCE OTHER DIMENSIONS; WHILE FOR THE PSYCHOLOGIST THEY REPRESENT THE WORKINGS OF THE UNCONSCIOUS MIND.

**ABOVE** Whatever we think we know about dreams is forgotten when we fall asleep and enter the strange reality of the dream world, where physical laws are suspended and a different reality takes place.

## SLEEP PATTERNS

Through a night of around seven to eight hours of undisturbed sleep, we experience two alternating types of sleep: orthodox or slow-wave deep sleep, and paradoxical or light sleep. Orthodox sleep lasts for about 90 minutes, and is followed by a shorter period of paradoxical sleep. Paradoxical sleep is marked by rapid eye movements (REM) and it is during this type of sleep that we dream. This alternating cycle goes on through the night, with the REM phase gradually increasing in length with each subsequent cycle, until after about seven or eight hours' sleep it can last for up to half an hour or more. As we get older, the length of time we spend in REM sleep diminishes, while at the other end of the scale, it has been found that young babies spend extended periods of time in REM.

## THE ROLE OF DREAMING

Scientific research also indicates that in the later stages of gestation the unborn child exhibits signs of REM activity in the womb. This has led to the

suggestion that dreaming is somehow linked with human growth and development. Similarly, laboratory testing has shown that if you deprive people of REM sleep, the subject becomes unwell very fast. Within a few days, unpleasant symptoms such as depression, anxiety, nausea, irritability and general disorientation are experienced. Irrespective of whether or not we remember them, it seems our dreams play an important part in health and wellbeing. It has even been suggested that we sleep in order to dream.

## A LITTLE DEATH

Many believe that our dreams are also linked with spiritual growth. In some esoteric traditions for instance, sleep is regarded as an intermediate stage between life and death. Every night we experience a "little death" as we fall into unconsciousness, and dreams are regarded as gateways into altered states of mind. Learning how to navigate the world of dreams becomes an important preparation for when the soul will eventually leave the body permanently at death. Initiates are taught how to prepare themselves for sleep and dreaming, learning how to influence the dreaming state and to bring back experiences from the dream world.

## THE POWER OF THE UNCONSCIOUS

This dream world is not something that exists outside of ourselves but resides deep within. In psychological terms, it is regarded as a product of the unconscious mind.

The unconscious may be described as the deepest level of the psyche in which impulses are held in a dynamic, but repressed state. In contrast to the relatively small proportion of things of which we are aware, the unconscious is a massive storehouse of memories, dreams and reflections, both personal and, some believe, transpersonal. By bringing unconscious material up from the hidden depths of the mind and out into the open, our dreams are a way of gaining greater self-knowledge. They are a way of increasing our conscious awareness and becoming wise. From this perspective, dreams are no longer seen as messages from gods or other independent agents outside of ourselves, but as messages from within.

**LEFT** Sometimes we don't remember our dreams but that doesn't mean they aren't continually occurring in our sleeping minds.
**BELOW** Do babies still in the womb dream? And if they do, where on earth do their dream images and impulses come from?

## THE LANGUAGE OF DREAMS

In order to interpret these messages from the unconscious, we need to understand the language of dreams. During the day, the conscious mind is in control and we negotiate the everyday world through reason and logic. At night, the unconscious mind takes over and enters the dream world, using visual imagery, symbols and metaphors. These can elicit a deep emotional response. To understand our dreams we need to listen with the heart rather than the head, developing our intuition while temporarily suspending judgement and disbelief.

We are such stuff
As dreams are made on;
and our little life
Is rounded with a sleep.

WILLIAM SHAKESPEARE, THE TEMPEST

## ANIMALS' SLEEP

Dreaming does not seem to be confined to human beings. Different animal species also exhibit signs of REM sleep and dreaming. Cats, for instance, enter deep-wave sleep about 30 minutes after sleep onset. In that condition, their neck muscles are fully relaxed and slight twitching of the rest of the body may be observed. Although we do not know what the cat is experiencing, we assume that it is a vivid dream.

# DREAMING THROUGH HISTORY

Since time immemorial, our dreams have been a source of awe and wonder. At various points in history, they have been seen as messages from the gods, and supernatural experiences involving visions of the future, as well as indications of the state of our physical and mental health. Dreams have been used to shed light on the past, gain understanding of the present, and even to predict the future. This has not only been true for individuals, but also for whole nations. Some dreams have even changed the course of history.

In this section we will look at how dreams have been regarded through the ages, in the ancient and classical world, in India and the Far East, in Europe and in traditional societies. We will also look at the important role they have played in some of the world's major religions, including Buddhism, Christianity and Islam.

# SINCE THE DAWN OF TIME

HOW LONG IS IT SINCE WE BEGAN DREAMING? WE HAVE NO SURE WAY OF KNOWING, BUT STRETCHING BACK INTO THE MISTS OF PREHISTORY, CAVE PAINTINGS IN FRANCE FROM THE NEANDERTHAL PERIOD SEEM TO INDICATE SOME SORT OF DREAM DRAWINGS ABOVE THE HEADS OF THE HUNTERS. THOUSANDS OF YEARS LATER WHEN PEOPLE BEGAN TO DISCOVER WAYS OF WRITING, THEY NOTED DOWN THEIR DREAMS. WE KNOW THAT DREAMING WAS AN IMPORTANT PART OF LIFE IN THE ANCIENT CIVILIZATIONS OF SUMER, ASSYRIA, BABYLONIA AND EGYPT. DREAMS WERE ASSOCIATED WITH DIVINE OR SUPERNATURAL POWERS, AND TEMPLES WERE DEDICATED TO THE GODS OF DREAMS.

## THE FIRST DREAM RECORDS

Clay tablets dating back to around 3000 BC provide some of the earliest surviving writings of the human race. These tablets include the dream books of the Assyrians and Babylonians, discovered at Nineveh in the library of Ashurbanipal (c.669-626 BC), an Assyrian king. Other similar tablets were discovered during excavations of a pyramid-type temple at E-zida, in Mesopotamia, on the top of which was a shrine to Nabu, the Sumerian god of wisdom. The tablets' cuneiform script reveals fragments of the Babylonian epic of Gilgamesh, the legendary warrior king of Sumer. They also tell us about Gilgamesh's dreams and how his mother, the goddess Ninsun, interprets them. Her interpretation is often credited with being the first dream analysis, or at least the first for which we have a written record.

## THE DREAMS OF GILGAMESH

Night after night, the aggressively powerful warrior king of Sumer, Gilgamesh, was troubled by bad dreams. Disturbed, Gilgamesh takes the dreams to his mother, who tells him that someone as powerful as himself is about to enter his life. She predicted that his struggles to gain supremacy over the newcomer will fail, but that the two men will become close companions and together achieve great feats. Later on in the epic, Ninsun's interpretation proves correct when Gilgamesh meets Enkidu, a "wild man" (an embodiment of an uncivilized, "primordial" human) who does indeed become his friend and helps bring Gilgamesh back down to earth. Further on in the tale, Gilgamesh is warned in another dream of the death of Enkidu, which also comes to pass.

**ABOVE** Gilgamesh, the warrior king of the Sumerians, is recorded as being the first person in history ever to seek an interpretation for the dreams that were troubling him.
**RIGHT** Early cave paintings have a strange, almost dreamlike quality about them; are they portraying everyday life or are they drawings of dreams from the dawn of time itself?

## PORTENTOUS DREAMS

The primary interest in dreams at this time seems to have been in the salutary warnings they could provide about the future, although dreams were also used as a form of gambling, where the dream symbols were used to predict lucky wins. Furthermore the Assyrian and Babylonian dream books also reveal a concern with the dangerous aspect of dreams, allegedly sent by demons and spirits of the dead. To protect themselves from such harmful influences, people built temples to Mamu, the Babylonian goddess of dreams, and propitiatory rites were practised in her name. An Za Qa, the god of dreams, was recognized and worshipped by the Sumerians, Assyrians and Babylonians.

## MYTHOLOGY OF DREAMS

Looking at the mythology of any ancient civilization has been likened to reading a dream. That is because these stories represent what are sometimes referred to as the "cultural pattern dreams" of that civilization. In other words, the gods and goddesses, the heroes and villains, and the shapes and symbols of the stories are the same ones that people would have dreamt of night after night. These characters represent what are known as "archetypal" images, presenting us with the themes and concerns that have always struck a chord deep within the heart and soul of humankind. Irrespective of time or place, these stories are able to teach or remind us of universal truths.

**ABOVE** In Babylon vast temples were built dedicated to Mamu, the Babylonian goddess of dreams; and dream interpretation was elevated to the status of a religion.

### THE GODDESS ISHTAR

Throughout the ancient world, the Moon was worshipped in various forms. The Babylonian goddess Ishtar was known as Ashtarte in Canaan, Isis in ancient Egypt and Artemis in ancient Greece. Like the moon in its waxing aspect, the goddess is a symbol of fertility and all life emanates from her, yet like the waning or dark moon, she is also the destroyer, the one who disappears into the darkness. However, like the crescent moon, the goddess is reborn and appears once again in her beneficent aspect.

The story of Ishtar's descent into the underworld, where she is tortured and bleeds to death before being revived by the twins Plant and Water of Life, is a myth of regeneration, symbolizing the cyclical nature of life and the passage between worlds.

And the goddess Ishtar appeared to each man in a dream, saying: 'I will march before Ashurbanipal, the king whom I have created'.

BABYLONIAN LEGEND

**ABOVE** Egyptian pharaohs were accorded the status of gods and were therefore linked with dream travel.
**ABOVE RIGHT** The city of Thebes, source of a papyrus thought to be the first dream record.

## ANCIENT EGYPT

Like the Babylonians, the Egyptians also regarded dreams as warnings, although they believed they came from the gods rather than from spirits or demons. The Egyptians viewed dreams as a portal, a gateway to another world which they passed through every night. Here in this other world they could travel in their astral or "dream body", gathering knowledge of far distant places, conversing with the gods and meeting with the spirits of the dead. In general, dreams were regarded as helpful, although they could also be malevolent. In order to avert disaster the gods demanded penance and sacrifices, although they would also answer questions put to them by the dreamer in a practice known as "dream incubation".

## DREAM INCUBATION

The practice of dream incubation was widely observed throughout the ancient world, although our first record of it comes from ancient Egypt. Throughout the land, a number of temples, known as "serapeums", were dedicated to Serapis, the god of dreams and dreaming. The most famous of these was at Memphis, dating back to around 3000 BC.

Thebes was another important site. It was in such temples that dream incubation was practised. This was an intensely ritualistic procedure intended to encourage an especially informative dream from the gods. Dream incubation seems to have been very popular and was used for a variety of purposes, including seeking remedies for particular illnesses, obtaining guidance on relationship and/or personal issues and predicting what the future had in store. The practice was often dedicated to Imhotep, the god of healing.

## INCUBATION RITUALS

Ritualistic preparations for dream incubation were extremely complex and could last for several days. Typically the incubant (the dreamer) would take part in purification practices, such as fasting, bathing and abstaining from sex, they would also make prayers and offerings to the gods. Sometimes harmless snakes were placed around the dreamer's bed at the serapeum and the dreamer would then go to sleep with his or her request in mind. Through their own rituals, while the dreamer slept, the temple priests often helped to "seed" the dreamer's request. At times a "stand-in" dreamer was used in place of the

## THE DREAM OF THOTMES IV

One very early prophetic dream dates back to around 1420 BC. It is recorded on a sheet of granite and held between the paws of the great sphinx at Giza where it can still be seen today (right).

While sleeping next to the sphinx, Thotmes dreamt that he would one day be ruler of Egypt and have a long and prosperous reign. However, for the dream to come true, the gods told Thotmes that he had to clear away the sand from the statue. At that time, the sphinx was neglected and beginning to disappear under the sand.

When Thotmes awoke he did as he had been instructed and then vowed to keep the sphinx clean and well cared for, for the rest of his life. Thotmes later went on to become one of Egypt's pharaohs.

person who was seeking help. The stand-in would be someone who was known to be a gifted dreamer. When the dreamer or the stand-in awoke, the dream would be related to the oracles or priests for their interpretation.

### DREAM INTERPRETATIONS

Ancient Egyptian papyri reveal some of the conclusions the Egyptians reached about dream interpretation. One document, dating back to the 13th dynasty (1770 BC), concludes that if a woman dreams of kissing her husband, trouble lies ahead. This is an example of "opposites", in which it is thought that a dream means the reverse of what it appears to suggest.

One of the most famous dream records of the Egyptian era is the "Chester Beatty" papyrus, which was inscribed around 1350 BC. It came from Thebes and contains references to around 200 dreams, many of which date from an earlier period. Particularly interesting are the details of three modes of interpretation, which anticipate principles used by Freud centuries later, these are the detection of hidden associations, the use of opposites, and the use of visual or verbal puns.

### DREAM PUNS

Puns in the world of dream interpretation are rather like games of free association, where one thing reminds us of another. Sometimes these "meanings" are catalogued and get handed down in dream dictionaries, where they appear as utter nonsense to later generations, whose cultural references and language are completely different. For instance, the Chester Beatty papyrus reveals that in ancient Egypt to dream about bare buttocks means the dreamer is about to lose his or her parents. This may seem absurd until we realize that the word used for "buttocks" closely resembled the word for "orphan".

### DISPOSING OF BAD DREAMS

For dealing with a recurring bad dream, the ancient Egyptians had a curious ritual. On waking after another night of the same dream they would blow out their breath into a special receptacle – usually a wooden cup – which was then thrown into the fire. This symbolic act represented "burning" the dream, its negative power would be destroyed by the fire so that it could never return to haunt the dreamer.

# THE CLASSICAL WORLD

ONEIROLOGY IS THE STUDY OF DREAMS. THIS WORD IS DERIVED FROM "ONEIROS", THE WORD FOR DREAMS IN THE ANCIENT GREEK LANGUAGE. LIKE THEIR KNOWLEDGE IN SO MANY AREAS, THE ANCIENT GREEKS' UNDERSTANDING OF DREAMS WAS ESPECIALLY SOPHISTICATED AND SEVERAL WELL-KNOWN THINKERS OF THE DAY DEBATED AND GAVE THEIR INSIGHTS ON THE SUBJECT. THIS INFORMATION WAS LATER EXTENDED AND CLASSIFIED BY THE ROMANS TO GIVE US A WIDE BODY OF KNOWLEDGE FROM THE CLASSICAL WORLD. BOTH CIVILIZATIONS USED DREAMS AS A FORM OF PREDICTION AND AS A WAY OF GAINING INSIGHTS INTO THE MIND OF THE DREAMER.

### GATES OF HORN AND IVORY

The earliest mention of dreams in Greek literature is from Homer. We have little information about Homer or his life, but many historians date his era as some time in the 700s BC. We know that at this time there was widespread belief in the divine origin of dreams, which were regarded as messages to humanity from Zeus, communicated by Hypnos, the god of sleep and his son Morpheus, the god of dreams. However, not all dreams were necessarily reliable. Homer distinguishes between true and false dreams, writing that true dreams come through a "gate of horn", and false through an "ivory gate". Such distinctions were not merely of theoretical interest, as to act on a false dream as if it were true could have disastrous consequences. Centuries later

**BELOW** Homer, seen here being honoured by the gods, made the distinction between true and false dreams, and talked of the danger of being unable to distinguish between the two.

for instance the Persian leader Xerxes' dreams falsely convinced him that an attack on Athens would end victoriously. Acting on this advice Xerxes led his army to destruction in 480 BC.

### HOMER'S ODYSSEY

In his epic work *The Odyssey*, Homer enlarges on the idea of true and false dreams through the character of Penelope, who remarks that dreams are awkward and confusing, for what is in them does not necessarily come true. She says: "There are two gates through which these insubstantial visions reach us; one is of horn and the other of ivory. Those that come through the ivory gate cheat us with empty promises that never see fulfilment; while those that issue from the gate of burnished horn inform the dreamer what will really happen".

### SIGNIFICANT AND NON-SIGNIFICANT DREAMS

Influenced perhaps by Homer's ideas, the ancient Greeks also distinguished between two types of dream: the significant and the non-significant. Significant dreams were the ones which came from the gods. These were the ones that people wanted to have when they were about to undertake an important project, such as a business venture, a voyage or a new relationship. The non-significant dreams were more personal to the dreamer. The gods played no part in these and the way they are reported makes them sound more like the sort of dream we experience, for the most part, today.

### DREAMS AND HEALING

The tradition of healing temples and dream incubation is one that was continued by both the Greeks and Romans, especially for acquiring information to treat disease. In ancient Greece famous sleep temples at Oropos and Epidaurus were dedicated to Asklepios, the god of medicine, although it is believed that hundreds more temples existed throughout the ancient and classical world. The temples were situated in places of natural beauty, surrounded by fragrant plants and herbs, natural springs or shady forests. Another common feature was the serpent, and today the ruins at Epidaurus show us the pit where snakes were kept for healing and incubation purposes. This association of snakes with healing developed into the familiar symbol of the "caduceus", a healing staff entwined by two serpents. Today this symbol is widely used by many healing professions.

## HIPPOCRATES

Known as the father of modern-day medicine, the Greek doctor, Hippocrates (460-377 BC), accepted that some dreams were of divine origin and could prophesy events. He endeavoured to put this capacity to scientific use by using the symbolism of dreams to diagnose the dreamer's state of health, associating the microcosm of the human body with the macrocosm of the universe. In his *Treatise on Dreams*, for instance, Hippocrates asserts that bright

stars in a dream indicate good health, whereas to dream of dim stars precedes illness. Dreaming of flowing rivers, he states, indicates problems with the urinary system, while dreaming of floods points to an excess of blood and the need to "bleed" the patient. Such dreams are referred to by Hippocrates as prodromal, from the Greek word *prodromos*, meaning "running before".

**ABOVE** Hippocrates, the Greek physician, believed dream interpretation was connected to physical sickness – if you dreamt of a specific sickness or disease it meant that you were suffering from it in real life.

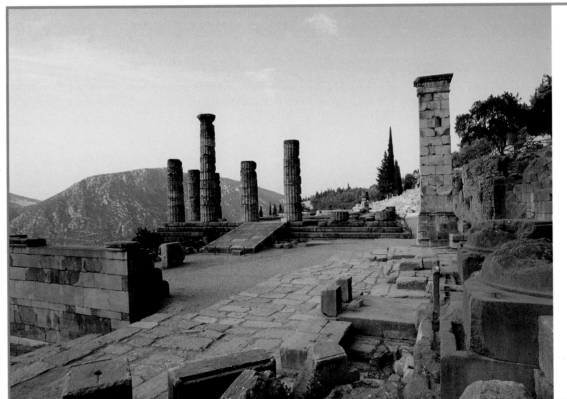

## THE DELPHIC ORACLE

The word "oracle" also means "answer" and oracle dreams were incubated at the famous site in Delphi (left), widely believed in ancient times to be the centre of the world. The site was situated on sulphurous hot springs and its entrance bore the inscription "know thyself". Hallucinogenic plants, such as henbane and jimsonweed, were burned to put the seer of the oracle into a trance, and make them ready to receive dreams and visions from the gods.

**ABOVE** Some Greek philosophers would have nothing to do with dream interpretation, whereas others were convinced that dreams had mystical importance. The two groups debated the issue endlessly.

## THE PHILOSOPHERS

It would be wrong to assume that all Greeks subscribed to the mystical significance of dreams. Many famous thinkers challenged this notion and their ideas have been highly influential in the way dreams are regarded by Western society. Heraclitus (450-375 BC) is generally regarded as the first person on record to proffer a purely rational explanation. Far from being a communication from the gods, he asserted, someone's dream world is entirely personal to them. It has nothing to do with anything outside of the dreamer's mind and is simply an ordinary experience, having less significance than anything that happens while in waking consciousness. However, perhaps more than any other thinker, it is Aristotle (384-322 BC) who comes closest to our modern way of looking at the meaning of dreams.

## ARISTOTLE'S CONTRIBUTION

From his observations of sleeping animals, Aristotle concludes that it is not only humans who have dreams. He uses this as evidence to counter any theory that dreams have any divine or cosmic pattern or that they have any particular significance. He also notes that since all external sensations are reduced or absent during sleep, subjective sensations must be highlighted. He goes on to assert that dream images can have an influence on subsequent behaviour. In that sense dreams can be prophetic, as our thoughts are influenced by what we have seen during sleep. He also claims that the insights

## THE EMPEROR'S DREAMS

After Calpurnia's prophetic dream about her husband, Julius Caesar, Caesar's heir, the emperor Augustus (above) (63 BC-AD 14), made a law declaring that anyone having a dream about the emperor's welfare should announce it in the marketplace. According to another historical text, Tranquillus' *Lives of the Caesars* Augustus set such store by dreams that he made a fool of himself. He went about Rome begging for alms because it had been predicted that he would do so in a dream.

available from dreams are like objects reflected in water: when the water of the mind is calm, the images are easy to see, when the water is troubled, the reflections become distorted. He says that the more the mind can be calmed before sleep, the more the dreamer can learn. Aristotle's theories were outlined in three seminal works: *On Dreams*, *On Sleep and Waking* and *On Prophecy in Sleep*.

## DREAMS AND THE HUMAN PSYCHE

In his theories, Aristotle also links the hallucinations of the mentally ill, the illusions of ordinary people and the content of dreams and fantasies, concluding that they may all share a common origin – an idea which was later developed by the 20th-century psychologist, Carl Jung. Plato (427-347 BC), another of the Greek philosophers, also had ideas about dreams which predate 20th-century psychology. He describes the human psyche as possessing "a lawless, wild beast nature which peers out in sleep". As we no longer exercise rational control while sleeping, our lust and rage can enjoy free and full expression. Centuries later, such a view would be central to Sigmund Freud's ideas about defining human personality and behaviour.

## PROPHETIC DREAMS IN ROME

Accounts of prophetic dreams have occurred throughout history with some of the most well-documented being those foretelling the death of the dreamer or someone close to him or her. The citizens of ancient Rome seemed particularly fascinated by the possibility of this phenomenon and there are several reported instances of such dreams. For instance, the Roman historian Plutarch (AD 45-125) tells us that Calpurnia, the wife of Julius Caesar (100-44 BC), dreamed of Caesar's assassination by Brutus the night before it happened. Similarly the day before Caligula was assassinated, in AD 41, he reputedly dreamed that he was standing beside the heavenly throne of Jupiter, when the god gave him a push with his big toe, causing the emperor to fall to the earth.

## DREAM DICTIONARIES

While the Greeks may have brought elements of logic and reason to the world of dreams, it took the orderly Romans to catalogue and classify the information. One of the most outstanding contributions was Artemidorus' five-volume *Oneirocritica* (The Interpretation of Dreams). A Roman soothsayer of the 2nd century AD,

Artemidorus travelled extensively throughout the Roman Empire, researching into dreams and drawing on knowledge from earlier times. His work includes more than 3000 dream reports from his interviewees, and is today acknowledged as the first true dream dictionary ever written.

Artemidorus suggests that dreams are entirely individual and that the contents are relevant only to the dreamer. The dream symbols and imagery that are found in these personal dreams are both cultural and individual, and are influenced by such aspects as the dreamer's health, state of mind and occupation. Artemidorus notes two broad classes of dreams: insomnium are dreams about everyday things and somnium are those that concerned the future. His approach is thorough and systematic and some symbolism is identified. For instance, dreaming of ploughing the earth is regarded as a sexual symbol, while a dream of a mouth represents the dreamer's home. More than a century later, a second *Oneirocriticon* appeared, compiled by Astrampsychus. This one contains such axiomatic statements as "to wear a purple robe threatens a lengthy disease".

**ABOVE** The assassination of Julius Caesar by Brutus was said to have been foreseen in a dream by his wife, Calpurnia. This detail of the story has survived, and has continued to fascinate people, from ancient Rome to modern times.

She dreamt tonight she saw my statue,
Which like a fountain with an hundred spouts
Did run pure blood; and many lusty Romans
Came smiling, and did bathe their hands in it.

WILLIAM SHAKESPEARE, JULIUS CAESAR

# India and the Far East

While the civilizations of the Near and Middle East attributed dreams to a divine agent, in India and the Far East they were regarded as having an inner source. In China dreams were thought to emanate from the soul, while in India and Tibet they were associated with a state of mind. In all these civilizations, dreams were inextricably linked with the philosophy, spirituality and mythology of their cultures. In the Far East, in particular, surviving texts reveal a sophisticated understanding of dreams, an understanding echoed in the oral traditions of many indigenous peoples.

### THE ATHARVA VEDA

According to legend, the 52 great Rishis (seers) of ancient India travelled to the highest mountains of the Himalayas seeking guidance to help humanity. During their meditations they believed that they discovered how the universe works. This knowledge was eventually transcribed into the Vedas, the sacred books of the Hindus, which scholars date between 1500-1000 BC. One of these texts, the *Atharva Veda*, contains many references to dreams, providing information about how they occur, what purpose they serve and how to interpret them.

### LUCKY AND UNLUCKY DREAMS

When trying to make sense of complex information, a first response is often to classify it into opposites. This holds as true for dreams as for anything else. Where other ancient cultures distinguish between good and bad, divine or demonic, and true or false dreams, the Vedas focus on the distinction between "lucky" and "unlucky" dreams, having particular

interest in a dream's predictive power. For instance, the *Atharva Veda* comments that showing passivity in a dream is a bad omen, whereas an aggressive dream is favourable. However if the dreamer receives any injury, this is considered an ill omen. The omen is made worse if the injury, such as an amputation of a limb, is something that could occur in waking life. The effects of unlucky dreams can be countered by performing purification rites, such as burning incenses and ritual bathing.

### TIMING AND PERSONALITY

For the first time, the personality type of the dreamer is taken into account in dream interpretation. For instance, a depressed person is more likely to have depressing dreams, while a hyperactive sort is more likely to have manic dreams. The *Atharva Veda* also theorizes that a person's dreams occur in cycles throughout the night, with the most important dreams occurring towards the end of the dreaming cycle or later on in

### HINDU DEITIES

During the Vedic period a pantheon of Hindu deities developed. A lot of these gods and goddesses have strange, dream-like qualities to them. For instance, Ganesh is the elephant-headed god of wisdom and "remover of obstacles", and the god Shiva has four arms, four faces and three eyes. Shiva wears the skin of a tiger and has a snake entwined around his neck, representing two powerful demons that he has defeated. In his fight against a particularly powerful demon, Shiva calls on the goddess Kali, the "dark side" of his consort Devi, to help him. Kali (shown left) is usually depicted wearing a girdle of severed arms and a necklace of skulls. Her bloodthirsty tongue lolls from her mouth and she carries a sword in her left hand. Intoxicated by her murderous killings, she dances on the bodies of her victims.

the night. In fact the later on in the night a dream occurs, states the Vedas, the more likely, as well as the more quickly, it is to come true.

## THE TWO WORLDS

The Vedas also contains texts known as the Upanishads, philosophical works that expose spiritual truths. One of the most elaborate and important of these is known as *Brihadaranyaka*, sometimes described as a "cosmic meditation". This text declares that essentially there are two states, one in this world and one in the other. A third intermediary state exists: the state of sleep and the land of dreams. It is while we are in the intermediary world that we have the capacity to perceive the real world and the next simultaneously. In this context, the dreaming state is considered to be more important than the waking state because it is then that we have access to realms of knowledge and experience denied to us when we are awake. To this end, techniques such as yoga and meditation were developed to help us "attain" or become more open to this other world, experienced as a place of heavenly bliss.

**ABOVE** The Hindus believe we can attain enlightenment during our dreams, only for it to evaporate when we wake.

**ABOVE** To the Buddhists this whole world is a waking dream. Once we perceive this we can really wake up to a new reality. But might not this also be another dream?

## THE FAR EAST

It was not only in India that dreams were linked with spirituality and states of mind. An important Chinese Taoist manuscript, known as the *Lie-tsu*, distinguishes between six different types of dreaming: ordinary dreams, day-residue dreams, dreams of waking, dreams of fear, joyful dreams and terror dreams. Taoism, and later, Buddhism, were hugely influential throughout the Far East. Both of these spiritual traditions assert that the worlds we see in our dreams are more or less identical to the worlds we will experience after death.

## THE BARDO

*The Book of the Dead* is an ancient Tibetan Buddhist text. Written to help prepare the soul for death, it describes death as a dream-like condition. When the soul leaves the physical body it must pass through the "Bardo", which has three distinct illusory states.

**RIGHT** The Tibetan *Book of the Dead* is a very ancient manuscript written on wooden tablets. In it a dialogue with the dead, who are said to have entered the bardo, the dream state between the living and the dead, is carried out.

As we pass through each state we face a multitude of self-created thought forms which may be pleasant or fearful, according to our thoughts and expectations. By becoming aware at any time that what we are experiencing is an illusion, the soul is elevated to a higher plane and avoids the constant cycle of death and rebirth. Consequently, learning to remain conscious while sleeping, being aware that we are dreaming while still in the dream, is seen by Tibetan Buddhists as a vital part of the spiritual preparation for death. Today in the West this state or technique is referred to as "lucid dreaming".

## P'O AND HUN

In ancient China, it was believed that we possess two types of soul. The material soul, or "p'o" motivates us in daily life and is implicit in our physical make-up. This soul dies when the body dies. Additionally, we possess an eternal soul, or "hun", which survives us at death, leaving the physical body and the material world for a different plane of existence.

Every night during sleep, the hun temporarily separates from the dreamer's resting body to travel the world of dreams. This concept is similar to the idea many Western esoteric traditions hold today of the dream body and astral travel. As the dreamer sleeps, the hun communicates with spirits, demons and ghosts, bringing back memories of its nightly travels to the dreamer.

## THE CITY OF DREAMS

In ancient China, people believed in a divine City of Dreams. Known as Ch'eng Huang, the city was thought to hang halfway between heaven and earth and is the place we go to when asleep. To enter the celestial city the dreamer had to pass through the "moongate", which necessitated being pure in mind and body. Once safely inside the city, the dreamer could leave their body and astral travel anywhere in the world. In this context, it is interesting to note that the Chinese had a god of the South Pole, a geographical region they had not actually discovered. Did the Chinese know of its existence because they had travelled there in their dreams?

## BEDROOM RITUALS

To pass through the moongate easily, rituals were practised before going to sleep. These included lighting incense and proceeding around the bedroom in an anti-clockwise direction, beginning in the east and moving through south, west and north before getting into bed. It was also important to make sure the bedroom was decorated in auspicious colours (typically red and gold), and to make sure that nothing hung over the bed which could interfere with the exit of the spirit body. Consequently it was thought inadvisable to sleep under such things as beams, canopies, mirrors or lights. Similarly great care had to be taken to ensure that the spirit body could safely return to the dreamer's physical body. Playing tricks on a sleeping person, such as altering their physical appearance in some way, or else waking someone up too abruptly was believed to be dangerous. The returning soul needed to be able to recognize the sleeping body and it also needed time to re-enter the body. If the soul could not return for some reason, the sleeper would die.

**ABOVE** The Chinese believe that every part of the natural landscape is ruled by mythical creatures who protect it. **ABOVE LEFT** The Chinese landscape has a dreamlike quality.

## DREAMS AND ASTROLOGY

Written around **AD 640**, the earliest Chinese book of dream interpretations is the *Meng Shu*. It suggests that many factors should be taken into account before interpreting a dream. These include the time of year and astrological factors such as the position of the planets. It was also believed that external stimuli could be reflected in dreams. Sleeping on a belt, for instance, might produce dreams of a snake.

## MU JEN DOLLS

In ancient China, great faith was placed in Mu Jen, the wooden man, or dream doll. For instance, if a child was suffering nightmares, the parents would "give" the dream to the Mu Jen doll, and he would then be sent away, taking the bad dream with him. Alternatively, if a dreamer wanted to make her wish come true, she would whisper it to the doll and then place him under her pillow as she slept. It was believed that during sleep the Mu Jen would come to life and be a "sacred warrior", capable of granting a person's wishes, protecting them from harm, and generally acting as a friend and helper.

# EUROPEAN TRADITIONS

THE CUSTOM OF SLEEPING AT HOLY PLACES TO INCUBATE PARTICULAR DREAMS WAS NOT CONFINED TO THE ANCIENT AND CLASSICAL WORLD. THROUGHOUT EUROPE, THE PAGAN CELTS AND THE EARLY CHRISTIANS ALIKE PRACTISED THE SAME PROCEDURE, SLEEPING AT SHRINES TO ENCOURAGE VISIONS AND DREAMS OF HEALING POWER. FOR THE CELTS, THESE SACRED SPOTS WERE ASSOCIATED WITH NATURE SPIRITS, AND FOR THE CHRISTIANS WITH THE SAINTS AND MARTYRS OF THE EARLY CHURCH. AS THE INFLUENCE OF THE CHURCH BECAME MORE WIDESPREAD HOWEVER, DREAMS WERE REGARDED WITH INCREASED SUSPICION UNTIL, BY THE MIDDLE AGES, THEY WERE LARGELY SEEN AS THE DEVIL'S WORK.

## CELTIC WISDOM

The Celts believed that all things possess an immortal soul, which exists through many lifetimes, learning from its experiences on the earthly plane in its journey towards perfection. To ascertain the will of the gods and help the soul along its way, many methods of prophecy and divination were used. The natural world was believed to be an infinite source of magic and spiritual wisdom, and symbolic significance was given to such things as the shape of clouds, a particular animal or plant species, as well as the portents of dreams. Dreams were interpreted by the druid, which literally means the "oak seer", or "one who sees with the aid of the oak". In fact, trees were especially important, and specific qualities were attributed to each species. Dreams were incubated in sacred groves, where the dreamer could ask the spirit of the trees for healing and assistance.

## THE EARLY CHURCH

Traditional Celtic lore was frowned upon by Catholic doctrine, but theologians of the early Church also began to comment on their dreams. In his treatise *On the Making of Man* (380 AD), Gregory

**BELOW RIGHT** Dreams were part of the religious and artistic world of the Celts and artefacts from this era reflect this.
**BELOW** Dreams to early cultures were powerful messages from the gods, from nature, and from deep within. They were never to be ignored.

### THE SALMON OF WISDOM

Stories about the source of all knowledge are practically universal. These symbolic tales have a rich, dream-like quality to them.

In the Irish Celtic tradition, the well of Nine Hazels is the dwelling place of the Salmon of Wisdom. The Salmon became wise when he imbibed the hazel nuts that fell into the well from the nine hazel trees. It is said that whoever catches and eats the salmon, will be imbued with its wisdom and filled with "imbas", or inspiration. Finn Eces, an elderly druid, captures the salmon and asks his young apprentice, Fionn mac Cumhail, to cook it for him. While it is cooking, some liquor from the fish splashes on to Fionn's thumb, and it is he and not Finn who gains the inspiration from the well.

of Nyssa asserts that dreams occur when the intellect and senses are at rest during sleep. The actual dream content is determined by the dreamer's memories of activities during waking life and his or her physical state. In other words, an individual's nature is revealed in his or her dreams. In Nyssa's view, dreams are most commonly motivated by the passions, expressions of our "brute" nature which should be rigorously held in check by the intellect if we are to remain pure. Because the intellect is "off guard" during sleep, our passions can be given unbridled expression in our dreams. A little later, St Augustine (354-430 AD) noted that certain aspects of his mind were beyond his control, and he worried that God might hold him responsible for his dreams.

## THE MIDDLE AGES

It was not long before the Christian Church associated human passions, especially sexual desires, with the devil or Satan. In their dreams, people were vulnerable to the temptations of the flesh: they could sin while asleep and not even know it, risking their souls to eternal damnation and the terrors of Hell. They therefore should practise great vigilance against the devil and all his works, as he was believed to intervene in human affairs in order to possess people's souls. A regime of devout prayer and austerity was recommended and any who continued to "sup with the devil" were branded as witches, facing persecution, torture and a terrible

death. Consequently the capacity to have vivid dreams was greatly feared and dream divination became linked with sorcery. It was at this point that dream divination in the West became anathema and consequently went underground, until its secular revival centuries later.

**ABOVE** Dreams are mysterious markers of landscapes that affect us very deeply – archetypes aren't just people but also symbolize aspects of ancient cultures.

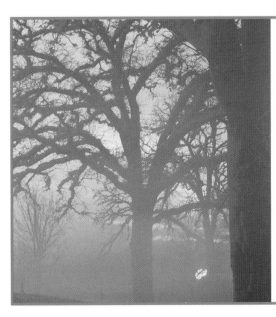

## TREE LORE

The Celts ascribed a symbolic meaning to trees. The oak, or "godhead" tree, held divine power and significance. Sleeping next to an oak tree could inspire prophetic dreams. Other important trees were the hazel, used as the druid's staff; holly, its red berries symbolizing the food of the gods; and ash, denoting health and immortal life.

### THE DEVIL'S HELPERS

One of the dangers facing the dreamer was a nightly visitation from one of the devil's helpers. A succubus is a demon who assumes a female form and has sex with sleeping men. She then collects the semen, using it in magical rites to produce an "incubus", a male demon, satyr, faun or devil. Any man unfortunate, or some would say, wicked, enough to attract the attentions of a succubus was destined to follow the ways of the witch forever. By this means, Satan was said to "increase his horde, his progeny and to spread the diabolical craft of the witch".

---

### THE SHEPHERD AND THE SUCCUBUS

The 16th-century author, Nicolas Remy, reports that a young shepherd who was found guilty of witchcraft began his evil ways by being seduced by a succubus while attending his flocks. It was said that whenever he fell asleep in the warm afternoon sunshine, he would dream of his demon lover, who took the form of a dairymaid with whom he was in love. She would allow the shepherd to fulfil his sexual desires with her provided that "he acknowledged her as his Mistress and behaved to her as though she were God Himself". The shepherd claimed that "she so possessed me that from that time I have been subject to no will but hers".

---

**ABOVE** Today we are much more forgiving of people who suffer or enjoy sexual excitement while asleep but to the ancient Church such people were very wicked indeed, and were inevitably accused of Devilish practices.

Witches, it was claimed, had sexual intercourse with incubi in order that they could give birth to the children of demons.

### NOCTURNAL INTERCOURSE

The word "incubus" means "to lie on", and it was believed that any heavy feeling in bed, such as a weight pressing down on your chest, especially if accompanied by nightmares, was a sure sign that an incubus (or succubus) had attempted to have nocturnal intercourse with you. Today we know that dreaming affects the body as well as the brain. For both men and women, the body regularly shows signs of sexual arousal (sometimes to the point of orgasm) during sleep, even when erotic dream content is absent. Given the religious fervour of the Middle Ages, it is not altogether surprising that the idea of a demon lover was believed to account for this phenomenon.

## FORERUNNERS OF THE MODERN AGE

Although St Augustine was concerned about his inability to control his dreams, it was hundreds of years later before the idea that something goes on inside us that we know nothing about was clearly formulated. Von Leibniz (1646-1716) compared the workings of the soul to the circulation of blood through the body: it is something that happens even though we are unaware of it. A little later, a German physicist, G.C. Lichtenberg (1742-99) made the first link between unconscious mental activity and dreaming.

At the beginning of the 19th century, signs of a renewed interest in dreams began to gather momentum. Robert Cross Smith from England became very successful as an astrologer, practising under the pseudonym of "Raphael". In 1830, he published *The Royal Book of Dreams,* which gave the reader interpretations of particular kinds of dream. However, it is through the work of a French doctor, Alfred Maury (1817-1892), that we begin to enter a new age of dream interpretation. From his study of more than 3000 dreams, Maury concludes that external stimuli are often responsible for what we dream about. Recent memories appearing in dreams, especially of the day before, are referred to as "day residues", and Maury discovered that stimuli such as noises and smells often register as we sleep and become included in our dreams.

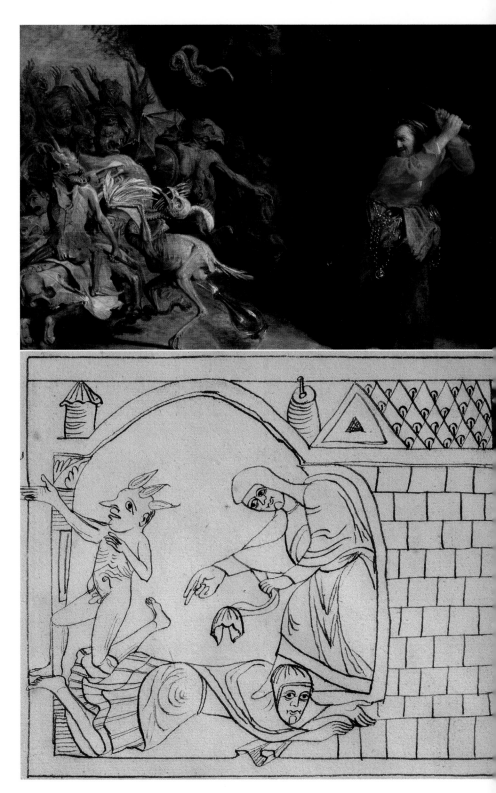

**ABOVE RIGHT** Much of the accusations levelled against so called witches by the Church involved detailed, nightmarish descriptions of the devilish creatures the women were said to have under their control.
**RIGHT** The only way to redeem a witch or possessed person was to exorcise the malignant spirit and extract a confession from the accused.

### MAURY'S DREAM

In one of his dreams, Maury dreamt he had been condemned to death by the guillotine. As the blade was falling, he woke up to find the top of the bed had fallen and hit him on the back of the neck at the exact time the guillotine would have struck him. This gave weight to Maury's theory that dreams happen so quickly that they are almost concurrent with the external stimulus that produces them.

### THE DREAM DEMON OF MORAY FIRTH

Legend has it that in the 16th century, a demon lover lived near the banks of the Moray Firth River in Scotland. The lover seduces a young girl, but the lovers are caught when the girl's parents overhear sounds of lovemaking coming from her bedchamber. The parents call the priest and together break down the bedchamber door to find the girl fast asleep in the embrace of a "monster horrible beyond description". The priest recites from the gospels, whereupon the evil demon gives a terrible cry, setting fire to the furniture in the room and vanishing upwards, carrying the roof of the bedchamber with him.

# INDIGENOUS PEOPLES

TRADITIONAL SOCIETIES ACROSS THE GLOBE HAVE DREAMING TRADITIONS THAT STRETCH BACK INTO THE MISTS OF TIME. IT SEEMS THAT DREAMS HAVE ALWAYS BEEN PART OF THE FABRIC OF LIFE FOR PEOPLES AS DIVERSE AS THE AUSTRALIAN ABORIGINES, THE INUIT FROM THE ARCTIC REGIONS AND THE PEOPLES OF AFRICA, AS WELL AS THE NATIVE AMERICAN INDIANS. EACH CULTURE HAS ITS OWN THEORY OF DREAMING AND PARTICULAR TECHNIQUES FOR INTERPRETING DREAMS. THEIR DREAMS AND SYMBOLS RELATE TO A PARTICULAR WAY OF LIFE, YET THEY ALL HAVE SOMETHING IN COMMON. THEIR DREAMS ARE RESPECTED AS COMING FROM A REVERED SOURCE AND ARE SEEN TO CONTAIN IMPORTANT INFORMATION.

**ABOVE** To the Aborigines of Australasia nothing is more sacred, more important, or more meaningful than the dreamtime, when the world was first created out of the seeds of the spirit ancestors.

## THE DREAMTIME

Hundreds of thousands of years ago, the Aborigines travelled from Asia to the northern shores of Australia. Here they split into groups and moved around the land in search of water. They travelled great distances, and their legends say that as they did so they deposited the spirits of those yet to be born along the way, leaving marks on the landscape, on the rocks, mountains and other geographical features, to signpost the places they had been. According to legend, these ancestors were mythical figures, spirit beings who emerged from the earth, sea and sky and who took on various forms, particularly of animals. They were given symbolic names such as Red Kangaroo, the Blue Lizard or the Bell Bird Brothers. This era is known as the "dreamtime", when the ancestors created the landscape and set the pattern for the future. For centuries the Australian Aborigines have followed in the footsteps of their ancestors, tracing the paths trodden by these giant beings and marking their sacred sites with ritual, song and legend.

Those who lose dreaming are lost.          AUSTRALIAN ABORIGINAL PROVERB

The dreamtime is like a "cosmic dreaming energy" which can be set free if the ground is rubbed or stroked at the exact spot where the ancestor left the world at death and went into the ground. In ritual dances, these sacred sites on the landscape are struck and the power of the ancestors is brought back to life from the sleep of death. If no-one remembers or honours the dreamtime, the stories say, we shall remain trapped in the earth when we die and will cease to be.

## THE DREAM IS LIFE

The dreamtime of the Aborigines is a complex concept: it is at once a creation myth, a whole series of fables and an entire spiritual philosophy. For the native Australians, the whole of life had its evolution in the dreamtime, and for them everything around us is brought to life by the dream. They do not perceive time as a linear process but rather see humans as existing in an eternal "now", where past, present and future exist simultaneously. The world as they see it is a magical place imbued with

supernatural forces, and we are at all times "dreaming the dream" so that it can become impossible to differentiate between the waking and the dreaming state.

## AFRICAN SOCIETIES

The Bushmen of the Kalahari hold a similar viewpoint, seeing the whole of life as a dream and believing that they are the ones being "dreamed". Similarly, the Pagiboti people of Zaire consider that dreams are sent from their ancestors and believe that the spirits of the past have access to wisdom that can help with daily life. For instance, hunting is important to the survival of the Pagiboti and they believe their dreams can give them important information that can help them be successful: to dream of encountering an animal in the forest is regarded as a good sign. Many other African societies set great store by dreams, believing that they are linked to destiny. All aspects of life, from cures for sickness to political decisions, can be based on dream advice.

**ABOVE** According to the Aborigine creation myths we are all holders of the dreamtime.
**ABOVE LEFT** The Aborigines' sacred art consists of pictorial representations of the dreamtime and how the world was created.

### THE DREAM SMOKE OF ULURU

The two Bell Bird Brothers were hunting emu at the rock pool near Uluru, the most sacred of all Australian Aboriginal sites (right), when their prey was disturbed by a young girl eating grubs. On her head she carried a sacred bundle which fell to the ground – the indentation is still to be seen at the base of the rock – but the brothers managed to catch the emu. They killed it and cooked it but Blue Lizard came and stole it. In punishment the Bell Bird Brothers set fire to Blue Lizard's hut and he was burned alive. The smoke from the fire can still be seen across the face of Uluru, and it is the smoke from this fire that sets us dreaming.

This story indicates one of the reasons why Uluru is so important to the Australian Aborigines. Take the rock out of their control and they lose their power of dreaming, and by implication, the power to live.

## NORTH AMERICAN INDIAN TRADITIONS

Like other traditional societies, Native American cultures find it difficult to define the border between the waking and the dreaming state, and the ability to dream is highly valued. Each of the great tribes has its own understanding of dreams and a complex dream culture exists. Iroquois traditionalists, for instance, have a strong belief in dream precognition and respect the ability of a gifted dreamer to provide information vital to the survival of the people. Because Iroquois culture is built on warrior values, any sign of being taken care of in a dream is greatly feared, as it is believed that it will undermine

**ABOVE LEFT** Through dream journeys the shaman is able to connect with the animal world.
**ABOVE RIGHT** The shaman is the guide through the dream. Without the shaman our dreams are dangerous places to go.

bravery. Where a dream indicates trouble or disaster, it is believed to be possible to change its outcome by playacting the event that the community wishes to avert. In fact drama and ritual play an important part in Iroquois dream culture. Each year people travel great distances to attend a festival where dreams are acted out in a theatrical performance known as the *Ondinnonk*. According to the Iroquois, big dreams occur either because we have an out-of-body experience during sleep or because we receive an interesting "dream visitor". These are the dreams that put us in touch with our deepest spiritual source and contain vital information for health and wellbeing.

The Navajo pay particular attention to the diagnostic aspect of dreams, seeing them as tools to pinpoint illness, particular mental states and emotional disturbances. Dreams can also reveal a ritual cure for what is wrong, and if this is carried out in waking life the dreamer will return to health. For instance, there is a story of a sick girl

**LEFT** Ritual dances can be followed to interpret the dream in song and music. This is a valuable tool in dream interpretation but one that is specific to a culture, to those who understand the steps.

## THE FOUR DIRECTIONS

Each of the four directions is associated with a particular element and quality. The element of the North is air. North is associated with the power of the mind and clear-thinking. Water belongs to the South and is associated with feelings and intuition, while the power of the West revitalizes and renews the physical body. Its element is earth. The power of the East triggers enlightenment and spiritual realization and its element is fire. This Navajo sand painting uses the four elements in its symbolic representation of abundant crops.

It is believed that positioning the bed in a particular direction allows the dreamer to "work" with the qualities of its associated element.

dreaming of nine feasts and being persuaded by the medicine man that if she has these feasts in reality, she would recover from her illness.

## HOPI DREAM PROMPTERS

For the Hopi, a dream is viewed as a message from spirit guides who can appear in the form of an animal or other guises. Waking up and not remembering a dream is seen as losing something essential and people go to great lengths to ensure that this does not happen.

A commonly used dream prompter is a squared circle, a symbolic device used to aid dream recall. A circle is drawn on a square piece of cloth or leather. The circle is then divided into four quarters to represent each of the four directions: North, South, West and East. The square is then placed by the side of the bed. An item of symbolic value is placed in each of the four quarters – for instance, a tiny pot of water, a bunch of fresh grass, a lit candle and some burning incense – these items represent each of the four elements of water, earth, fire and air. Sleeping next to a dream prompter is believed to enhance dream recall.

## THE INUIT SHAMAN

The Canadian Inuit culture is similar to those found in other northern regions, such as in Russia and the northern Scandinavian countries, where survival is challenged by the extreme climate. The Inuit believe that *anua* (souls) exist in all people and animals. Individuals, families and the tribe follow a system of taboos to ensure that animals will continue to make themselves available to the hunters, and rituals and ceremonies are performed before and after hunting expeditions to encourage success.

The shaman is the spiritual leader of each tribe. He is able to interpret causes of sickness or lack of success in hunting. In a manner similar to shamans or medicine-men in other cultures, he enters a trance-like state with the aid of drum beating and chanting. This allows him to travel out of his body, traversing great distances to determine the causes of sickness and other community problems, and to bring back solutions. In this dream-like state the shaman is imbued with magical powers and can move about outside of the dream.

### CULTURAL PATTERN DREAMS

Anthropologists have suggested that the dreams of traditional societies can be broken down into four types: "big" dreams are those that possess cultural significance; prophetic dreams predict or give advance warning of events; medical dreams promote diagnosis and healing; and "little" dreams are purely personal to the dreamer. Although all dreams are valued, the ones held to be the most significant are the big dreams. These powerful dreams are also known as "cultural pattern dreams" or "official dreams".

The dream world is the real world. SENECA INDIAN HEALER

# SACRED DREAMING

THROUGHOUT THE ANCIENT WORLD, THE CONNECTION BETWEEN DREAMS AND SPIRITUAL BELIEF WAS CLOSELY INTERWOVEN. DREAMS SEEM TO HAVE PLAYED A SIGNIFICANT ROLE IN THE SHAPING OF MANY OF THE WORLD'S MAJOR RELIGIONS, APPEARING AS PART OF THEIR HISTORY AND IN THEIR HOLY TEXTS. MANY OF THESE DREAMS HAVE A REVELATORY OR VISIONARY QUALITY TO THEM, WITH RICH SYMBOLIC IMAGERY AND METAPHOR. THESE EXPERIENCES ARE NOT THE SAME AS THE ORDINARY DREAMS MOST OF US HAVE MUCH OF THE TIME – ALTHOUGH IT IS POSSIBLE TO EXPERIENCE A DREAM OF SUCH PROFOUND SIGNIFICANCE THAT LIFE CAN NEVER BE THE SAME AGAIN.

## BUDDHIST ENLIGHTENMENT

For a long time before the birth of Gautama Buddha (c.563-c.483 BC), many predictions had been made that a "chosen one" would arrive. While she was pregnant, Gautama's mother dreamt that she was carrying a shining, silvery white elephant with six tusks. Interpreters regarded the dream as an announcement of the chosen one's arrival. Elephants had holy status in India: the Hindu god, Ganesh, remover of obstacles, is depicted with an elephant's head, while the unusual colour and appearance of the elephant in the dream was also seen as significant. Later on in the Buddha's life, his father, a nobleman, had a dream in which his son left the family to become a monk. This came to pass when Gautama was 30 years old, when he left his family, renouncing his worldly status to seek enlightenment.

## BIBLICAL VISIONS

Dreams also figure largely in both the Old and New Testaments. In the Old Testament, important dreams often coincide with critical times in the development of Judaism. For instance, while in exile in Egypt Joseph interprets the Pharaoh's dreams. The Pharaoh

**BELOW** Gabriel, a universal archetype who appears in several different traditions, played a significant part in the dreams of Mohammed, who dreamt that they journeyed together to the seven levels of heaven.

## HINDU BELIEFS

The Hindu religion has its own interpretation of what dreams are all about and believes that some dreams come from the dreamer's own emotional nature, some from hidden fears, and some from playing back experiences in daily life. Certain dreams, however, come from the gods. These dreams only appear to very religious people, such as this sadhu (right), who live a disciplined life, or sadhana, getting up before sunrise and practising austerities.

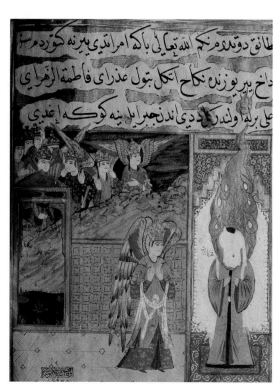

And He said, 'Hear now my words: If there be a prophet among you, I the Lord will make myself known unto him in a vision and will speak to him in a dream'.                    OLD TESTAMENT, NUMBERS 12:6

**RIGHT** Joseph became a dream interpreter to the Pharaoh, and in this role became one of the most important people in the land. The Egyptians believed that dreams were messages from the gods.

dreams that seven fat cattle are eaten by seven lean ones, and then that seven ripe ears of corn are destroyed by seven blighted ones. Joseph realizes that both dreams mean the same thing: they predict seven years of plentiful harvest followed by seven years of scarcity, which will destroy the bounty of the previous seven years. The Pharaoh acts on Joseph's interpretation and during the bounteous years builds up large stores of grain. The interpretation not only saves the populace and the ruling system, but Joseph is promoted to a position of great political influence.

In the New Testament, divine messages are often relayed in dreams. The angel Gabriel appears in a vision to the pregnant Mary, announcing that she will give birth to a child of the Holy Spirit. The angel also visits Joseph in a dream, telling him to accept Mary's pregnancy and to name the baby Jesus, because he will save his people from their sins. Dreams also contain warnings. For instance, Joseph is told to take his family to Egypt in order to escape Herod's jurisdiction that all newborn male infants should be slain. Later the same angel returns to Joseph, informing him that it is safe to return after Herod is dead.

## ISLAMIC DREAMS

Dreams also seem to have played an important part in the building of Islam. It is said that Mohammed (c.570-632 AD) had visions of the archangel Gabriel, who appeared to him when he was alone at night, praying and meditating. During one such

visitation, the angel dictated the first chapter, or Sura, of the Koran, the holy book of Islam. The Arabic root for the word *Koran* means "address" or "recitation". According to tradition, Mohammed could neither read nor write, but the Koran was recited word by word by him just as he had received it from Gabriel. Later Mohammed had a dream or vision that he journeyed in the company of Gabriel and other angels. He was taken to holy places and to the seven levels of heaven and hell, meeting important religious leaders and prophets from the past. This experience, referred to as the Night Journey, has inspired many writers and artists.

**ABOVE** Angels have appeared to many in dreams – are these dreams or visions? Moments of madness or divine communications? One of the most well known angelic dreams is Mary's, as she is told of the coming of Jesus.

---

### THE TALMUD

The body of Jewish civil and ceremonial law, the Talmud, divides dreams into three types: dreams of prophecy, dreams of nonsense, and dreams that originate from a person's thoughts and experience during the day. The way a dream is interpreted helps determine its outcome, and actions such as fasting or reciting special prayers are recommended as atonement for a bad dream.

# THE NATURE OF DREAMS

A dream is a series of pictures or events that occur in the mind. Generally dreams are experienced as we sleep, although it is possible to enter a dream-like state while awake. These images seem to be based on the dreamer's thoughts or experiences although certain dreams seem to bear little or no relation to the dreamer's normal life. Precisely how and why these images occur and what relevance they may have is a subject that has inspired a great deal of research and provokes much debate.

In this section we shall explore the nature of dreams, looking at some of the most influential ideas from science and psychology, drawing particularly on the work of Freud and Jung. Some modern approaches to dreaming are discussed before going on to investigate paranormal phenomena, dream travel and out-of-body experiences. Other dream states in the "twilight zone" are examined before finishing with a look at lucid dreaming. Although we may not have one single, comprehensive theory about dreaming, there can be few who would deny it is a fascinating subject.

# Scientific Research

THE RELATIONSHIP BETWEEN THE BODY AND MIND, THE BRAIN AND SLEEP HAS ALWAYS BEEN A PUZZLE, YET SCIENTIFIC RESEARCH INTO DREAMS IS A RELATIVELY RECENT PHENOMENON. EARLY RESEARCH IN THE 19TH CENTURY SUGGESTED THAT EXTERNAL STIMULI, SUCH AS NOISES AND SMELLS, CAN INFLUENCE DREAM CONTENT AND CERTAIN DREAM EXPERIENCES WERE GIVEN A PHYSIOLOGICAL EXPLANATION. HOWEVER IT WAS NOT UNTIL THE PHYSICS OF ELECTRICITY WAS UNDERSTOOD AND EEG (ELECTROENCEPHALOGRAM) INSTRUMENTS WERE INVENTED THAT SCIENTISTS BEGAN TO DISCOVER HOW THE BRAIN WORKS, TRANSFORMING OUR KNOWLEDGE OF SLEEP AND DREAMS.

### EEG INVESTIGATIONS

In the early 1950s at the University of Chicago, Kleitman and Aserinsky made a breakthrough in sleep research using EEGs. They found that when a person was asleep the brain had periods of intense activity, demolishing the widespread idea that during sleep the brain was resting. They also found out that blind people have vivid dreams in colour.

Another important dream researcher was Kleitman's pupil, William Dement, to whom we owe the term "REM (rapid eye movement) sleep". REM occurs after periods of slow-wave or deep sleep, at regular intervals throughout the night. REM is characterized by visibly detectable movements of the eye behind closed eyelids together with a change in brainwave frequency. It is during REM sleep that we experience dreams.

Dement's research team found that if someone is woken in or immediately after REM sleep they usually have good recall of their dreams. On the other hand, if even as little as five minutes has elapsed before they wake, they usually have little or no memory of their dreams.

### PHASIC AND TONIC DREAMS

We now know that REM sleep falls into two types, generating two different types of dreams. Firstly there is the phasic component. This is characterized by jerky eye movements, spasmodic limb and facial twitching and sudden breathing changes. When volunteers are woken from this sort of REM sleep, they typically describe their dreams as being strongly visual, active and "real". Phasic REM and its accompanying dreams tend to occur later on in the sleeping period. Nightmares are associated with this type of sleep.

The second type of REM sleep is known as tonic and is accompanied by muscle relaxation and

## PHASIC AND TONIC DREAMS

REM sleep has two components, each having its own dream characteristics.

**phasic dream** I was running down a metal tunnel. It was very cold and hard and my feet made a noise on the floor as I ran. There were vibrant colours inside the tunnel and I felt I could reach out and touch them. Behind me I could hear the echoing roar of rushing water and it made me tremble. I wasn't afraid but I did feel very anxious – you know the sort of feeling, where you think the worst is going to happen at any minute. It was pretty overpowering.

**tonic dream** I was sitting in a temple meditating. There was a monk beside me and I could sense what he was thinking. There was a feeling of calm and peace all around and I drifted away in the swirling incense smoke. I felt weightless and insubstantial.

sometimes sexual arousal. Tonic REM takes place earlier on in the sleeping cycle. It is calmer and more restful, and tonic dreams are more passive and "feely". When woken, the dreamer typically reports such things as "I was feeling floaty" or "there was a feeling of peace".

## DATA THEORIES

Although we now know much more about the brain, scientists remain divided as to the exact purpose that dreaming serves. In the 1960s, some dream researchers thought that while we are asleep the brain, like a computer, is "off-line". This does not mean it has shut down, but is that is going through a process of reassessing, filing and updating data from the day's activities. Many dreams certainly seem to fall into this category.

Some researchers took the analogy even further by suggesting that the brain, like the computer, discards redundant information through the process of dreaming. In the 1980s, Crick and Mitchison called this process "reverse learning". Dreams, they reasoned, help the mind to jettison an overload of data which could otherwise cause confusion. Dreams are like a rubbish-bin of the mind and have no particular meaning. From this perspective, we dream in order to forget.

## UNDERSTANDING THE BRAIN

The brain has two hemispheres: the left side is associated with logic and language, while the right is more connected with intuition and creativity. It seems that dreaming is associated with right brain activity. Scientists have also discovered that dreams flow along visual and verbal "pathways" or nerve channels to the brain. We also know that the brain emits different types of electrical signals or waves. Of these, the following four types are of interest to sleep researchers. Beta waves (30-13 hertz) are associated with normal waking activity, with waves near the top end of the scale (30) signalling states of extreme agitation. Alpha waves (12-8 hertz) are produced during rest, while theta waves (7-5 hertz) are produced on the point of sleep. Delta waves are the longest and slowest (4-1 hertz) and are produced during deep sleep or in the womb. It is usually when alpha moves into theta that dreaming begins.

**ABOVE** The more we understand the function of the brain the better able we are to understand our dreams and thus not only our emotional impulses but also, perhaps, our spiritual function.

**BELOW LEFT** Our dreams may be a simple way of us downloading all the data we have picked up during the day and may have no meaning at all.
**BELOW** On the other hand dreams may be imbued with mystical importance and we would be lost without them – lesser beings indeed.

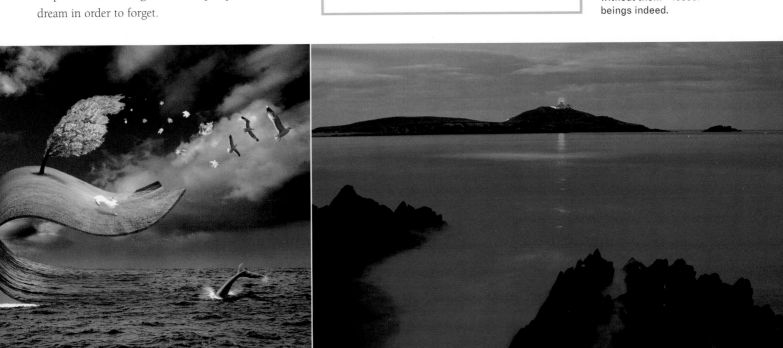

# FREUDIAN PSYCHOLOGY

WHILE PEOPLE HAVE ALWAYS BEEN INTERESTED IN THE WAY THE MIND WORKS, IT WAS NOT UNTIL THE 20TH CENTURY THAT OUR UNDERSTANDING WAS REVOLUTIONIZED. THIS BREAKTHROUGH CAN BE ATTRIBUTED TO THE WORK OF SIGMUND FREUD (1856-1939), AN AUSTRIAN NEUROLOGIST AND THE FOUNDER OF PSYCHOANALYSIS. FREUD "DISCOVERED" THE UNCONSCIOUS AND DESCRIBED DREAMS AS THE "ROYAL ROAD" TO ITS UNDERSTANDING. WHEN HIS *INTERPRETATION OF DREAMS* WAS PUBLISHED IN 1900 IT WAS HIGHLY CONTROVERSIAL, YET HIS IDEAS PERMEATED ALMOST EVERY ASPECT OF WESTERN CULTURE. BECAUSE OF FREUD, DREAMS WERE ONCE AGAIN TAKEN SERIOUSLY.

## THE CONSCIOUS AND THE UNCONSCIOUS MIND

According to Sigmund Freud, the conscious part of the mind represents a small fraction of the whole. It is like the tip of the iceberg, with the unconscious lying below the surface of the water. Like the iceberg, part of the unconscious is near the water's surface. Freud refers to this level as the "pre-conscious" and it is relatively easy to get in touch with. The deeper levels, however, are more difficult to access. It is a journey into the dark.

The unconscious is not static but dynamic. Freud believed that underneath our social exterior, the tip of the iceberg, at rock bottom we are a seething mass of instincts and unspeakable desires, most of which relate to sexuality and aggression, or our biological drives. He refers to this part of the psyche as the "id". Any experiences, thoughts or desires that are either too painful to allow, or that will contradict our self-image are either denied by the rational, conscious part of the personality (referred to as the "ego"), or repressed by an internal "censor" (also known as the "superego"). The unconscious is a bubbling cauldron of our personal and social taboos, yet it also provides the underlying motivations for our behaviour, of which we are largely unaware.

## THE ROLE OF DREAMS

Freud believed that the unconscious cannot be studied directly but can only be inferred from clues in a person's behaviour, speech patterns and also their dreams. Dreams are symbolic representations of our unconscious needs, wishes and conflicts. Freud describes them as being in essence "the hallucinatory fulfilment of a forbidden wish". He asserts that dreams not only represent current wishes but are also the irrational expressions of infantile wishes, usually of either a sexual or an aggressive nature, that are left over in our subconscious from early childhood.

Because the wish is perceived as dangerous by the censor, it is expressed in the dream in a disguised or symbolic form. Freud believed dreams have two aspects: a latent content (the repressed desire) and a manifest content (the dream itself). So, for instance, repression of sexual desires (latent content) leads us to dream in metaphors of sexual imagery (manifest content): to dream of a chimney is to dream of an erect penis, to dream of a cave is to dream of a vagina. In other words, dream symbols are coded

**BELOW** Sigmund Freud was the first modern Western scientist to make a detailed attempt to understand and interpret dreams, and his legacy continues to this day.

*Anyone who behaved while awake in the way the situations in the dream present him would be regarded as insane.*

SIGMUND FREUD

**RIGHT** Freud believed that dreams mask what is really going on in our subconscious, and we have to strip away the scaffolding to discover the true, to him invariably sexual, meaning of the dream.

messages, having sufficient ingenuity to slip through the tight webbing of the censor's net. Freud believed that this subversive activity was necessary because it allowed the sleeper to go on sleeping. Without such disguise techniques, the content would be so disturbing that the dreamer would be woken from sleep. This leads to Freud's description of dreams as "the guardians of sleep and not its disturbers".

## APPROACH TO INTERPRETATION

Freud's approach to dream interpretation is to look for the underlying meaning, or the latent content, behind the dream. To help his patients identify the latent content of their dreams, Freud developed the technique of word association, known as "free association", where words and ideas derived from the dream are freely associated without being censored. This technique forms the basic method of psychoanalysis.

### DREAM DISGUISES

Central to Freud's theory is that dreams use "disguise" techniques to hide the latent content from the internal censor. This is how he accounts for the peculiar and irrational nature of the manifest dream. These are the different disguise techniques that Freud identifies:

Condensation dreams use a kind of shorthand, coalescing or "condensing" different ideas together into a single image which is often unusual or bizarre.

Displacement dreams are when a potentially disturbing idea is redirected or "displaced" on to another person or object so that it becomes less disturbing. For instance, a young man harbours feelings of murderous rage towards his father. In his dream, he sees his father being killed by a stranger, whereby his aggressive desires are displaced on to the stranger.

Symbolization dreams are where a neutral image is used to represent a potentially disturbing, usually sexual, idea. For instance, putting a key into a keyhole is interpreted as a penis entering a vagina.

Representation dreams are when thoughts are converted into visual imagery.

**ABOVE** Freud believed that all dream imagery is symbolic in content, and that the symbolism is universal rather than personal. For example if you dream of holes in the ground, tunnels or caves (above left) you are dreaming about the vagina. Similarly, if you dream of chimneys or towers (right) you are dreaming of the penis.

# PSYCHOLOGY AND JUNG

FOR OUR CONTEMPORARY UNDERSTANDING OF DREAM INTERPRETATION WE ARE INDEBTED TO THE WORK OF CARL GUSTAV JUNG (1875-1961), A SWISS PSYCHIATRIST AND FOUNDER OF "ANALYTICAL PSYCHOLOGY", WHO MADE THE STUDY OF DREAMS AND THE UNCONSCIOUS HIS LIFEWORK. JUNG WAS A ONE-TIME PUPIL OF FREUD, AND WAS IN AGREEMENT ABOUT THE IMPORTANCE OF UNCONSCIOUS PROCESSES IN THE CAUSE AND TREATMENT OF MENTAL ILLNESS AND IN THE PRODUCTION OF DREAMS. GRADUALLY HOWEVER, JUNG BECAME DISSATISFIED WITH FREUD'S THEORIES AND PROPOSED THAT DREAMS PLAYED AN IMPORTANT PART IN THE HEALTHY FUNCTIONING OF THE PSYCHE.

## JUNG'S BASIC PHILOSOPHY

It was Freud's emphasis on sexuality and the overly biological orientation of his theories that gradually alienated his pupil, Jung. Freud's is a deterministic, and some would say, pessimistic, view of human behaviour. In a sense, he argues, we are little more than machines, driven by blind forces arising from our biological inheritance, over which we have little or no control. In contrast, Jung believed that human beings possess the capacity for growth and fulfilment and regarded sexual energy as part of a much more general, innate drive towards psychic health and wholeness. Jung calls this process individuation and describes it as the most important task any person can undertake in life – the attainment of harmony between all the aspects of the psyche, which makes us one and whole.

Essentially Jung saw life in terms of a spiritual journey and, far from being a dangerous melting pot of repressed and forbidden wishes, he saw the unconscious as a friend and guide to help us on our way. Jung applied these principles to his own life and used his dreams to help him make decisions, resolve uncertainties and move him along his path to self-realization.

## THE PURPOSE OF DREAMS

Jung saw the psyche as self-adjusting, helping us to reconcile opposing parts of our nature and restore inner balance, and believed that dreams had an important part to play in this process. Dreams have a compensatory function, alerting us to imbalances in our personality and allowing us to change. They also have a teaching function, where certain aspects of the personality that need revising can be given attention. Jung believed that dreams are a way of communicating, of bringing levels of unconscious information into conscious awareness. They express the current state of the dreamer's unconscious and, Jung believed, they also provide clues as to future potential – a view that contrasts with Freud's more backward-looking perspective.

## APPROACH TO INTERPRETATION

Unlike Freud, Jung never published a systematic theory of dream analysis because he believed that every dream carried its own meaning and must be interpreted individually. For Jung, the dream itself is the content and its symbols are subject to subjective interpretation. Rather than leading the person away from the dream by free association, Jung's method is to stay focused on the content of the dream itself. Through amplification or "direct association" he

**BELOW** During his life, Jung estimated that he interpreted around 80,000 dreams. He found that the details of a dream were not only relevant to the dreamer, but were sometimes part of a bigger picture relating to the world we live in.

---

### JUNG'S DREAM OF HIS FATHER

Following a dream of his dead father, Jung became interested in the spiritual dimension to life.

"Six weeks after his death, my father appeared to me in a dream. Suddenly he stood before me and said that he was coming back from his holiday. He had made a good recovery and was now coming home. I thought he would be annoyed with me for having moved into his room. But not a bit of it! Nevertheless, I felt ashamed because I had imagined he was dead. Two days later the dream was repeated. My father had recovered and was coming home, and again I reproached myself because I had thought he was dead. Later I kept asking myself: 'What does it mean that my father returns in dreams and that he seems so real?' It was an unforgettable experience and it forced me for the first time to think about life after death."

---

*The general function of dreams is to restore our psychological balance.*                    CARL JUNG

encourages the dreamer to explore all their
associations with a particular image, returning to the
image itself again and again.

## THE COLLECTIVE UNCONSCIOUS

The other important area where Jung diverges from
Freud is in the way he conceptualised the
unconscious. Although many dreams are expressions
of a personal unconscious and related to the
individual psyche of the dreamer, Jung noticed that

there were other dreams that do not fit into this
category. These make use of symbols which have no
particular personal significance for the dreamer, but
have a "universal" quality about them. Through his
studies of religion, art, anthropology and mythology,
he concludes that many of these symbols stem from
some common source – the "collective unconscious"
the largest and deepest area of the psyche. He refers
to these universal symbols as "archetypes" and
argues that their meaning transcends the personal.

**ABOVE** To understand our
personal archetypes is to
unlock the power of our
dreams and to be truly
released.
**ABOVE LEFT** Jung
encourages the dreamer
to explore their own
dream, and discover its
meaning for themselves.

**LEFT** Archetypes can be
traced back thousands of
generations, and traces
may even be seen in the
landscape, where the first
human cultures in our
history drew the
creatures of their
imaginations.

# DREAMS AND PREMONITIONS

TALES OF PROPHECY AND FORESEEING THE FUTURE ARE AS OLD AND DIVERSE AS HUMANITY ITSELF. WHILE ORTHODOX SCIENCE INSISTS THAT PSYCHIC PHENOMENA DO NOT EXIST, DREAMS CONTAINING INFORMATION FROM OTHER PEOPLE OR NEWS FROM THE FUTURE AS WELL AS DREAMS OF PROPHECY AND WARNING HAVE ALL BEEN RECORDED AT VARIOUS TIMES. SIMILARLY THERE HAVE BEEN MANY INSTANCES OF DREAMS BEING USED AS A DIAGNOSTIC TOOL FOR HEALING PURPOSES. HOWEVER WE ACCOUNT FOR SUCH PHENOMENA, THERE IS A BODY OF EXPERIENCE WHICH CANNOT SIMPLY BE DISCOUNTED OR READILY BE ABSORBED BY OUR RATIONAL, SCIENTIFIC WORLD VIEW.

### PRECOGNITIVE DREAMS

An estimated 40 per cent of reported psychic experiences concern knowing the future in some way, with dreams being the most common way for premonitions (precognitions) to appear. Precognitive dreams are ones where the dreamer somehow receives information about the future which subsequently turns out to be verified by events. This information could not have been obtained or inferred by any other means.

Traditional societies typically take precognitive dreams seriously, believing that they may contain information that could be vital to the survival and wellbeing of the community. In modern society, many precognitive dreams have been linked with major disasters, including the sinking of the *Titanic*

in 1912 and the Japanese attack on Pearl Harbor in 1941. Dreams of earthquakes, volcanic eruptions, and transport disasters on land, sea and air, as well as the assassinations of public figures have all been foretold in dreams. There are also instances of particularly gifted dreamers using knowledge gleaned in their dreams or in a dream-like state to help the police solve crimes.

Significant historical figures have also dreamt of their own destiny. For instance, Ghengis Khan, Oliver Cromwell, Napoleon Bonaparte and Adolf Hitler all had prophetic dreams of their success in battle, while the US president Abraham Lincoln saw his dead body laid out in a coffin two weeks before he was assassinated. Although Lincoln took the dream seriously he was unable to avoid its fulfilment. On a lighter note, there are also many instances of people dreaming racehorse winners or lottery numbers, sometimes on a sufficiently regular basis to make money from it.

**BELOW** Are we to take notice of precognitive dreams? There have been cases where the veracity of such dreams is utterly convincing to the dreamer, but does that mean it is really possible to dream the future?

### THE SLEEPING PROPHET

Perhaps one of the most spectacular revelatory dreamers of recent times was Edgar Cayce (1877-1945). Known as the "sleeping prophet", Cayce was able to diagnose illness, prescribe treatments, and correctly describe people he had never seen while in a sleep or trance-like state.

Cayce practised clairvoyance for 43 years and by the time he died, he had gathered together around 30,000 diagnostic reports and case studies containing testimonies from his patients and doctors that vouched for the accuracy of his diagnosis and treatments. Cayce also used his psychic abilities to help the police identify and track down criminals.

Dreams must be heeded and accepted, for a great many of them come true.          PARACELSUS

## OTHER TYPES OF PSYCHIC DREAMS

These are also relatively common types of psychic dream phenomena.

**dreams of apparitions** These dreams involve the deceased, whether you know the person or not. The theory suggests that the person appears in the dream in order to convey a personal message. This message is not necessarily for the dreamer. For instance, it is common for apparitions to appear to people who didn't know them very well, giving them a message to pass on to the loved ones of the deceased.

**clairaudient dreams** These dreams involve sounds in which you can clearly hear information.

**empathic dreams** These dreams involve clear and sympathetic feelings or sensations about an event that is occurring as you dream it.

**clairvoyant dreams** Events occur at the same time as a dream experience of the same event. There is absolutely nothing you can do about changing or preventing anything you see in a clairvoyant dream, although the information can be used to help people.

**telepathic dreams** Communication is made directly from one energy source to another without any mechanical assistance of any kind. These dreams tend to show us people and events not in our immediate environment. Such dreams sometimes occur when someone is either in danger or in an unusual predicament.

## SCIENTIFIC RESEARCH

The problem with premonitions is that the knowledge of the event appears to precede the cause, which in conventional science is impossible. It also raises the principle of free will. Arguments are put forward that the events could be inferred, that the dream was not specific enough, or that they are just coincidences. However research suggests that there is some evidence for foreknowledge. Tests have been conducted where participants guess which card will be shown next, or which light on a panel will come on next, and correct predictions happened surprisingly often.

**RIGHT** Perhaps dreams are a way for our subconscious to experiment with our hidden fears, rather than any kind of premonition of oncoming disaster that might be creeping up behind us.

# NIGHT TRAVELLERS

THE QUESTION ABOUT WHAT HAPPENS TO US WHEN WE ARE ASLEEP IS ONE THAT CONTINUES TO PUZZLE US. SCIENTISTS ARE NOW ABLE TO EXPLAIN THE PHYSIOLOGICAL CHANGES THAT TAKE PLACE IN THE BODY AND ALSO TO MONITOR BRAIN WAVE PATTERNS TO INDICATE STAGES OF SLEEP. PSYCHOLOGISTS CAN EXPLAIN SLEEP AND DREAMING IN TERMS OF UNCONSCIOUS PROCESSES AND RECOGNIZE ARCHETYPAL DREAM SYMBOLS AND PATTERNS. YET NEITHER SCIENCE NOR PSYCHOLOGY CAN ACCOUNT FOR OUT-OF-BODY EXPERIENCES (OBE), WHERE A DREAMER LEAVES THEIR PHYSICAL BODY YET STILL RETAINS CONSCIOUS AWARENESS.

## ASTRAL PLANES

Some people believe that dreams are our jumbled and distorted memories of our experiences in the astral kingdom, in which we have wandered while our physical body was sleeping. The astral planes are the supposed non-physical worlds that exist beyond time and space as we know it. Almost all esoteric traditions believe in the astral world in some form or another and that adepts can learn how to "astral travel", or journey into this realm at will.

The astral world is not regarded as an "imaginary" world in contrast to the physical reality of this one, but one that exists in parallel. In fact many spiritual traditions turn the argument on its head, saying that it is our present world that is illusory, and the astral world that is our spiritual home.

**BELOW** Many cultures believe we leave our body at night and go travelling on the astral plane – in some societies it is the job of the shaman to guide the dreamer and bring them safely back to their body.

## THE ASTRAL OR DREAM BODY

In the West, the concept of astral bodies largely originated with Paracelsus, the 16th-century alchemist and healer. Paracelsus was convinced that we are influenced by the sun and moon and planetary constellations, but was not sure how. He came to the conclusion that stellar influences were exerted through what he called the "astral" or invisible energy body that surrounds the physical body. The astral body is roughly the same size and shape as the earthly one, but can detach from it and move about independently.

Psychics who are able to see the astral body maintain that it is connected to the physical body via a "silver cord". When we die, this cord is finally broken and the dream body no longer unites with the physical body.

## FLYING DREAMS

During sleep, the astral or dream body lifts away from the physical body to explore other dimensions, but remains connected by the cord. The astral body can travel vast distances, but if the dream body strays too far, the physical body jerks it back again, which may register in sleep as a sense of falling, the sleeper sometimes abruptly waking from the "jolt" with feelings of disorientation and even physical symptoms, such as headaches and nausea. Some commentators believe that dreams of flying are related to psychic out-of-body experiences, the dream body floating weightless into the air, defying the laws of gravity. Such dreams are usually marked by a sense of euphoria and are rarely forgotten by those who have experienced them.

A man dreamt that he slipped out of his flesh just as a snake sheds its old skin. He died the following day. For his soul, which was about to depart from his body, provided him with these images.

ARTEMIDORUS

## OUT-OF-BODY EXPERIENCES

The concept of the dream body may help to explain what is happening in an out-of-body experience (OBE). There are many well-documented instances where people have described not being "in" their bodies, but outside them, having no physical sensation but otherwise being able to see and hear what is going on. Some people have reported these experiences at the edge of falling into or out of sleep, describing themselves as "floating" near the ceiling while seeing themselves in bed. There are also many instances where people have reported OBEs while under anaesthesia. As they "float" above their physical body on the operating table, they are able to watch the proceedings and later are able to recount accurate details of what took place.

Many other people have experienced OBEs as a result of a near-death experience or shock. Such experiences are generally life transforming and seem to indicate that we have a level of consciousness that exists independently from our physical condition.

## SCIENTIFIC STUDIES

Volunteers who have claimed to be able to generate out-of-body experience at will have been clinically tested. During a reported OBE, EEG readings reveal a change in brain wave patterns from a relaxed alpha rhythm to beta. Beta waves are the ones produced during normal waking activity. Similarly the breathing and heart rate both showed signs of increase, suggesting that some activity or stimulus, similar to a waking condition, was going on in the body. REM was absent, although there were more eye movements than in the usual non-dreaming (orthodox) sleep.

These findings seem to indicate that the sleeping subject was in a relaxed state but with a considerable degree of alertness. They were not, in fact, asleep. Physiological changes and changes in brain wave patterns indicate that something is happening, but more research and validated evidence is needed before science can describe something that "proves" an OBE.

**ABOVE** Are our dreams a tunnel from this world to the next? Or are our minds perhaps simply experimenting with fears that we avoid when we are awake but still need to confront?

**ABOVE LEFT** Do dreams give us a little taste of what it is like to be dead? Many claim they do and until it actually happens to us there is no way of being sure.

# THE TWILIGHT ZONE

A DREAM IS AN ALTERED STATE OF CONSCIOUSNESS THAT WE FALL INTO DURING SLEEP. HOWEVER THERE ARE OTHER DREAM-LIKE STATES EXPERIENCED WHILE AWAKE OR ON THE BORDERS BETWEEN SLEEP AND WAKING. THESE INCLUDE DAYDREAMS AND HALLUCINATIONS, AS WELL AS HYPNOGOGIC STATES (OCCURRING AT THE EDGE OF SLEEP). ALL ARE CHARACTERIZED BY VIVID IMAGERY AND HEIGHTENED SENSITIVITY. THROUGH TRAINING AND DISCIPLINE, SOME PEOPLE ARE ABLE TO ENTER THESE STATES AT WILL, AND CERTAIN PLANTS AND HERBS HAVE BEEN USED TO ASSIST THE DREAMER'S ENTRY INTO A TRANCE-LIKE STATE. OTHER PEOPLE MAY EXPERIENCE THEM THROUGH MEDITATION.

## HYPNOGOGIA

As we relax and drift into sleep, our brain wave pattern lengthens and slows down, changing from beta to alpha, and finally to theta. During this nodding-off stage, we can experience what is known as "hypnogogic" imagery, a series of vivid pictures or surreal imagery that bears little or no relation to waking memories. The imagery doesn't have the narrative quality of most sleeping dreams, but consists of a series of shifting and seemingly unconnected pictures that appear as if from nowhere: an animal, a face or a figure, an eye, a swirling rainbow of colours – the variety is infinite. The same process can also happen in reverse, emerging from sleep into drowsy wakefulness, where the fleeting visions may be referred to as "hypnopompic" imagery. Sometimes these persist into full consciousness when we are fully awake.

**BELOW** As we begin to fall asleep, or sometimes during deep meditation, where the brain slows down, we go through a hypnogogic stage, where our mind tries to make sense of all the images in our head.

This state, also known as hypnogogia, is not only associated with sleep, but may occur in other situations where the brain wave pattern slows down sufficiently and we "switch off", such as during meditation, or even through boredom – as on a long stretch of motorway driving for instance.

## HALLUCINATION

The Latin root for the word "hallucination" means "to wander in the mind", while the word "sleep" is derived from the Old English meaning "a vision". While visions, hallucinations and trance-like states are not the same as a sleep-induced dream, they nevertheless represent a dream-like experience where the boundaries between normal waking life and another dimension dissolve and merge. Within these blurred boundaries, there is a fine line between sanity and madness. For instance, people

> But the dreamers of the day are dangerous people, for they dream their dreams with open eyes and make them come true.
>
> T. E. LAWRENCE

who suffer extreme states of mental illness, or who have misused certain drugs can become overpowered by hallucinations to such an extent that their grip on conventional reality breaks down, and is never really recovered.

## SHAMANIC DREAMING

In many traditional cultures, the ability to enter a trance consciously and safely is a skill that is cultivated for the good of the wider community. The role of the dreamer, typically filled by the shaman or priest, is to travel "between the worlds", in search of a vision that can assist or advise his or her people. In fact the word "shaman" may be translated to mean "one who is exalted or lifted up". The shaman has the ability to step outside of their being in ecstatic trance, and is able to enter the dream world at will. While present in the other world they will be able to communicate with the "dream guides" and to bring back gifts of wisdom and healing.

**BELOW LEFT** Is sleep the same as an hallucination? Research on the brain suggests that the two states are very different although they share similar language, imagery and themes.
**BELOW RIGHT** The shaman needs to know how to explore the world of the dreamer, and this requires a rigorous and lengthy training.

### SACRED HERBS

There are many plants and herbs that are known for their mind-altering effect. Some, such as fly agaric (*Amanita muscaria*) stimulate hallucinations, others such as peyote (*Lophophora williamsii*) produce out-of-body experiences, while cannabis (*C. indica, C. sativa*) and morning glory (*Ipomoea*) produce euphoria. Dramatic and vivid dreams can be induced by the infamous opium poppy, shown right, (*Papaver somniferum*). It was while under the influence of opium that Coleridge is alleged to have "visioned" his Kubla Khan poem. In many cultures, including our own, these plant substances have degenerated from their traditional sacred use by initiates in search of higher states of consciousness, into drugs used to escape the realities of everyday life. Most of these drugs are highly addictive and their use is illicit.

To become a shaman involves years of arduous training that typically involves lengthy periods of solitude, fasting and other "tests" designed to build inner strength and preserve sanity in preparation for when the ego's defences are dropped. Certain plants and herbs, as well as incense, talismans and objects of "power", are used to assist the dreamer in entering a trance-like state.

# LUCID DREAMING

In 1913, Frederick van Eeden, a Dutch psychiatrist, coined the term "lucid dreams" to describe the state of being aware that you are dreaming, while in the dream state. He based this on his experience of his own numerous lucid dreams. Centuries earlier in ancient Greece, Aristotle had also concluded that during sleep "there is something in consciousness which declares that what then presents itself is but a dream". What happens in the consciousness of the dreamer is something we barely understand, but it seems that lucid dreams introduce us to the part of ourselves that creates our dreams.

**ABOVE** A lucid dream is one in which we know we are dreaming. They can be very terrifying and unsettling, but if controlled can become liberating and empowering.

**ABOVE** There will always be clues in a lucid dream that will give the game away and become the trigger that lets us know we are in a dream – minor or major things that are utterly impossible in waking life.

## DIRECTING A DREAM

Frederick Van Eeden describes a lucid dream he experienced on the night of 9th September 1904. His experience indicates that not only did he retain a level of conscious awareness in the dream, but also that he was able to direct the dream's content and action to some extent.

"I dreamt that I stood at a table before a window. On the table were different objects. I was perfectly aware that I was dreaming and I considered what sorts of experiments I could make ... I took a fine claret glass from the table and struck it with my fist, with all my might, at the same time reflecting how dangerous it would be to do this in waking life; yet the glass remained whole. But lo! When I looked at it again after some time, it was broken. It broke all right, but a little too late, like an actor who misses

his cue. This gave me a very curious impression of being in a fake world cleverly imitated but with small failures."

## SPONTANEOUS LUCIDITY

In general, people who have good recall of their dreams report at least one experience of being in a lucid dream, while for those who regularly record and work with their dreams the experience seems more familiar and frequent. However, we are not really sure what it is that turns a normal dream into a lucid experience. The most common trigger seems to be that the dreamer recognizes a dream-like

For lucid dreamers nothing is impossible!

STEPHEN LABERGE

quality to the events taking place. Sometimes this is when the dreamer becomes aware of a fantastic element, such as a talking dog or being able to fly, while others come to recognize the sensation of the dream state and seem to "just know" they are dreaming. People who record their dreams regularly appear to actually incorporate their recognition of dreaming into the dialogue and action of the dream.

## VIRTUAL REALITY

Many people are attracted by the notion of lucid dreams because the idea strikes us as a kind of virtual reality. Once you know that you are in a dream, perhaps you can control the action and influence the course of events – go places, do things, meet people and generally have the kind of experience you want. Because the dream world is not bound by logic or the rules of physics, it is possible to do or be anything that you desire. You can travel through the universe, turn yourself into an alligator, meet a long-lost lover or enjoy an extravagant luxury. This creates an exhilarating sense of freedom and expansion beyond everyday life.

## PERSONAL DEVELOPMENT

Many Western therapists regard lucid dreaming as an essential skill on the path to inner development. Charles Tart, an American psychologist, suggests that we use the freedom in lucid dreams to seek or create a wise guide whom we can call upon for advice relating to our spiritual and psychological growth. Lucid dreams can also provide an opportunity to try out new strategies that are different to our habitual responses. By seeing all aspects of the dream as part of yourself, it is possible to stand outside of the role you are playing in the dream, analyse it and change it if you so wish. For instance, instead of fleeing in the face of a tiger, you can try turning around and facing it head on. A recent study indicates that lucid dreamers may have a stronger sense of their individuality and personal power, and may be less likely to succumb to group pressure or conform to society's expectations.

## LEARNING TO LUCID DREAM

The most important key to learning how to generate lucid dreams is your level of motivation. The second is being adept at recalling your dreams, something which comes through practice. However, the following techniques may also be used to encourage lucidity:

**pre-sleep suggestion** As you drift to sleep, repeat a request or statement in your mind about becoming lucid in your dreams.

**periodic questioning** Develop a "critical-reflective attitude" to your state of consciousness while awake, asking yourself "could I be dreaming now?" at regular intervals throughout the day.

**rehearse dreaming** Sit down and pretend that you are dreaming. Use your imagination to create a dream.

**if this were a dream** Several times a day, stop and ask yourself "if this experience were a dream, what would it mean?"

**meditation** People who regularly practise meditation techniques seem to have more lucid dreams.

**dream groups** It is possible to join up with other people who are interested in exploring their dreams. People with an established forum in which to discuss their dreams tend to become regular lucid dreamers.

# The Sense and Substance of Dreams

Every night we all dream. What we dream about can be hard to remember, or when we do remember, may be difficult to comprehend. During sleep the brain is active and our dreams are perceived through the deeper layers of the unconscious mind. The unconscious does not communicate in words or through reason, but uses visual images to stimulate intuition and feeling. When we wake we are left with a residual "sense of" something that stays with us through the day, an imprint in our memory like a footstep in the snow.

This chapter looks at some of the characteristics of dreams, the importance of archetype and symbol, and the logic and landscape of the dreaming world. This information will help you start to make sense of your dreams and of what they are about.

# JUNGIAN ARCHETYPES

In his investigations into the collective unconscious, Jung formulated several archetypal forces or principles. These may not be definitive, but they nevertheless remain a handy and convenient tool for making sense of our dreams.

## THE PERSONA

The conscious personality, the Persona, is akin to Freud's concept of the ego. It is the person we present to the outside world, the mask we wear in order to protect our most real and vulnerable self. To find the Persona in our dreams is to look for a symbolic representation of "me".

We have many guises and wear many masks depending on the social role we are playing. Responsible parent, respected professional and rebellious teenager are just a few examples. Appearing naked in a dream is an indicator that the mask has slipped, our Persona is absent and we are literally naked before others, physically, emotionally and even spiritually. If we feel the mask is tarnished we may appear as a scarecrow, a tramp, or a degenerate. If we feel the mask is too firmly in place we may wear armour or a visor.

## THE SHADOW

Jung described the Shadow as a "splinter personality". Anything that does not fit with how we like to see ourselves is pushed into the background, repressed into the unconscious. Yet no matter how hard we try to keep it under control, every now and again it erupts, like a wilful and disobedient child. The Shadow is our dark side, our "sinful" nature that we judge and condemn as wrong and bad. It is our temper tantrums, black moods, anger, violence, lust, greed and unspeakable desires. It is the things we fear and hate the most.

We are very afraid of the Shadow, for it has the power to rip away the mask and reveal our true face. In our dreams it may appear as a shadowy figure, a cloaked evil-doer, a malignant force threatening to overpower us. Yet Jung did not perceive the Shadow as inherently evil, merely "somewhat inferior, primitive, unadapted and awkward". It does things in the old way, as Jung put it, and its messages are often actually for our own good.

## THE ANIMA AND ANIMUS

We each wear the mask of our gender. Yet within every man and woman resides the seed of the opposite sex. "Anima" and "Animus" were the terms coined by Jung to personify the "inner woman" and the "inner man", or the feminine part of a man's personality and the masculine part of a woman's.

Both the Anima and Animus are shaped by the child's experience of his or her mother and father. Broadly speaking however, the Animus is the hero within, practical, adventurous, independent and self-assured. The Anima is the heroine, both goddess and seductress. She is sensitive, compassionate, sensual and instinctive. It must be remembered that these are psychological attributes rather than characteristics of men and women as such. When these qualities are not integrated into the psyche, we project them on to other people, particularly our partners, in our desire for that perfect person who, we believe, will make our dreams come true.

## THE TRICKSTER

Hard to define because he is always one step ahead,
the Trickster leads us a merry dance as we follow
pipe dreams. He is the shape shifter, the joker in the
pack and the jester or clown. His is the leering,
jeering face in the carnival, painted and seductive.
He is the Pied Piper, the Lord of the Dance who
offers us delight and pleasure, but if we follow his
call we will end up a laughing stock, with dust in
our mouths.

Although a mischievous fraudster and saboteur,
the Trickster's antics can also be corrective. With
great skill he pricks the balloon of our inflated sense
of self, mocking our vanities and self-obsessions,
ridiculing our ambitions and desires. Not of this
world, the Trickster is also the shaman, the one who
can enter the realm of magic and interpret our
dreams. He represents our intuitive side.

## THE DIVINE CHILD

A symbol of innocence and purity, the Divine Child
embodies birth and growth, potential and latent
energy. The Divine Child is a link between past,
present and future, a mediator who brings healing
and wholeness, and possesses enormous
transforming power. Symbols for the Divine Child
include the changeling, the jewel, the flower and the
chalice. By becoming the Divine Child ourselves we
strip away all our preconceptions and judgements,
as well as our ideas and goals. The Divine Child is a
return to innocence, a readiness to be reborn
without the mask.

## THE LITTLE PRINCE

The following extract is from Antoine de Saint-
Exupéry's novel *The Little Prince* in which he
describes a dream-like landscape and an archetypal
Divine Child figure.

"Look very carefully at the landscape so as to be
sure to recognize it ... And if you should happen to
come upon this spot, please do not hurry on. Wait a
little, exactly under the star. Then, if a child comes
towards you, if he laughs, if he has golden locks and
if he refuses to answer questions, you will surely
guess who he is."

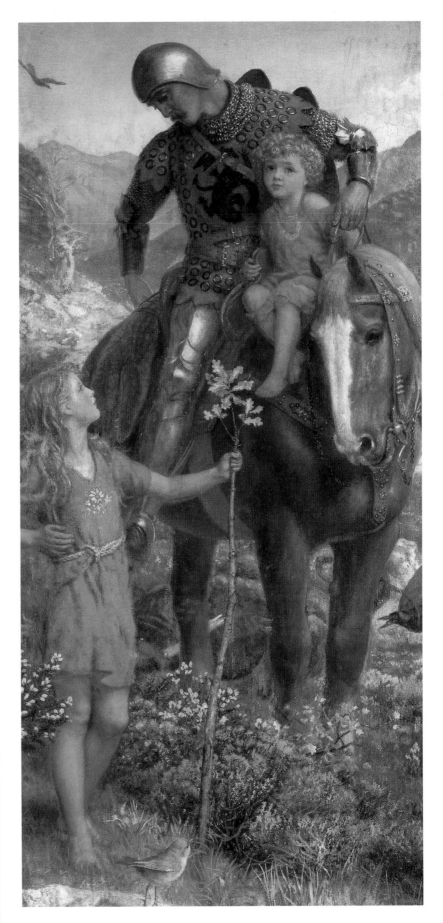

**ABOVE** The image of the Divine Child is a very powerful
one and it has inspired painters and poets for
centuries. Here it is contrasted with the archetype of
the hero, the youthful aspect of the Father.

# DREAM LOGIC

LOGIC IS NOT THE FORTE OF THE DREAMING MIND. IN OUR DREAMS THE IMPOSSIBLE BECOMES POSSIBLE AND THE NONSENSICAL APPEARS PERFECTLY NORMAL, AS PEOPLE, ANIMALS, OBJECTS AND PLACES BEHAVE IN BIZARRE AND UNACCOUNTABLE WAYS. FREUD ONCE REMARKED THAT ANYONE WHO BEHAVED WHILE AWAKE AS THEY DO IN THEIR DREAMS WOULD BE REGARDED AS INSANE. IN THE WORLD OF DREAMS, THE NORMAL RULES OF LOGIC, REASON AND "COMMON SENSE" ARE THROWN TO THE WINDS AS EVENTS APPEAR TO KALEIDOSCOPE INTO A THEATRE OF THE ABSURD. YET STRANGE THOUGH IT MAY SEEM, OUR DREAMS DO IN FACT HAVE A CURIOUS LOGIC OF THEIR OWN.

**ABOVE** All our dreams have their own curious dream logic, stemming from our own personal logic. Once we crack the code all our dreams can be understood.
**ABOVE RIGHT** It is useful to look at other people's dream logic but bear in mind they might only match yours slightly, more likely they will bear no resemblance at all.

## FREUD'S DREAM LOGIC

Intrigued by the absurdity of dreams, Freud began his investigation into how dreams work. His work claims that dreams express an element of logical connection in four different ways: simultaneity, contiguity, transformation and similarity.

When two elements in a dream are presented close together, simultaneity suggests that an intimate relationship exists between the two. Dream combinations are not randomly formed but have meaning within the dream. Contiguity is when dream elements occur sequentially, and transformation is when one thing turns into another. Similarity is the direct or indirect association between things in the dream.

The work of American psychologists Hall and Nordby adds the idea of "relative consistency" to Freud's ideas, noticing that dream motifs have a certain frequency and uniformity about them.

## YOUR DREAM LOGIC

Other people's ideas may be helpful when practising dream interpretation, but they will not necessarily fit with everyone's dreams all of the time. We all have our own unique dream logic which may be completely different from anyone else's. If you are keeping a dream record, see if you can find a consistency of pattern to your dreams. It may be that you always appear as yourself or always as someone else. Your dream logic is a bit like Woody Allen films. You may see a different film each time but the style is consistent and recognizable. You get to know your way round as you study the subject.

## MICE AND SPIDERS

Your unique dream logic invariably extends to your dream symbolism and will most likely influence the type of archetypes you are working with. These represent what you need to "bring to the surface"

What is life? An illusion, a shadow, a story. And the greatest good is little enough: for all life is a dream and dreams themselves are only dreams.   PEDRO CALDERON DE LA BARCA emotionally and indicate the sort of imagery you feel more or less comfortable with. For even in the depths of the most awful nightmare, you will find yourself being terrorized by the sort of thing that you already know you find scary. In a sense this is a comforting thought, because you will not frighten yourself in your dreams with an image that is totally alien. If it is mice and spiders that scare you in waking life, then they are the most likely creatures to pop up and scare you in your dreams. Conversely if it is the Bogey Man, ghosts or monsters that terrify you, then that is what will stalk the nightmare corridors of your dreaming mind.

## BLOOD IN THE TAPS

Your own curious dream logic is likely to remain fairly constant over the years and you will gradually come to know your dreams, and yourself, pretty well. Once you know your own dream logic you can to a certain extent ignore what is following those predictable patterns. For instance, if someone dreams that water comes out of the taps, then their logic is following a natural course. If, however, they

**ABOVE** Whatever scares or disturbs you in your waking life is likely to scare you just as much in your dreams. The nightmares that frighten you will carry images that you have an instant fearful reaction to.

always dream that blood comes out of the taps then that is their unique dream logic. Neither dream is good or bad, right or wrong. They are merely the unique expressions of two different dreamers whose minds are processing their unconscious material while they are asleep.

## DREAMS AND EVERYDAY LIFE

There does seem to be a close relationship between what happens in our "real" lives and what happens in our dreams. The situations may change but the rules governing them tend to be the same as in everyday life. For instance if you are always concerned with what people wear, then it is likely that clothes and the way they are worn will be just as important in your dreams. If, on the other hand, you are more interested in what people say, then it is likely your dreams will follow a similar pattern.

# DREAM SCENERY

DREAMS HAVE TO BE SET SOMEWHERE, TO HAVE A PHYSICAL SITUATION THAT THEY TAKE PLACE IN. THIS IS THE DREAM SCENERY, SIMILAR TO THE BACKDROP OF A THEATRE STAGE. THE LOCATION AND PROPS PROVIDE A CONTEXT FOR THE DREAM AND GIVE CLUES ABOUT THE ACTION THAT IS TAKING PLACE. FOR MOST OF US MOST OF THE TIME, THE CHARACTERISTICS OF THIS BACKDROP REMAIN MUCH THE SAME AS IN EVERYDAY LIFE. IT IS UNUSUAL FOR DREAMS TO BE SET IN A LANDSCAPE WHERE, FOR EXAMPLE, EVERYTHING IS PERMANENTLY UPSIDE DOWN. IT IS MUCH MORE LIKELY THAT THE SCENERY WILL BE THE RIGHT WAY UP AND THE DREAM ACTORS AND PROPS BEHAVE ACCORDING TO THE NATURAL LAWS OF PHYSICS.

## SURREAL LANDSCAPES

Now and again of course, dream settings and characters do not obey natural laws. Trees may appear upside down, the sky may be green, the sea a brilliant shade of yellow, cats may swim and people may fly weightless above the ground. Within the context of the dream, all of these things appear perfectly normal. It is only when we wake that they strike us as odd, as the rational mind tries to make sense of the illogical and therefore impossible.

These surreal dreams are often the ones that stick in the memory and usually have particular significance for the dreamer. The landscape is what we would focus on when trying to interpret the dream, although the conclusions we reach will depend on each individual.

According to Freud, the landscape of our dreams can be interpreted, and represents the uncharted territory of the unconscious mind and our repressed sexual longings.

**BELOW RIGHT** Once we are immersed in the dream the landscape will appear real; it is only when we wake that it seems odd. It may be a symbolic or real place, or even both.
**BELOW** Interpreting the landscapes in your dreams will depend on what significance they have to you in real life. Tall buildings would have suggested the phallus to Freud, but to you they might represent anything from soaring ambition to intimidation.

> Then suddenly I ... fly slowly over the lane, over the houses, and then over the Golden Horn in the direction of Stamboul. I smell the sea, feel the wind, the warm sun. This flying gives me a wonderfully pleasant sensation... P. D. OUSPENSKY

## INTERPRETING THE LANDSCAPE

In a Freudian world, soft round or curvy shapes and narrow indentations represent the female form. For instance, hills represent a woman's breasts, belly or womb, and a dark doorway or passageway, her vagina. Alternatively, hard, upright or elongated shapes represent the male form. Mountain peaks, tall buildings, a train and an aeroplane are all phallic symbols. Only you can decide if these ideas have meaning for you in the context of your dreams.

Jung did not interpret the dream landscape in the same way as Freud, yet he nevertheless believed that the place where the dream is staged makes a tremendous difference to the way the dream is interpreted. A dream that is set in a wood or forest has quite a different feel about it to one that is set in a living room or office. Some dream experts believe that dreams staged in a man-made setting are more based on the concerns of the personality, while those dreams that are set in nature come from the deeper reaches of the soul.

## MOODS AND FEELINGS

It is not only the physical nature of the dream setting that is important, but the mood or atmosphere it inspires. The dream landscape has the power to provoke feelings and emotions in the dreamer. Although the scenery may look the same as it does in ordinary life, it may take on a curious surreal quality, appearing melting and hypnotic, as deeply experienced and more real than real. People in a state of hallucination have reported similar occurrences, experiencing a world where walls are sad or happy, trees can sing and dance, and crockery can throw itself at you in a fit of angry pique.

Yet dream scenery does not need to take on a life of its own for it to inspire mood and feelings. Some of the most lasting impressions of our dreams

**LEFT** Dream landscape not only refers to natural scenery, but to any context in which your dream takes place, inside or out. You might dream about your own living room – it would still be your dream landscape.

### COMMON DREAM SETTINGS

Research indicates that the most frequent dream setting is a building, usually a domestic residence, with the living room, bedroom or kitchen being the most common place. The average number of characters in a dream is three, with strangers appearing slightly more often than friends or family members. Predominant dream activities are action-based, such as walking or running, followed by talking, sitting, socializing and playing. The most common emotions are apprehension and anger, followed by happiness and excitement.

are fragments of a landscape dimly remembered. Beautiful, awe-inspiring, tantalizing or downright peculiar, the dream setting is not only a backdrop for the action to take place, but is an integral part of the dream's content and the message it is trying to convey to the dreamer.

**BELOW** The dream setting allows us the freedom to imagine that anything can take place; that anything is possible, it doesn't have to be real or feasible, and it is important to examine why you have dreamt it like this.

# NIGHTMARES

ALMOST EVERYONE KNOWS WHAT IT'S LIKE TO HAVE A NIGHTMARE. THE CHINESE DESCRIBE THEM AS DREAMS OF TERROR AND DREAD, WITH THE POWER TO JOLT US OUT OF SLEEP. WITNESSING ACTS OF HORROR OR BEING IN SOME KIND OF DANGER ARE THE MOST FREQUENT NIGHTMARE SCENARIOS. THESE ARE USUALLY ACCOMPANIED BY FEELINGS OF HELPLESSNESS AND PARALYSIS, OF BEING LOST OR OUT OF CONTROL AND AT THE MERCY OF AN EXTERNAL AGENT OR EVENT. FOR THOSE WHO SUFFER FROM FREQUENT NIGHTMARES GOING TO BED IS FILLED WITH FEAR. SLEEP IS NOT RENEWING AND REFRESHING, BUT IS MORE LIKE GOING INTO A STRESSFUL SITUATION, NIGHT AFTER NIGHT.

### THE SUBJECTIVITY OF NIGHTMARES

Although we share a broad consensus about what is frightening, the content of our nightmares is always subjective. What is frightening in one person's dream world may seem innocuous in someone else's. What makes a nightmare upsetting is how it feels, the emotional experience, rather than the symbols or events in themselves. Consequently people who are emotionally sensitive seem to be more likely to experience nightmares than those who can shrug unwanted thoughts and feelings away. This may help explain why people with a creative bent, as well as young children, seem to suffer more frequent nightmares than other people.

### WHY WE HAVE NIGHTMARES

Although nightmares are unpleasant, they may have a positive intention. They can be a message from the unconscious mind, a way of alerting us to something that is going on in our waking life that we need to become more aware of. When this is the case, the nightmare may recur, growing progressively more frightening until we understand what it is about and can root out the cause. Sometimes nightmares may be signs of illness and/or drug reactions, so do check with your doctor to eliminate this possibility.

### CREATIVE VISUALIZATION

When nightmares become a real problem, and begin to disturb your waking life too, there are self-help measures you can take to reduce their frequency and intensity. The following suggestions are based on the techniques of creative visualization. Use them to begin to learn how to tap into the powers of your imagination in order to create change.

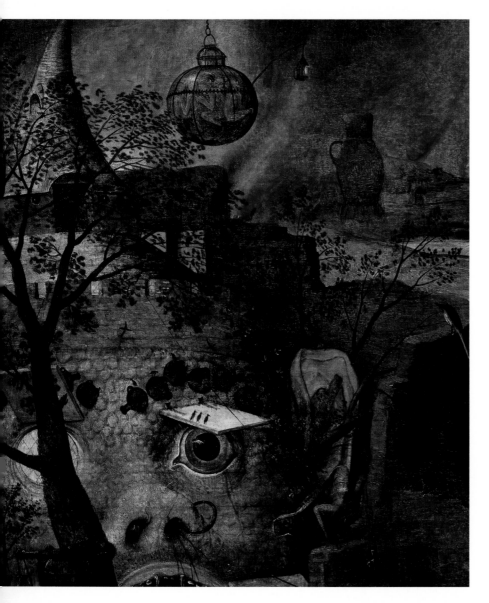

**LEFT** The more sensitive we are, the more artistic and creative, the more likely it is we are going to have nightmares. If you suffer from them, you might take some comfort from that fact.

> To sleep: perchance to dream: ay, there's the rub:
> For in that sleep of death what dreams may come...
>
> WILLIAM SHAKESPEARE, HAMLET

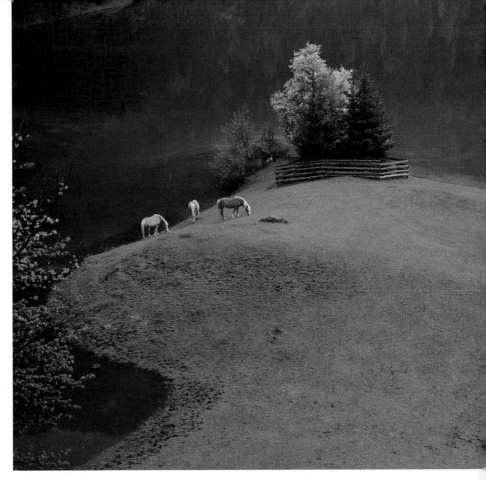

## CREATING AN IMAGINARY SCENE

Some people are able to visualize very easily; for others it might take some practice. You are trying to develop your ability to experience a mental escape from the scenes of your nightmares. Aim to make your imaginary scene such a strong image in your mind that it travels with you into your dream, and becomes your refuge over which you have control.

1 Sit in a quiet place where you feel safe and won't be disturbed. Close your eyes, breathe gently and allow yourself to relax.

2 Now imagine yourself in a beautiful place. This may be outside in nature, or indoors. It can be a real or an imaginary place. Visualize the scene as fully as possible, noticing the objects or scenery that surround you, any sounds or smells, whether it is warm or cool. Notice how you feel and what you are wearing. If you find yourself stopping at various points as you go through your imaginary scene, take notice of where you stop and then start again. It may take a few stops and starts to develop the scene in your mind's eye, but with time and regular practice it will come.

3 When you are comfortable with your scene, experiment by making small changes in it. For instance, you could change the colour of the walls, or add an animal that you like, or maybe a doorway or pathway. Continue to practise until you feel confident that the power of your own imagination has been added to your collection of skills. If at any time you start experiencing a negative reaction to what you are imagining, stop the scene and start again.

## WORKING WITH NIGHTMARES

When you are able to create an imaginary scene and play about with it at will you are ready to use the technique with your nightmares. For some people, nightmares arise as a result of an actual trauma. Traumatic events can be too much for us to deal with at the time, so for the sake of preserving our sanity, they get pushed into the basement of the unconscious. Later the unexplored material may resurface in our dreams, perhaps so that any leftover memories and feelings associated with the event can be worked through and healed in relative safety. You may need to seek professional help when dealing with these sorts of nightmares.

1 Write down a recent nightmare. After you have written it down, allow yourself to change the nightmare in any way you wish, writing out a new and less threatening scenario.

2 Using your creative imagination, visualize the new dream you have written. See the scene in as much detail as possible. Let it play through your mind for 5-10 minutes, as if it is a new dream that you are actually experiencing.

3 Imagine this new dream at least once a day for a week, preferably before going to sleep. It is best to work with one dream at a time and not more than three a week.

After three months you should see some improvement in your nightmares. If no change is happening, change the dream again, creating a different scenario.

**ABOVE** The beautiful imaginary place that you create in your mind can take many forms. If you always return to the same place it can become more and more real, with a potency that can overcome the nightmare.

# WORKING WITH DREAMS

There are many different kinds of dream. Some are at a relatively superficial level. These are largely concerned with daily trivia and seem to represent a cataloguing of the day's events. Others seem to bubble up from the deepest, darkest corners of the psyche and are not so easily understood. These are the ones that usually strike us as important in some way, even if we cannot be sure why. Learning to capture these "dreams from the deep" and finding ways to decode their meaning is what the following pages are all about.

Keeping a dream diary, working with dream tools and using your dreams for problem-solving as well as learning how to control your dreams are some of the different ways you can work with your dreams. With these keys you will be able to unlock the secrets of your dreams. This will bring a greater understanding of yourself and your relationships and increase your capacity to live life to the full.

# DREAM RECALL

MANY PEOPLE CLAIM THAT THEY DO NOT DREAM. IT IS MUCH MORE LIKELY THAT THEY ARE UNABLE TO REMEMBER THEIR DREAMS. OUR DREAMS TEND TO SLIP AWAY, LIKE A THIEF IN THE NIGHT, BEFORE WE HAVE CHANCE TO APPREHEND THEM. YET OUR DREAMS ARE THE ONE PLACE WHERE WE CAN RELAX, WHERE WE CAN BE OURSELVES. OUR DREAMS ARE RIPPLES IN THE POOL OF OUR UNCONSCIOUS, THE PLACE WHERE THE WORRIES AND ANXIETIES THAT WE SO SUCCESSFULLY HIDE FROM THE WORLD MAY SURFACE IN SAFETY. DREAMS CAN GIVE US VALUABLE INSIGHTS INTO OUR LIVES, AND TO GET THE MOST OUT OF THEM, WE NEED TO TRAIN OURSELVES IN THE ART OF DREAM RECALL.

**ABOVE** Talking about dreams is a good way to defuse them, but also to begin to understand them. Women tend to talk about their dreams more than men, and express more of an interest in others' dreams.

## DREAM JOURNALS

One of the best and easiest ways for remembering dreams is to keep a dream journal. It's worth keeping a special book or note pad and using it only for recording your dreams. Keep the book and a pen by your pillow and write in it as soon as you wake each morning. When you wake up, make as little physical movement as possible – even turning over can be enough for the memories to evaporate before you have had chance to record them. Lying still, in the same position as when you woke up, often increases dream recall. Keep your eyes closed. Not only will there be less distraction this way, but many people are often able to see the dream again.

If you can't remember any dreams, then just jot down feelings or thoughts that spring to mind. These may well be echoes of your last dream, a sort of dream vapour trail, and may be enough to trigger further memories of your dreams. If you wake up from a vivid dream in the middle of the night, it is a good idea to record it straightaway before going back to sleep. Some people keep a torch by the bed to save putting the bedside light on.

## RECORDING DREAMS

There is no single, right way to record your dreams. You may want to jot down key words or feelings, or make a note of the people or events. Some people prefer to write a narrative of their dream while others like to include pictures or sketches. If you can't remember the start of your dream, don't give up. Don't worry about sequence; working backwards or from the middle can lead you to remember more details. Sometimes you'll be halfway through

**RIGHT** The more we keep a journal the more likely it is to actually influence our dreams – we begin to dream the journal. This makes analyzing and understanding our dreams much easier.

remembering a dream when you'll remember something from dreams you had previously forgotten. Even fragments of dreams are valuable and can contain useful information. Writing in the present rather than the past tense can help you re-live the dream as you record it.

You might want to record your dream on one side of the page and leave the other side blank for comments and interpretation later on. It is, however, a good idea to record the date and the place where you had the dream and to generally include as much detail as possible; some people like to include the phase of the moon for instance. If you can't write the dream in your journal immediately you wake up, then make a note of the things you remember the most. These will jog your memory later on when you do have time to continue your journal.

## THEMES AND PATTERNS

As you keep your journal, images, incidents and even emotions will slowly build over time to create a picture of your unique psychic identity, but you should keep the journal for at least a month before you try to make any sense of it. When you look, you may notice recurring themes or patterns in your

dreams. Perhaps a recurring vision of being chased, or falling from a high place, or being confined in a small place for instance. Or it might be a symbol, such as a flower, a road, a boat, or a particular animal that keeps cropping up. Recurring themes often indicate there is something in your life that needs your attention, perhaps a part of you that wants expression. You could also look for links between your dreams and events that happened recently. Identifying a pattern can make us better equipped to deal with life.

**LEFT** Dreaming of a particular symbol and seeing it crop up repeatedly might indicate an important theme that you need to work on.

**ABOVE** Recurring themes often indicate recurring worries. By paying attention to what the dream is trying to say to us we can help alleviate the stress.

A dream is an answer to a question we haven't yet learned how to ask.    FOX MULDER, THE X-FILES

# DREAM TOOLS

IN MANY PARTS OF THE WORLD, GREAT STORE IS SET BY DREAMS, FOR INSTANCE MANY AFRICAN SOCIETIES BELIEVE THAT DREAMS ARE LINKED TO DESTINY. DREAMS ARE SEEN AS A VEHICLE FOR THE SPIRIT WORLD TO COMMUNICATE WITH THE DREAMER, GIVING IMPORTANT INFORMATION RELATING TO HEALTH, ENEMIES OR THE FUTURE. AMONG NATIVE AMERICANS THERE IS A WIDESPREAD BELIEF THAT A "SACRED POWER" SPEAKS TO YOU IN YOUR DREAMS. THIS POWER WILL OFTEN APPEAR AS AN ANIMAL. IN SUCH SOCIETIES DREAMS ARE TAKEN SERIOUSLY AND DREAM TOOLS ARE USED TO ASSIST THE DREAMER IN A VARIETY OF WAYS, ESPECIALLY FOR PROTECTION FROM BAD DREAMS AND TO ASSIST IN DREAM PROGRAMMING AND RECALL.

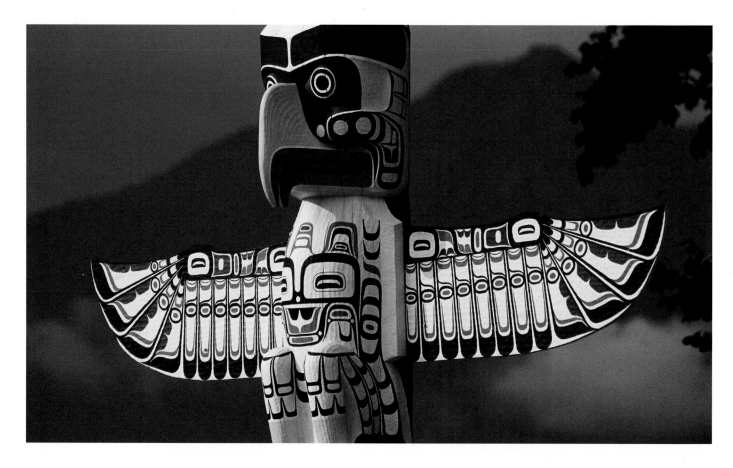

**ABOVE** We have access to a wide range of tools to help us interpret our dreams, including those used by other cultures.

## DREAM WISDOM

People have always suspected that the inner universe of our dreams is a source of infinite wisdom. Throughout history, dreams have been used for healing, to stimulate invention and discovery, as well as inspiring great literature and works of art. They have also been used to predict the future and bring spiritual revelation. For most of us most of the time, our dreams do not fall into these epic categories, yet increasingly we are recognizing them as a valuable source of self-knowledge. Once we have accepted that dreams are an important part of our life, we will find that they become more potent and revealing. This means that we should prepare ourselves for the best possible dreams that we can have.

## THE DREAM DOCTOR

The Cuna Indians of Central America see dreams as having an identity or power, with bad dreams signifying an impending disaster or illness. A disturbing dream would be taken to the "dream doctor" or medicine man for interpretation and a "prescription" to make it better.

Typically the prescription is an object into which special "power" or spells have been worked. The dream tool is then taken to bed by the dreamer to work its magic through the night and nullify the bad effects of the dream. Dream dolls and spearheads are the Cuna's most common dream tools, but stones, pegs, crosses and miniature weapons, such as axes or knives, are also used.

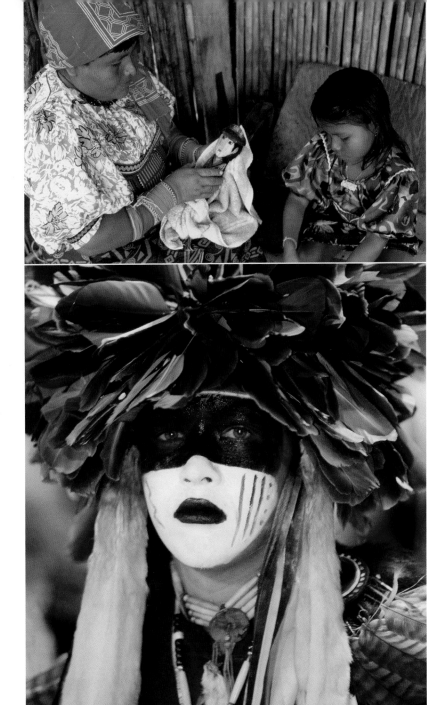

**RIGHT** A Cuna Native American woman, with a young girl beside her, takes care of a dream doll. As a potent dream tool the doll will be an integral part of the owner's daily life, linking the waking and dream worlds.

The dream doctor may also make up a powder containing a special wood mixed with black date palm and rub it over the dreamer's eyes to protect them from the effects of the bad dream. Through these actions it is believed that the dream's power is negated or "earthed".

## SKY AXES

The Cuna Indians live on the islands off the Atlantic coast of Panama, and their lives are very much influenced by the weather and the natural elements. Violent storms during the night frequently disturb their sleep, and a favourite dream-doctor cure is to sleep with a "sky axe". Sky axes are real axe heads that have been found at the old burial ground sites of the Cuna people. The Cuna Indians believe that these axe heads help protect their dream spirit guides from the power of thunder by making the spirit guides invisible.

As we would expect, the dream tools used by the Cuna Indians and other indigenous peoples are intimately related to a specific culture and lifestyle. However, we can adapt the principle of dream tools to suit our particular circumstances and create our own tools to assist our dreaming.

## YOUR OWN DREAM TOOLS

If you want to create your own dream tools, you need to choose objects that have special meaning for you. This could be an item that has special significance in your everyday life, or a childhood toy, a memento from a lover, a gift from a friend, or a treasured photo. If it is nature that inspires you, look for natural objects such as a piece of driftwood, a pebble from a favourite beach, a piece of tree bark or a fragrant flower. Dream tools can also be chosen to tie-in with the kind of dream you are trying to have or recall, maybe in answer to a particular question or on an important theme in your life. For instance, if work is an issue, then choose an object to symbolize what it is that you do: a tool for an engineer, a mixing spoon for a chef, a pen for a writer, or a thermometer for a nurse for instance.

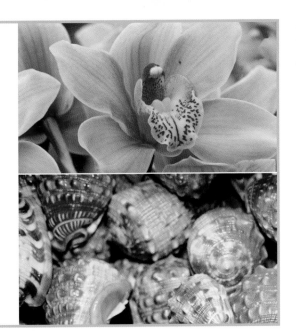

**ABOVE** Like other Native American traditions, the Fox and Sauk tribe uses costume and ritual to help people recall and interpret their dreams.

## EMPOWERING YOUR DREAM TOOL

Before a dream tool can work its magic, traditionally it is "empowered" by the dream doctor with special spells. You can do this yourself using colour and visualization. Use red for dreams of passion and adventure, blue or lilac for healing, green to be shown new pathways in life, and orange when looking at relationships. If you are working on communication issues, choose deep blue; for power and authority use purple; or work with yellow when seeking an answer to a health question. You could also use any other colours that intuitively spring to mind as being the ones that are most appropriate for you at the time.

To work with the colour, visualize your dream tool surrounded in coloured light, wrap the tool in a piece of the right coloured fabric or tie coloured ribbons on to the object. As you do so, spend some time visualizing the colour in your head, and mentally surround the item with it. When it is ready, take your dream object and put it under your pillow. It may help you have the sort of dream you want or else help protect you from bad dreams.

## DREAM CATCHING

In Native American culture, dreams are seen as messages from sacred spirits in the night sky. Certain tribes also believe in the idea of the Great Dream. In the womb, everyone has their own great dream but this gets forgotten at birth. This dream bestows gifts

such as courage, creativity, humour or empathy upon the individual and gives a vision for the best pathway through life. From a young age, children are encouraged to "catch" and explore their dreams and young men will fast until they have a vision of their "song of life". Dream catching plays an important part in initiation ceremonies, where the initiate makes a magical or sacred circle around himself to "capture" the messages from the dream spirits in the space inside the circle. The dream catcher tool is a symbolic representation of this magical or sacred circle.

## CATCH YOUR DREAMS

Dream catchers not only capture the good spirits, but also filter out any negative or unwanted powers. They consist of a cobweb-like structure on a circular frame, usually with beads or feathers attached to it. This structure symbolizes the "web of life"; in other words, it shows how all aspects of life are not separate but are intimately connected to one another. At the centre of the web sits Iktome, the spider, and keeper of dreams. Iktome is often represented by a coloured bead or shell. The dream catcher is hung near the sleeper's bed. The good dreams pass to Iktome, who holds them for the dreamer. The bad dreams are ensnared in her web and can be emptied away in the morning.

Dream catchers can be made in many shapes and sizes. They are not only useful but are also bright and colourful and make an interesting decoration in a bedroom. Children find them especially appealing and many parents have experienced positive results with children who suffer nightmares or who are afraid of the dark. Remember to empty the dream catcher each morning by tapping any unwanted dreams into the waste bin. Do this with the child, or encourage them to do it for him or herself.

## MAKING A DREAM CATCHER

A good way of protecting yourself from disturbing dreams is to make your own dream catcher. It may also help you gain more insight into where you should be going in life and show you the best choices to help you achieve your ends. A dream catcher is a very personal thing and there is plenty of scope to make it in a way that appeals to you.

YOU WILL NEED

- a thin and bendy piece of wood about 60cm (2ft) long. A freshly cut piece of bamboo or hazel is ideal.
- a length of twine, such as fishing line or strong cotton thread
- feathers, a few beads and some coloured ribbons for decoration

1  Curl the bamboo or hazel into a circle and fasten it with twine wrapped around. Some people like to cover the whole of the wood in ribbon before they start, but it is up to you.
2  Cut off any sharp ends of wood at the join and wrap some ribbon around it.
3  Tie one end of the twine onto any point on the circle and tie it to the opposite point of the circle. Cut off the long end of twine.
4  Tie another piece of twine across the middle of the circle, at right angles to the first piece.
5  Attach four shorter pieces of twine between the four tying-on points to form a square. From the middle of one of the shorter lengths, attach a piece of twine to the two tying-on-points on the other side of the circle. Repeat for the other short lengths. This gives you a sort of "cat's cradle" effect. Experiment until you have a pleasing criss-cross of lines resembling a spider's web.
6  Add a bead in the centre to represent the spider.
7  Finish by decorating the dream catcher with some ribbons hanging from the bottom of the circle. Add some feathers and beads to these downward-hanging ribbons.

When your dream catcher is finished you can empower it in the same way as with a dream tool. Hang your dream catcher at the window of your bedroom, or above the bed.

**ABOVE** The dream catcher is a Native American device that filters your dreams so that only the pleasant ones get through.

## DREAM GUIDES

Sometimes an ally or guide will appear in our dreams. In Native American culture, animals often symbolise these guides or helpers, with each person having their own totem or "power" animal. To find your totem animal, ask to be shown in a dream, or devise a dream journey to find it. This involves a visualization in which you see in your mind a path that you begin to walk down. As you walk, take notice of the scenery and the details around you, then open your mind and call for your power animal. The animal could be anything, from a wolf to a beetle, when it arrives greet it warmly, touch it and give it love. Be aware of what it feels like and feel the love it has for you. Remember, the greater the detail the more real it will be. Your dream guide might be an animal that you feel an affinity with in real life, you might love horses, for example, or feel inspired by the traditional north American wolf or bison, but don't try and manipulate the choice, let the animal make itself known to you.

# DREAMS AND RELATIONSHIPS

WE ARE SOCIAL BEINGS AND OUR INTERACTIONS WITH ONE ANOTHER AFFECT US DEEPLY. RELATIONSHIPS OF ONE KIND OR ANOTHER WEAVE THE FABRIC OF LIFE, FORMING A RICH TAPESTRY. SOME OF THESE RELATIONSHIPS ARE RELATIVELY SUPERFICIAL, WHILE OTHERS HAVE THE POWER TO AFFECT US AT A DEEP EMOTIONAL LEVEL – FOR GOOD OR BAD. OUR DREAMS CAN GIVE US GREAT INSIGHT INTO OUR RELATIONSHIPS WITH LOVERS, FRIENDS, FAMILY OR COLLEAGUES. THEY CAN HIGHLIGHT AREAS OF TENSION, REVEAL THINGS, ANSWER OUR QUESTIONS AND HELP US COME TO TERMS WITH OUR FEELINGS. WE CAN USE OUR DREAMS AS A "WAY IN" TO HELPING IMPROVE THE RELATIONSHIPS THAT MATTER TO US MOST.

**ABOVE** Dreams about relationships can act as a way in to understanding them more. Don't dismiss even the most banal ones, as they still could be a way of accessing how you really feel about people close to you.

## MAKING SENSE OF IT ALL

Sometimes it is tricky to disentangle the messages carried in a dream. Another person appearing in a dream may be representing an aspect of the dreamer's own psyche rather than themselves. Other people may also appear in disguise as an animal or an inanimate object for instance. We also have to remember that our dreams are not our everyday lives being acted out. They are an attempt by the unconscious to comment on and try and make some sense of what is going on for us. They can reveal what is frightening or worrying us, what is making us happy or sad, jealous or angry, and what we need to further growth and development.

When using your dreams to work on relationships, avoid the temptation to come up with a quick and easy interpretation. You need to tread

carefully and keep asking yourself "have I got this right?" It may also be helpful for close friends or partners to work on their dreams together, checking the meaning of the dream with one another. This can be an exciting journey of discovery and strengthen the bond that is between you.

Of course it isn't just our lover that we might dream about. All sorts of other relationships are reflected in our dreaming – children, friends, colleagues, even enemies or mere acquaintances. How we view our relationships in our dreams can indicate how we really view them on a waking level – without the need for any social niceties. We may find that the relationships no longer sustain or support us, or that they need some care and attention. What our dreams can tell us is dependent on how honest we are with ourselves.

Personal relations are the important thing for ever and ever.

E M FORSTER

## DREAM DETECTION

A good place to start doing some relationship work is to play "dream detective" and begin by asking some basic questions about the dream. By working through them, you will gain a lot of insight into what the dream is trying to tell you, which is very different from interpretation. The questions can be used to investigate any type of relationship that you wish to explore, not only sexual partnerships.

### DREAM QUESTIONNAIRE

Asking the following questions may help to unlock the symbolism of your relationship dreams.

1   What exactly are you doing in the dream? How are you doing it? Describe your thoughts and feelings as you do it.

2   What aren't you doing in the dream? Is there anything specifically missing from the dream that is important, anything that you feel you should or want to be doing?

3   Imagine the dream is a play being acted out and you can rewrite any section of it. Which bits would you re-script and why? With regard to what you are doing, how would you replay the action of the dream differently?

4   Is there anything in the dream that remains unfinished or that you would like to know more about? Is there anything in the dream that brings up conflicts that you feel have not been dealt with in the dream?

5   How do your actions (and those of anyone else in the dream) parallel your actions in daily life? How far are they similar and how far are they different? If they are different, can you think of any reasons why this might be so?

6   If this dream were a film or play, what sort of film or play would it suggest to you? For instance, would it be a romance, a thriller, a comedy, a farce or an adventure story? How does this correspond with daily life? How is it different?

7   If this dream were an educational device for relationship training, what message would it be teaching? What are you learning from the dream? Does it provide any useful insights into the relationship?

8   How will you apply these insights from the dream to your everyday life? What will you do with the information you have gained from the dream?

**ABOVE** The relationships we have with peers are often some of the most formative and influential of our lives.
**LEFT** Once we become parents our emotional lives take on a whole new depth. This could well be reflected in our dreams.
**BELOW** Close friendships can be sustaining and supportive, but can also create angst and turmoil in our lives. Examine your dreams for clues to how you really feel about those who are closest to you.

# PART TWO

# THE DREAM LEXICON

There is nothing in our dreams that we cannot conceive of, or even that we haven't already experienced in some form or another. Our dream images and feelings are generated by our unconscious, for our own benefit. In our dreams, our unconscious talks to us directly, one to one. We are the dreamer and the dream – the playwright, director, actors and audience, rolled into one.

The lexicon that follows is different from a traditional dream dictionary in which individual elements are listed alphabetically with a set meaning attributed to each. Rather, it aims to provide a vocabulary that will enable you, the dreamer, to start interpreting the key symbols and metaphors of your dreams in a way that makes sense to you. To tease out the meaning of your dreams, you need to understand the simple relationship between the feelings and issues your unconscious is working with, and what is being shown to you symbolically. We know better than anyone else what our own dreams mean, and how to respond to the subtle nuances and quirky associations that our dreams carry.

# ABSTRACT QUALITIES

The properties of the countless people, objects and ideas that we encounter in our dreams can be highly significant when we are trying to work out what our dreams mean. We may focus on particular qualities because they are so dominant, or because they are distorted or unusual. Abstract concepts such as time and space, power or number, may hold a particular relevance in your dream, either pointing to a literal preoccupation or working symbolically.

When properties that we would take for granted are changed it is almost certainly significant. To work with these elements you need to note what it is that has changed and consider the qualities and meaning of that object as it is in real life as well as how it is in your dream. Occasionally in our dreams abstract concepts are so important that we divest them of all associations, then we can focus on the feelings that such dreams generate.

# Science and Numbers

ABSTRACT QUALITIES

Sometimes the universe appears orderly and rational, and at other times it seems random and chaotic. In dreams of science or ones in which numbers seem particularly significant, we are trying to resolve these contradictions and make sense of the world around us; we want to impose our own sense of rationality and control over our lives. Science gives us a measure of control over the universe and stops us feeling quite so small or powerless. Together with numbers it puts us on a par with the gods, and can give us a feeling of control and powerfulness, which can be reflected in our dreams.

### A SCIENTIFIC APPROACH

The discipline and rationality of science makes it a strongly intellectual activity, as we push back the boundaries of knowledge with little regard for emotional or intuitive responses. Because science is much esteemed in our society, we may seek shelter behind its authority to avoid facing our emotions or dealing with irrationality. On the other hand, the strict scientific approach to understanding may seem unnecessarily restrictive to more expressive people.

In dreams that involve science it might well also be that we are abdicating responsibility for working out what makes the universe tick. We may not believe in a divine force so we hold fast to the idea that science will work it out for us.

### CALCULATIONS

Numbers provide a way of quantifying aspects of our world, and we may dream of them to give us a sense of control, rationality and certainty if these are lacking in our lives. We use them in calculations, so working with figures may indicate that you are trying to take a methodical and "calculating" approach to a situation, rather than following your heart or your intuition.

### NUMBERS AS SYMBOLS

Some numbers also have specific symbolic values based on cultural associations. We internalize these values and associations to some extent and may employ them in our dreams. The idea that numbers have mysterious powers has been explored in cultures around the world for millennia. In the West, numerology, as this theory is called, not only assigns particular numbers meanings but also associates them with colours and sound frequencies. If you are familiar with numerology, then such associations may reinforce the significance of the numbers, but you need to establish whether this feels true for you. Some of the values of the numbers in numerology have found their way into our cultural symbolic vocabulary and will probably seem obvious, such as One representing individualism or Two partnership, though others may not resonate particularly strongly for you.

Like all dream elements, numbers can have a personal significance as well as, in some cases, having gained symbolic value in the context of particular cultures. So for a devout Christian, Three could suggest the Holy Trinity; a musician may see it as the foundation chord of the scale, while for another

**BELOW** As children we play games with numbers. They are a part of our life from early on.
**BELOW RIGHT** Like all dream subjects, numbers have a personal aspect – what they signify can only mean something to us individually.

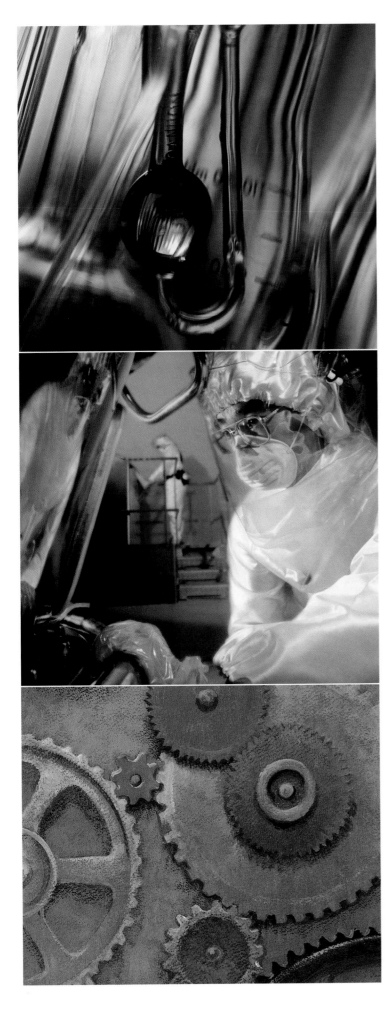

**LEFT** If we don't understand scientific principles, our dream symbols may present science in a negative, perhaps even intimidating, light. **MIDDLE LEFT** Doctors are part of the terrifying science dream symbolism and can appear or be used as distorted dream codes. **BOTTOM LEFT** We may use low-tech imagery such as cogs to represent time and science in our dreams.

person it may bring up the concept of the family trio of father, mother and child. Children often have strong emotional relationships to certain numbers, such as lucky Seven; a triple Six in the Christian tradition is the number of the Devil, while Thirteen has, over the centuries, come to represent bad luck so strongly that even in our modern, rational society there are streets with no house of that number. Even if you are not superstitious, the fact that these associations exist in our society is often borrowed by our mind to suggest something to us. If you relate to a given meaning on a deep and instinctive level then it is significant to you.

## NUMEROLOGY

The study of the symbolic value of numbers provides a way of understanding life by studying and exploring their esoteric significance as symbols of the energy of the universe. Numerology readings use numbers that are derived from your birth date and from the letters of your name, these numbers then provide understanding of personal traits that affect how you approach life. Sometimes the system of numerology is used for prophecy.

### NUMBER POWER

These are some of the basic characteristics that are assigned to each of the numbers One to Nine in numerology:

**1** unity, creation, independence, assertiveness, the self

**2** duality, emergence, compromise, discourse

**3** power, generative force, creative self-expression

**4** solidity, dullness, persistence, determination

**5** sensuality, pleasure, gregariousness

**6** perfection, harmony, balance, domesticity

**7** mysticism, psychic powers, magic

**8** materialism, success, justice, ambition

**9** spirituality, mental achievement, wisdom

# CAUSE AND EFFECT

FOR CENTURIES, PHILOSOPHERS, SCIENTISTS AND THEOLOGIANS HAVE GRAPPLED WITH QUESTIONS OF THE ORIGINS OF THE UNIVERSE, AND OF HUMANKIND'S PLACE WITHIN IT. THIS IS THE ULTIMATE QUESTION OF CAUSE AND EFFECT — THE EFFECT IS ALL TOO VISIBLE, BUT THE CAUSE STILL A MATTER OF GREAT DEBATE. ON A MUCH SMALLER SCALE, IN OUR EVERYDAY LIVES, WE ARE FACED WITH CAUSALITY ALL THE TIME — OUR ACTIONS HAVE CONSEQUENCES, WHICH IN TURN HAVE A KNOCK-ON EFFECT, AND WE ARE OFTEN AWARE THAT OUR LIVES HAVE TAKEN A DRAMATIC TURN BECAUSE OF WHAT SEEMED AT THE TIME LIKE AN INSIGNIFICANT OR UNRELATED EVENT.

## OUR ORIGINS

Creation myths and theories are part of every human culture. The Big Bang Theory, the Book of Genesis, the Egyptian and classical legends, the Buddhists' Seven Ages of the Universe – all attempt to address the big questions about existence, and all have entirely different starting points and conclusions in looking at the concept of our origins. Some people have a burning need to know how everything came into being and what was behind it. They may use dream time to look for the answers that will enable them to make their own sense of the universe, to formulate and test their belief systems, and to begin to conceptualize the primary force behind our creation. In fact these dreams may be an important way of revealing to us an underlying dissatisfaction with our beliefs, and a dislike of being adrift in uncertainty.

## THE RHYTHMS OF THE UNIVERSE

Causation is seen in the constant interplay of the forces of the universe, and all its physical routines – the sun rising and setting, the path of the stars through the night sky, the seasons, nature, beginnings and endings, life and death, birth and growth. Dreams that tackle such fundamental questions as why we are here, where we are going and what we want from life, cause us to sit up and take notice, change direction, even change our lives.

## THE FOUR SEASONS

The seasons of the year are a very potent symbol of change and the natural order of things. We use the cycle of spring, summer, autumn and winter as metaphors for the stages of our own life, and we also measure the years by the

**BELOW AND BELOW RIGHT**
How we came into being is a question that has been addressed through human history, from the creation myths of ancient Egypt (below left) to the Islamic prophets of the Middle Ages (below right). We still don't have all the answers, and our dreams will reflect this.

**ABOVE** Dreams of spring may symbolize new beginnings.
**ABOVE RIGHT** Summer dreams are often about enjoyment, relaxation, pleasure, warmth and love.

**ABOVE** Winter dreams may be about closing down, culmination, a decrease of desire and hope, endings and conclusions.
**ABOVE LEFT** Dreams of autumn may symbolize enrichment, fulfilment, bounty, harvest, and mellow fruitfulness.

turning of the seasons. The significance of nature in our dreams may reflect our feelings of being divorced from nature. Perhaps we live in cities and feel that we are unable to connect with the seasons visually and emotionally, but they still affect us on a very deep level, and if we don't acknowledge this it may surface in our dreams.

## EVENTS IN OUR LIVES

We ourselves are agents of change. Everything we say and think and do has an effect on our own lives and on those of others, and sometimes these effects are brought forcefully to our attention. You forget something at home and go back to get it, only to hear on the news that that brief delay meant that you narrowly avoided being involved in a car pile-up. You have a conversation with a friend about your hopes and frustrations with work, and they put you in touch with someone who can make your dream of running your own business a reality.

Awake or asleep, we may turn over in our minds questions of why things happened the way they did, and what might have been if we had done something differently.

Whether you regard these little triggers as chance or fate or part of some greater plan, they all have consequences great and small, and you may turn them over in your mind again and again. If these consequences are negative, you may be plagued by regret or guilt, and these feelings are likely to be played out in dreams by your unconscious mind. You may be trying to work through the events, to find a way to absolve your guilt, to discover that the events were not after all your fault, or wishing that things had happened a different way.

I shall be telling this with a sigh
Somewhere ages and ages hence:
Two roads diverged in a wood, and I –
I took the one less travelled by,
And that has made all the difference.

ROBERT FROST, *THE ROAD NOT TAKEN*

## LIFE-CHANGING DREAM

In my dream I was going to work. I was almost there when the lorry in front of me suddenly slowed to turn, and I sensed that I was going to have an accident. As I powered up the bike and overtook it, I congratulated myself on avoiding a crash. Then another lorry pulled out of a side road and I went straight into it. I could see my motorbike turning over and over in the air in slow motion. I was badly injured.

I was also badly shaken when I woke up, and as a result I gave up that job – I couldn't travel that road any more and my life changed direction completely.

# Strength and Weakness

In our competitive world, it is not surprising that dreams of strength and weakness trouble our sleep at times. Such dreams may take the form of conventional symbolism — the strength of a lion, a wrestler, iron chains or an electric storm, or the weakness and frailty of a tiny creature, an old or disabled person, a delicate spider's web. Or they may highlight your own personal strengths and weaknesses, either literal or metaphoric. What we think of as strength in our waking life may manifest completely differently in our dreams and we may be surprised by our own symbolism.

### COSMIC STRENGTH

The universe is immense, powerful and strong, and by comparison, we humans are almost absurdly tiny, vulnerable and weak. Cosmic dreams about strength underline the fact of this terrible fragility, as our unconscious tries to come to terms with the size, power, age and complexity of the universe.

We know where we begin and end as individuals, but any similar quantification of the universe is impossible. We know that we will die at some point in time, and that when we do so this immeasurable and intricate universe will continue in all its glory without a second thought.

Our passing and fleeting presence will leave not a trace in any way.

### SECURITY

Dreams about strength may be our way of investigating how safe we feel in our waking life. They may be our unconscious mind's way of getting us to do something about feeling insecure. If we live in a dangerous neighbourhood we are likely to have a constant background preoccupation with safety issues and a fear of being threatened unexpectedly; to address this our best course of action could be to learn assertiveness or how to be physically stronger, to build safe zones where we can let down our

guard, or to be more cautious about entering dangerous circumstances or places.

The insecurity that troubles us may be of a more personal nature – in our relationships rather than in the sense of our physical wellbeing – so we should look at why these relationships make us feel that way. Our dream might also be the start of a search for a guardian angel of some kind who will protect us from being overwhelmed by the strength and size of the universe.

### WEAKNESS

A dream of strength could be nature's way of drawing our attention to some aspect of our

**BELOW LEFT** Rather than the obvious images of power or strength, images of gentleness, such as a tiny baby, may be used as a symbol for true strength.
**BELOW RIGHT** In our dreams, conventional metaphors for strength may appear as clear or distorted images.

defencelessness and vulnerability. If we feel threatened by stronger forces then it makes sense to seek ways of becoming stronger so we are better able to fight off the threat, or of compensating in some other way if this is not possible. The dream is flagging up the fact that we feel weak or frail or naked and we are being urged to do something about that. Where the threat comes from in our waking life is up to us to determine. It might be that we need to find a way of coming to terms with the imponderables of an immense and powerful universe, or it might be more mundane issues, such as our work or our relationships, that are threatening to overwhelm us. Either way, if we feel threatened by strength in a dream then it is likely that there is something that is making us feel threatened or vulnerable in our waking life.

## PERSONAL STRENGTHS AND WEAKNESSES

It is probably physical prowess that first springs to mind when you think of strength, but just as important is the personal strength that we draw from being centred and knowing who we are. It may be that we express that centredness symbolically in an image of physical strength. We also describe as strengths and weaknesses the things that we do well or the things that we are not good at. And having a weakness for something means that we like it or are drawn to it so much that we cannot refuse it; although, say, having a weakness for chocolate may seem trivial, it could be a

**RIGHT** Powerful architectural forms may be used as symbols for strength in our dreams.
**MIDDLE RIGHT** An awareness of our mental strengths or fragilities may become apparent in our dreams and can cause worry.
**BOTTOM RIGHT** We may use immense symbols such as the power and strength of the entire universe to bring home a simple truth such as an acknowledgement that we are being used or abused in some way.

signpost to some other area of your life where you lack control. It is worth bearing all possibilities in mind when you are trying to understand your dream, as your mind may be using apparently frivolous concepts as a springboard for exploring more serious issues. How power manifests in our dreams can be a reflection on how secure we feel.

### A COSMIC DREAM

"I was alone in the vastness of space but I could feel the sheer size and strength of the universe closing in on me. Everything was black and I couldn't see what forces were pressing against me – it seemed as though it was the very walls of the universe that were crushing me out of existence. I couldn't fight against this sort of strength.

The dream was really quite terrifying, and I woke up feeling small and helpless. It made me realize that I was letting a lot of people walk all over me and needed to be much more assertive, to learn to say 'no' more often, especially at work."

# POWER DREAMS

POWER APPEARS IN MANY GUISES – FROM THE OBVIOUS FORMS AND TRAPPINGS OF POLITICAL OR MILITARY POWER AND WEALTH, TO PHYSICAL DOMINATION, OPPRESSION, VICTIMIZATION OR BULLYING, THE AUTHORITY OF AGE OR WISDOM, OR THE PERSONAL POWER OF A TRULY CENTRED INDIVIDUAL. POWER EXERTED OVER US CAN BE A SOURCE OF INSPIRATION, RESPECT, STIMULATION, ENCOURAGEMENT, DEFERENCE AND SAFETY. ON THE OTHER HAND IT CAN PROVOKE FEAR AND HOSTILITY. HOW WE FEEL ABOUT POWER AND INFLUENCE IN REAL LIFE WILL AFFECT HOW WE DREAM OF THEM. DOES POWER EXCITE OR DISMAY YOU? DO YOU FEEL INVIGORATED BY IT OR STIFLED?

**BELOW** A dream that involves a king figure, or even a godly one may well be a reflection of a feeling you have in your waking life that you are being dominated or controlled in some way.

Power can manifest itself on a cosmic level – divine, celestial, universal, collective – and also as an attribute of an individual or organization. Dreams in which power is a dominant theme tend to be unambiguous. We are likely to respond strongly to them and to remember them because of this. In them we may be enslaved or motivated; we may even be the source of the power itself.

Our society is highly stratified, and power in a social and political sense is an inevitable part of our lives. Monarchs and presidents wield it over their citizens, bosses over employees, parents over their children. Many people are preoccupied with power, seeking it, being dissatisfied with a lack of it, feeling the effects of the power that others wield. So it is not surprising that images of power crop up in dreams quite often. We may have power thrust upon us, such as when we are promoted to a position of responsibility, and be unsure of how to handle it or of how others will react. We may have bullied

someone and now be feeling guilty. If we pay attention to how power manifests in our dreams and how we respond to it, we may learn about how to deal with the real-life situation that is preoccupying us.

## NUCLEAR POWER

We have all grown up in the nuclear age, in which the possibility of being wiped out by nuclear weapons or by an accident at a nuclear power plant has seemed very real. Such power is immense, and used properly, it can enhance the quality of our lives, but if anything goes wrong, and the containment of this power fails or is breached,

---

### A DREAM OF GOD

"In my dream, God was sitting on a vast, unearthly throne. But rather than paying attention to being face to face with God, I was fascinated by the throne. Its construction was really important – it was made of some kind of metal, never seen on earth, which was grey flecked with red, and had a luminous transparency like crystal.

I realised that this throne was where the real power lay: whoever sat on it would become a god, and God Himself had only got his power from having been on it for so long. If anyone else sat there, they too would acquire that sort of power. There was no power in the person, only in the throne – the material trappings of power.

I'm not religious at all so I was quite surprised to have had what seemed at first like a religious dream, but I think it was more about knowing where power lies and how to access it than about the spiritual aspect of God. I'm very concerned with power and authority in my life as I am in the police force. My uniform represents these things, but it doesn't make me feel powerful from within; it also creates a negative reaction in some people, which I don't like."

disaster is virtually inevitable. The dreams of many people are affected by such fears, and they need to come to terms with the feeling of helplessness that this kind of threat generates. Because of the "all-or-nothing" feeling that nuclear war has, we may use it to represent in a more general or metaphoric sense the end of the world as we know it, or some personal calamity.

## THE POWER OF NATURE

Sometimes nature unleashes its power on a spectacular scale: lightening storms, floods, forest fires, hurricanes and avalanches all put us in our place in the universe. We try to minimize the damage done by these phenomena, but ultimately we are powerless. An impending natural disaster in a dream – the moment before a dam bursts or a storm breaks – may show us the potential power that we have in ourselves; how we express it may make the difference between greatness and destruction.

## COMING TO TERMS WITH POWER

In waking life or in our dreams, we might feel drawn irresistibly to some situation or event or person but cannot understand why. The power that draws us may be invisible and subtle but by careful analysis and observation we might begin to understand what is controlling us, and can assess what we are being manipulated or influenced by in our waking life.

By paying attention to power dreams we can literally empower ourselves in real life. Once we have pinpointed and understood the powers that we fear, find attractive or wish to develop in ourselves, then they can be tamed and put to use.

**ABOVE FAR LEFT** When you dream of power is it manifested on an individual basis, with a symbol of social control such as a monarch?
**ABOVE LEFT** Or does your dream of power involve forces such as those in large-scale industry?
**ABOVE** Or is it the power that might be unleashed by politicians and rulers that you fear you are unable to control?

**LEFT** Nature has such awesome power, such highly destructive force, that it may appear in our dreams as a frightening power indeed.

# COLOUR

THE MORE AWARE WE ARE OF COLOURS IN OUR LIVES, THE MORE WE ARE LIKELY TO DREAM IN COLOUR. BUT SOMETIMES IN A DREAM, COLOUR DEMANDS OUR ATTENTION, EITHER BECAUSE IT IS VERY STRONG OR BECAUSE IT IS UNNATURAL IN ITS CONTEXT. IN THIS WAY IT ACQUIRES SYMBOLIC VALUE, AND YOU SHOULD CONSIDER WHAT MEANING IT HAS FOR YOU. DO WE ALL DREAM IN COLOUR ALL OF THE TIME? THIS MAY SEEM IRRELEVANT IF YOU ALWAYS DO BUT WHAT IF YOU DREAM IN BLACK AND WHITE? HAVE YOU EVER HAD A DREAM THAT IS IN JUST ONE COLOUR? WHAT DO THE COLOURS WE SEE IN OUR DREAMS MEAN? ARE THEY REFLECTIONS OF OUR EMOTIONS OR OUR SPIRITUALITY?

Some colours we respond to in a very personal way, but many of the associations we have with particular colours are culturally informed – for example, white is worn by the bride on her wedding day in Western culture, but in the Far East it is the colour traditionally worn at funerals.

## CREATIVE POWER OF COLOUR

We may be surprised by the intensity of colours in our dream, by the inventiveness of our imagination. But everything in our dream expresses ourselves –

what we see is what we are capable of creating. These dreams can awaken in us a sense of our real power, can make us realize how impressive we really are, however much we get bogged down in our day-to-day lives.

## EXPRESSING OUR INNER BEING

A dream that focuses on fantastic colour and form – whirling patterns and shifting shapes – may resemble an "acid trip", or it could be that you are making spiritual contact with your inner self. In a rainbow, all the colours

are present, and are perfectly, naturally in balance. Strongly contrasting colours may signify either clear choices or a dilemma in some area of your life, while colours that merge and blend could signify an inner harmony, or, conversely, a lack of clarity.

Pay special attention if several dreams feature a particular colour, as this could be your unconscious trying to work with a particular issue that you are not addressing effectively in your waking life. Equally, if you stop focusing on this colour in your dreams then it could be that you have worked through something that was on your mind.

## COLOURS BY ASSOCIATION

It is said that the colours we see in our dreams reflect the state of our unconscious mind. So if blue predominates, we may be feeling emotional, while green could suggest an interest in nature or environmental issues. These are only two possible meanings though, and it may be that your mind has randomly drawn on a catchphrase such as "feeling blue" or the Green Party of environmental politics. In the same way, blue has even been suggested as an indicator of futuristic travel because of the phrase "taking off into the blue".

## COLOUR KEY

These are some associations people commonly have with particular colours. Remember though that your own personal experiences, as well as cultural differences, may mean that they do not always ring true to you – use them as a starting point to prompt your own feelings, rather than as fact.

**Red:** energy, fire, passion, love, sex, anger, danger

**Orange/yellow:** vibrancy, joy, life, sunshine, warmth, spirituality, jealousy

**Green:** calm, nature, illness, envy

**Blue:** peace, emotions, depression, space

**Violet/purple:** grandeur, royalty, rage

**White:** innocence, energy, emptiness, possibility, cleanliness, holiness

**Black:** death, mourning, depression, conformity, secrecy, obscurity

**ABOVE** Nature has her own colour symbolism which may not be for our benefit at all – flowers are coloured for the bees rather than for us.

**ABOVE AND ABOVE RIGHT** Natural colours, such as shades of green, have instant association with growth and renewal. If you dream of green your subconscious could be sending you a message about decisions that need to be made.
**RIGHT** Brightly coloured sweets attract children – do the colours have the same impact on you if you dream about them, or do they seem unpleasantly synthetic and confusing?

**ABOVE** The colour white in Western cultures is synonymous with purity and innocence. Dreaming of white weddings might therefore symbolize this.
**LEFT** Multicoloured objects in dreams may be a way for your mind to link with your emotions.
**BELOW** Perhaps there are no symbolic associations with colours in a dream. Vibrant shades might just be a way of your creative mind expressing itself.

The expression "seeing red", meaning to be angry, may well have come from the red mist you see before your eyes if in a severe rage, but it would be simplistic to say that this necessarily means that a dream involving the colour red always points to anger. Our conscious mind might make these easy associations of anger, violence, passion, fire and energy, but the red in your dream could also be the red of romantic love and passion, or a warning of danger. It could even be a "red herring" – perhaps before bed you saw the word "red", or a film in which colour was used for artistic emphasis. Perhaps you told your child the story of Little Red Riding Hood at bedtime. These triggers may lead your mind to cultural meanings that are commonly ascribed to the colour – the dangerous wolf is attracted by the girl's coat; her red coat may have pointed to the danger she was in.

## DREAM COLOURS

"I was standing on a hilltop, and could see myself from above, turning round and round in slow motion. I was so aware of the vividness of the grass, the sky, my clothes, everything, and the colours were so bright, that I felt I was being told something. I woke up wanting to paint those colours, although I hadn't picked up a brush for years. I took up painting again because of this dream, and I'm so happy just doing it."

# NATURE DREAMS

How we relate to the world around us and how secure we feel about being alive and part of our environment are revealed in dreams of nature. In nature we find the unspoilt, original state of our essential inner being, the truth of who we are as individuals. Landscapes, whether natural or urban, are highly evocative, and set the mood or tone of the dream. Together with the weather, they suggest the atmosphere and underlying impression of your dream, and give clues to your frame of mind, your disposition, your emotional states. The four elements, fire, earth, air and water, work as basic symbols for some key abstract concepts – principally passion, practicality, communication and ideas, and emotions. Animals and plants reveal some of our most primitive, instinctive feelings and fears, which arise from the deepest levels of our unconscious, and from the thoughts and understandings of the world that we formed during the years of our childhood.

# THE WEATHER

LIKE LANDSCAPES, THE WEATHER COLOURS OUR DREAMS EMOTIONALLY, GIVING BROAD CLUES TO HOW WE FEEL ABOUT OUR LIVES, AND WHAT SORT OF GENERAL MOOD WE ARE EXPERIENCING IN OUR EVERYDAY WAKING LIVES. WE GENERATE THE WEATHER IN OUR DREAMS AS A WAY OF EXPRESSING OUR FEELINGS. BECAUSE WHEN WE ARE AWAKE OUR MOODS CAN BE STRONGLY AFFECTED BY THE WEATHER AND THE SEASON, AND AS THERE ARE MANY WORDS THAT WE USE INTERCHANGEABLY TO DESCRIBE BOTH THE WEATHER AND OUR MOODS AND FEELINGS (STORMY, GLOOMY, SUNNY, HAZY, TO NAME JUST A FEW), THESE ARE RELATIVELY EASY SYMBOLS TO START WITH WHEN TRYING TO MAKE SENSE OF OUR DREAMS.

**ABOVE** Rain may symbolize our problems and worries raining down on us – or it might just be raining in our dream.
**ABOVE RIGHT** In your dream you may be relaxing, taking time out to enjoy the sunshine. Enjoy this dream holiday.

### FAIR OR FOUL?

Moods fluctuate, sometimes unpredictably, in much the same way as the weather. Usually the weather in a dream is congruent with how you are feeling, so calm, sunny weather could indicate a peaceful or happy disposition, while a storm could be expressing anger.

But it is worth taking a closer look at weather that seems to be at odds with your mood. You might be raging in your dream but if the background weather is calm and pleasant you can be fairly certain that your rage will soon pass. On the other hand, if you are being serene and reasonable in your dream but storm clouds are gathering and the temperature dropping, this could be a sign that you need to focus your attention on feelings that are being repressed.

### RAIN AND SNOW

As water is widely considered to be a symbol for emotions, rain and tears alike are richly evocative of your emotional state. Grey skies and rain clouds cast a gloomy shadow over your spirit, and could indicate that your unconscious is trying to work with feelings of depression or despondency. You may express your tears as rain – the gentle summer rain that clears the air and feels good, the light drizzle of a spring day, or the deluge of the storm. The rain can be cold and invigorating, or warm and welcoming, and an unexpected shower of rain could mean that you feel your enthusiasm or interest have suddenly been dampened. Any kind of rain can also have a cleansing and rejuvenating effect. Snow can be seen as rain in crystalline form. It

**ABOVE** Water represents emotions and rain is often linked to tears – if you dream of rain, is there someone you are crying for? If it is a natural expression of grief or tension then you might find a dream of rain is as beneficial as a good cry.

provides another way of expressing emotions, colder and clearer, but also often softer and gentler, and it dramatically changes the appearance of the landscape. It can mean the fun of playtime, but it can also be threatening – blizzards and avalanches show the emotions becoming overwhelming and out of control.

### STORMS

In the build-up to a storm, a hush descends on nature along with a feeling of anticipation of the power to be unleashed when the storm breaks. Dark, heavy clouds can be oppressive and threatening, and people who bottle up their emotions will recognize in the calm before the storm the moments before an emotional outburst.

Torrents of rain, dark, heavy clouds, and rumbles or claps of deep thunder all express the charged emotional content of the dream, whether anger or passion or outrage. Because storms can be dramatic, attention-grabbing events, they are likely to be central to the plot of the dream. Having a stormy dream gives you a safe opportunity to play out powerful emotions that may be too difficult or too dangerous to express in real life. Lightning gives dramatic moments of clarity as it illuminates the landscape. The passing of a storm parallels the end of an emotional outburst – you may feel relieved and invigorated by having put out your feelings, or you may be surveying the damage caused.

## MIST AND FOG

By contrast, dreaming of mist and fog, drizzle and gloom, all of which obscure the landscape, may suggest that you are unsure of how you feel about something. Pay particular attention to what you do in your dream to clear the air, to see the way forward, as this may give you clues to what you can do in your waking life to resolve a confusing issue. Weather that obscures things can also be hinting that you are in a state of denial about something, and you may need to ask yourself what it is you are not acknowledging.

**RIGHT** The seasons have their own rhythms which figure largely in our life. Do dark clouds in your dreams presage the coming of winter, or a storm? Does this resonate in your waking life?
**MIDDLE RIGHT** Nature is a powerful symbol, and a dream of sunshine is likely to hold pleasant connotations. It could also be a nostalgia for a lost golden age.
**BOTTOM RIGHT** Dreaming of a blanket of snow may symbolize a deadening effect in our waking life – all is cold and forgotten.

## THE SEASONS AND THEIR RHYTHMS

The rhythms of nature can be seen in the cycle of the seasons. As the year progresses and the seasons change, the days lengthen and shorten, the weather and the landscape changes, and plants grow, wither and die. These patterns can also have a profound effect on our outlook, behaviour, and lifestyles. The sequence of the seasons can also symbolize the progression from birth to death and the experiences that we have at different times of our lives.

---

### SEASONAL SYMBOLISM

**Spring** – birth and childhood, a time of innocence, growth, bursting forth, warming and reviving, love and romance
**Summer** – youth, vigour, warmth or heat (either giving or sapping energy), abundance, lushness, growth, happiness
**Autumn** – maturity, ageing, rich colours and experience, closing in, settling down, preparing for death, reflection
**Winter** – old age and death, barrenness, lack of colour, darkness, stillness, isolation, dryness and brittleness, loss.

---

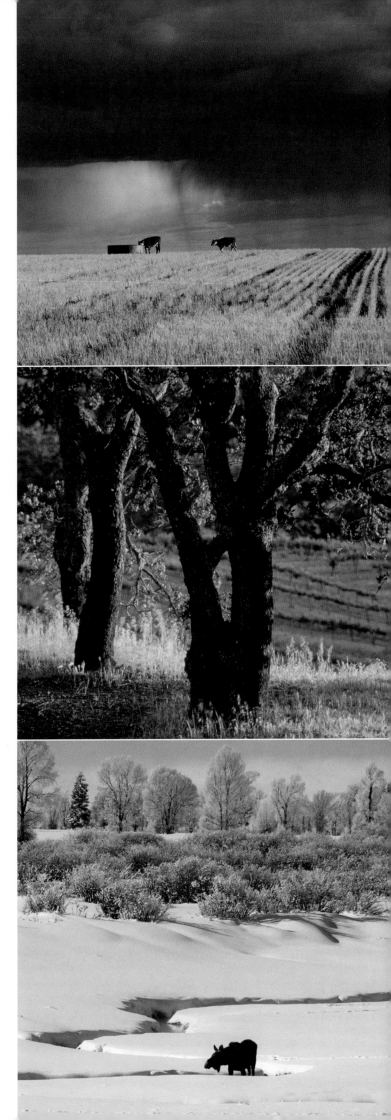

# THE ELEMENTS – FIRE

THE CLASSIC SYMBOL OF PASSION AND VITALITY. FIRE IN A DREAM CAN TAKE MANY FORMS. IT CAN BE THE RAGING BLAZE OF A FOREST FIRE, THE TINY FLAME OF A CANDLE, THE HEAT OF THE MIDDAY SUN IN AFRICA, A ROARING FURNACE OR BONFIRE, AN OPEN LOG FIRE – EVEN A MATCH OR THE GLOWING END OF A LIT CIGARETTE. FIRE IS THE ELEMENT ASSOCIATED WITH OUR NERVOUS SYSTEM AND WITH MOVEMENT. IT IS OUR ENERGY, WHETHER PHYSICAL, EMOTIONAL, CREATIVE OR INTELLECTUAL. WHAT IS BEING BURNT, HOW IT IS BURNING, AND WHETHER IT IS A PRINCIPAL ASPECT OF THE DREAM OR MERELY BACKGROUND ILLUMINATION ALL AFFECT THE MEANING OF THIS SYMBOL.

NATURE DREAMS

### SHAPES AND FORMS

Many things can produce a flame in our dream. An open log fire may represent romance and intimacy, or it could invoke feelings of comfort, of the warmth and cosiness of long, leisurely winter evenings, a warm haven protected from the cold outdoors. As a symbol of relationships, it can imply the security of a steady, warm love rather than an exciting and unpredictable new passion.

A bonfire, on the other hand, is usually livelier, more convivial and demonstrative. Bonfires are often celebratory events, and mark the purging of dead matter, of the accumulation of clutter in our lives. The ashy remains of an extinguished fire mark the end of a period of energetic activity, or of a passionate relationship.

### CONTROL

Fire is a difficult element, dangerous and unpredictable. How much control you have over the fire may suggest the amount of control you have over a volatile situation or relationship in your waking life. A fire that is out of control may be pointing to a lack of constraint, or to fears about a fraught situation in your life becoming overwhelming or having devastating consequences. Tending a fire may show how we keep control over things, but it could also suggest an urge to interfere with a natural process.

Various agents may have an influence on the meaning of fire. Water quenching the flames or air being blown in to cause an inferno can change how the fire burns and the effects that it has, and so alter its symbolic value.

### DESTRUCTION

Fire can often be seen as a destructive and irredeemable force; burning away or acting as a ritualized ending of some aspect or phase of your life. In its positive aspect, it purges, cleanses and purifies.

Whether what is being burned is valued or something you would like to get rid of is central to whether this is a traumatic destruction or one that gives a sense of relief and release. Your response to seeing someone burning books on an open bonfire, for instance, would say a lot about the nature of how you view learning, literature, culture, freedom of speech and so on. Many people prize books, holding them as a valuable source of information, inspiration and entertainment, and would be horrified by such destruction, but a person who cannot read may see this as a liberating dream. The destruction need not be dramatic, though – even blowing out a candle can symbolize the extinguishing of something.

### ILLUMINATION

Fire also brings light and hope, dispelling darkness and revealing aspects of your life that need uncovering, bringing them to light. The steady flame of the candle gives constant

**BELOW** Fire is a difficult element – dangerous and unpredictable. How much control we have over it in our dream may indicate how much control we feel we have in life.
**BELOW RIGHT** Looking at what is burning in our fire dreams may indicate what our fears are in waking life.

illumination but little warmth, while a bonfire flares up and burns fiercely, casting great dancing shadows, then dies down again when its flames are spent. How it burns and how much attention you give it can tell you about areas of your relationships that you may need to work on.

## CREATIVITY

The fire in a kiln or furnace or forge is immensely hot, and yet it is contained and controlled, and we put it to use to create things, both functional and aesthetic, that enhance our lives. We also use fire to prepare food. In these senses we can understand it as an expression of our creativity and productivity. By adding fuel to a fire we are giving our creativity greater expression.

## SMOKE

A by-product of fire, smoke can be toxic or suffocating, making you ill or unable to breathe, and polluting the environment. As such it could be trying to bring to your attention the need to escape from a suffocating or unhealthy relationship before it destroys you. If there is a lot of smoke you may have difficulty seeing your way forward.

In a positive sense though, smoke signals could be giving you a message, showing you where the fire can be found or warning you away from it, and the smell of a fire or incense can bring good associations or be used deliberately to enhance your mood and bring about a feeling of stillness.

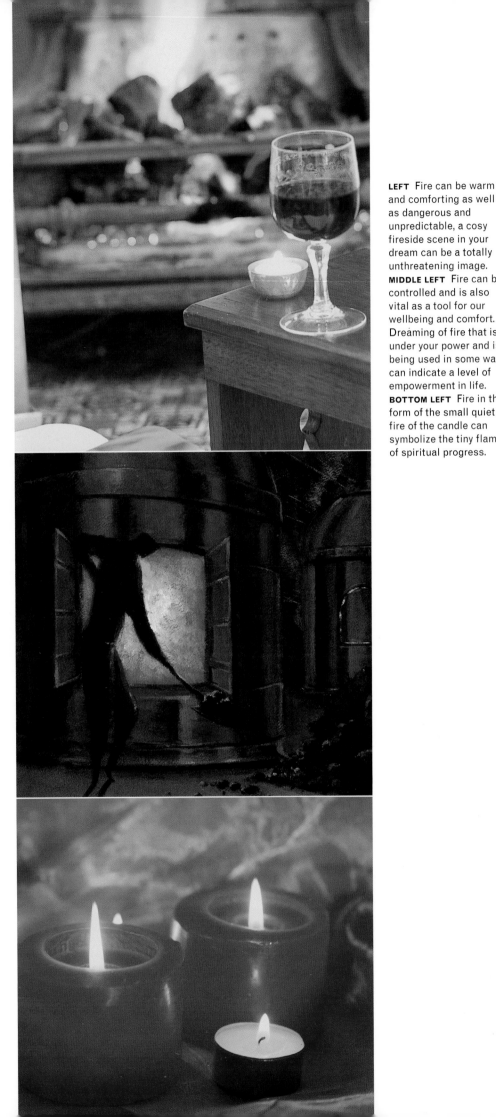

**LEFT** Fire can be warm and comforting as well as dangerous and unpredictable, a cosy fireside scene in your dream can be a totally unthreatening image.
**MIDDLE LEFT** Fire can be controlled and is also vital as a tool for our wellbeing and comfort. Dreaming of fire that is under your power and is being used in some way can indicate a level of empowerment in life.
**BOTTOM LEFT** Fire in the form of the small quiet fire of the candle can symbolize the tiny flame of spiritual progress.

# THE ELEMENTS – AIR

AIR IS THE VERY BREATH OF LIFE: WITHOUT IT WE SUFFOCATE AND DIE. IT HAS NO FORM, SUBSTANCE, SHAPE OR TEXTURE AND YET IT SURROUNDS US, REPRESENTING FREEDOM AND SPACE AND OPENNESS, BOTH IN A LITERAL WAY AND IN THE SENSE OF FREE AND OPEN COMMUNICATION. IT FILLS OUR LUNGS, GIVING US THE CAPACITY TO BREATHE, SPEAK, SING AND SHOUT – TO EXPRESS OUR EMOTIONS. AS ONE OF THE FOUR ELEMENTS, IT RELATES TO THE MIND AND THE INTELLECT, THE GENERATION AND COMMUNICATION OF IDEAS. WE CAN'T SEE AIR OR WIND, BUT WE CAN FEEL AND SEE ITS EFFECTS – DRIFTS OF SMOKE, LEAVES STIRRING, TREES BENT IN A GALE, CLOUDS SCUDDING BY OVERHEAD, BUBBLES IN WATER.

**ABOVE** We might not be able to see the air but we can see the creatures that use it and fly in it. If we dream of them, perhaps we are envying their soaring energy and freedom.

The current of air, whether it is a breeze or hurricane, is a vehicle for self-expression – like the air, our thoughts and emotions too are invisible but their effect is all too apparent at times. Smells are carried on the air, providing information about our environment and often generating an instant emotional response in us.

We should also look at how Air works in conjunction with the other three elements. Without air the fire cannot burn. Earth, water and air, together with the sun's warmth and light, bring forth plants that sustain all living creatures on our planet.

## THE INTELLECT

Traditionally, the element of Air symbolizes the intellect and our powers of communication. How clear the air is in our dream may show how clearly we are giving and receiving visual information and sounds. "Hot air" is a term meaning excessive verbiage, and we could see this as intellectual clutter. The mind does pick up puns, so dreams of hot air

**ABOVE** We can now use the air for recreational sports and doing so in our dreams could make us feel liberated and free. A dream of flying might mean we yearn for space and freedom.

ballooning, for instance, or jets of hot air, could well suggest communication overload to you – not surprising in this information age.

## WIND

Air is often manifest as wind, and in our dream we should look at what effect it is having, what role it is playing. Is it sustaining and helping us, like a cool breeze on a hot day? Do we work with it – flying, soaring or being borne aloft by it – or is it a powerful and harmful force, like the strong winds of a storm that blow us flat and bring destruction in their wake? As a symbol of intellectual and emotional direction and force, the wind in your dream is an outward manifestation of your internal life.

## SUFFOCATION

The lack of air is usually more noticeable than its presence, and suffocation is an important dream theme. Suffocating, feeling short of breath, or even being in a stuffy room may show that our emotional and spiritual expression is being stifled, or that our intellect is not being exercised sufficiently. Likewise, if we are ourselves choking someone or something, this may be pointing to unconscious guilt at choking the life out of a relationship, not allowing another person enough space and freedom, not saying what we want to say or not giving the other an opportunity to speak and be heard.

## OBSCURITY

Smoke, haze or mist all obscure the view, suggesting a lack of clarity in your thinking, or being unable to see your way forward. Equally, debris flying through the air could indicate distractions, a whirl of ideas, or being caught up with other people's ideas.

## HOLY BREATH

As we breathe we feel the air entering and leaving our body. The Hindus talk of *prana* – holy breath, cosmic spirit. The same is true of the Taoists of China who speak of *ch'i* – again a cosmic spirit or energy that flows like air – and feng shui – literally "wind and water", the two cosmic forces that shape the landscape in which we live and bring us health and life. In the Bible, the Holy Spirit is said to manifest in several forms, including as a wind and a flame.

### AN AIR DREAM

"I was standing on a high hill with the wind blowing all around me. Then suddenly I was being shot upwards at tremendous speed through a plastic tube on a column of air. In a flash the hill was far below me, getting smaller and smaller, more and more distant. I was aware of how important the air was. It was holding me, shooting me upwards. Without it I would fall back to the earth again and be killed.

As I realized I was reaching the top of the column I woke up and remember feeling incredibly grateful for the dream, and that I had to learn to breathe more deeply, to feel more alive."

**BELOW** Wind can be frightening and destructive as well as dangerous, and our dreams can reflect our fears of the untameable, wild and erratic manifestation of air.

**BELOW LEFT** The wind blowing through grasses is an evocative image. Are you dreaming of bending to forces that you find irresistible?
**BELOW** Smoke rising in misty swirls can be linked with holy breath, our spirit selves.

# THE PLANT KINGDOM

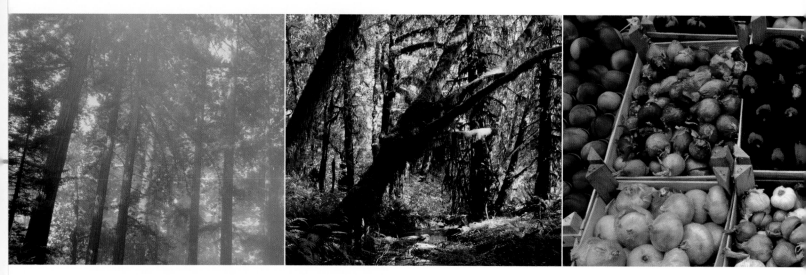

**ABOVE** Trees have always had the power to move us, fill us with wonder and awe.
**ABOVE RIGHT** Trees symbolize the power of nature and growth.

WITH ROOTS THAT SPREAD THROUGH THE DARK, FERTILE EARTH, AND LEAVES AND BRANCHES REACHING TO THE SKY FOR LIGHT AND WARMTH, PLANTS ARE PERFECT SYMBOLS OF THE RICH WORKINGS OF THE HUMAN MIND. LIKE THE UNCONSCIOUS, A PLANT'S ROOTS ARE DARK AND HIDDEN FROM VIEW, YET CAN STILL BE NURTURED WITH WATER AND FOOD, AND CAN PRODUCE A HEALTHY PLANT ABOVE GROUND. BRANCHES, LEAVES AND FLOWERS ARE THE VISIBLE MANIFESTATIONS OF OUR MINDS, AND TELL US ABOUT OUR MENTAL AND EMOTIONAL HEALTH.

**LEFT** The tree as a symbol of life, with its head in the sky and its roots buried in the earth, is deeply buried in our consciousness and permeates most cultures on earth with its resonance.

## TREES

Rooted deep in our unconscious and in the emotional landscape of our dreams, trees are often regarded as symbols of the past – of steady growth, age, experience, time and continuity.

Using this concept, we can see a wood as our family history and forests as the history of our society, culture, or ethnic group. Roots provide wisdom from the collective experience, and how you view trees may indicate how you feel about your own "roots".

Some tree species hold particular symbolic value, and around the world have long been valued as sacred or politically powerful icons. The oak, for instance, is seen as a symbol of longevity, strength, reliability and resilience. Down the ages the willow has had connotations of death or enchantment, and the evergreen holly with its scarlet berries has brought hope and cheer in the dark of winter. In ancient Britain certain trees were chosen as totems or symbols of tribal power – if one tribe ousted another, they uprooted a tree of the vanquished tribe and thrust it upside-down into the ground as a show of dominance. Such symbols may have lost relevance, but they are still embedded in our cultural consciousness and reappear in our dreams.

One of the key visual and conceptual symbols of the Jewish Kabbalah, used to investigate the mysteries of our spiritual life and

ABOVE Harvested food has many symbolic meanings. A cornucopia of produce can mean growth, plenty, vitality and sufficiency.

our relationship with God, is the complex diagram of the Tree of Life. A similar idea is used in the mythology of Native American Indian people, where the tree of life is what links heaven to earth. Shamans use this imagery in their journeys between worlds, and in their interpretation of dreams.

## FLOWERS AND VINES

Associated with pleasure, beauty and relaxation, flowers also denote giving and receiving. Cultivated garden flowers imply order and the application of discipline over creativity, while wild flowers are much more intuitive and express our artistic leanings. Dead flowers may indicate a need to look at underlying unhappiness. Climbing plants may show a need to escape from a situation, or a feeling of entanglement. Some, such as honeysuckle, clematis and vines, are said to represent our ambitions.

## FRUIT AND VEGETABLES

Ripe, juicy, seed-laden fruit is associated with fertility and readiness. Apples have associations of seductiveness because of the biblical temptation in the Garden of Eden, but equally they may symbolize the autumn, or the fruitfulness of our maturing unconscious. Over-ripe fruit may signify a loss of fertility, or a wasted opportunity.

Dreaming of vegetables shows a concern with nourishment, fullness and abundance – or the lack of those qualities if they are dried out or of poor quality. The shape of some vegetables may suggest sexuality, although the context of your dream will tell you whether this is true for you.

## GARDENING

Dreams about gardening may show you how you feel about work and career issues. Work and gardening alike may seem fulfilling or drudgery. We respond to gardens emotionally and the colour they bring into our lives, but weeds can choke out and destroy the life of our garden and distract us from its beauty. They may show that there are problems in our working life that need to be eliminated.

ABOVE If you dream of flowers you should try to remember their setting – are they contained within a controlled garden, or are they growing wild?
ABOVE LEFT What does a garden rose mean to you, natural beauty or excessive cultivation?

---

### GARDEN DREAMS

If you have a gardening dream it is worth looking at what you are doing and how you are doing it, to give you clues to how you approach the practical aspects of your life.

**Digging** Preparing the groundwork

**Weeding and pest control** Removing elements, allowing desirable elements to grow unhindered

**Planting** Nurturing, creating opportunities

**Harvesting** Reaping the benefits

**Grass cutting** Vital maintainance work

# THE CYCLE OF LIFE

No matter who or what we are, we all go through the same cycle of life, from birth through childhood, youth, maturity and old age to death. And no matter how we approach these different stages – whether we enjoy and welcome them or resent and try to avoid them – they are all inevitable, unless we die prematurely. How they appear in our dreams will reflect how enjoyable or difficult we find the whole experience, and dreams about the rites of passage associated with the different stages in the life cycle – about puberty, leaving home, getting married, having children, or retirement, for instance – affect all of us and show how we are in ourselves, whether we feel secure and at ease with where we are in life, or resentful and in denial. Indeed, these dreams are often the way we prepare mentally and emotionally for approaching rites of passage. They may prompt us to ask some of the serious questions about our existence that we may otherwise avoid –about those stages we have yet to go through, and especially about what happens to us when we die.

# DREAMS OF YOUTH

**ABOVE** Dreaming of puberty might mean that we are working through crucial life changes in our dreams.
**ABOVE RIGHT** Adolescent and teenage years can represent rebellion and flux, and if we dream of this stage it may be that in our waking lives we are trying to find the right course of action to take.

YOUTH IS A TIME WHEN WE THROW OFF BOTH THE CONSTRAINTS AND THE INNOCENCE OF CHILDHOOD, TESTING AUTHORITY FIGURES AND TRYING TO FIND OUR OWN WAY IN LIFE. IN OUR TEENAGE YEARS WE EXPERIENCE THE PHYSICAL CHANGES OF PUBERTY, DISCOVER OUR SEXUALITY, HANG OUT IN GANGS, SUFFER FROM INTENSE PEER PRESSURE, AND DISCOVER OUR POWER AS YOUNG ADULTS. BUT OUR OWN EXPERIENCE AS TEENAGERS — GOOD AND BAD — WILL BE REFLECTED IN OUR DREAMS AS MUCH AS THE STEREOTYPES OF THIS LIFE STAGE, SO DREAMS OF YOUTH WILL MEAN VERY DIFFERENT THINGS TO DIFFERENT PEOPLE.

## GROWING PAINS

Many people find adolescence to be a tumultuous and painful period, and some of us carry the scars for the rest of our lives. It is a time of transition from childhood to adulthood, and indeed the key take-home message of dreams about adolescence may well be metamorphosis. At this age we are not yet used to the changes in our bodies, and also often feel awkward and embarrassed at the errors we make in our quest to seem grown-up. To make things worse, we may be teased for the very mistakes we make and the changes we are going through, and withdraw as a result. Dreaming of youth later in life may mean that we are going through changes about which we feel uncertain or unconfident. We may be anticipating criticism or ridicule, or even fear that we will not be taken seriously by society. Even if your dream doesn't actually give you answers or guidance, it should be a useful way of making you aware of how you feel about the changes and what your fears are.

**RIGHT** The desire to be part of the "in-crowd" is probably at its most intense during youth, so if you dream about this it might reflect a feeling you have of being on the edge of things, of being not quite accepted.

## PEER GROUP

At the same time as we begin to rebel against the adult world and leave our childhood ways behind, we turn instead to our peers, with whom we can identify more strongly, for ideas, support and encouragement as much as friendship. Because the peer group becomes so important, many teenagers feel the need to conform – to adopt current fashions, have the latest gear, and even to use the right words, in order to be acceptable. In our youth we are testing out new roles, so there may be a lot of faking involved in our behaviour before we become settled in who we are. For this reason, dreams of adolescence may also be about inauthenticity, about following trends or trying to find a niche within an accepted set.

### EXTREMES AND IDEALS

Because we have so many new experiences as teenagers and young adults, this period of our lives may seem to be one of extremes, especially in our feelings and behaviours. We may be more passionately in love at this time than at any other later time in our lives, or be filled with despair when things don't go our way. It is a time when we are most likely to feel prepared to step into the unknown, travel the world on a shoestring or take up

dangerous sports. This is when we are at our physical peak, and feel able to do all these things because we have a sense of being invincible, immortal. It is also a time of pushing the boundaries – partying all night long, getting very drunk or experimenting with drugs – and exploring social or political ideals. We may still do all these things or have the same feelings later in life, but as a stereotype, we are more likely to associate them with being young, and youth may be the theme of our dream to represent our desire to try new things, to step back from the mundane practicalities of life and remind ourselves of our own ideals.

### LOOKING AHEAD

In our youthful explorations of the big wide world, we are in the process of finding where we belong in society and what we want to do with our lives. We leave school and have to make choices about work or further education, and begin to assert our own personal style and beliefs. While dreams about

youth may be about immaturity in yourself or others, they could also be about discovering and asserting yourself.

### NOSTALGIA

Looking back at our youth, we may feel nostalgic, remembering the freedom, the fun, the passion and excitement, and forgetting the more painful moments. We may even be reconstructing a youth that we never really had, perhaps one that seems more fun and interesting than our own. If we are afraid of growing old, we may be rejecting the stereotypes of middle or old age and clinging to youthfulness, rather than embracing the positive aspects our current stage of life can offer.

**ABOVE** If you dream of a lack of financial freedom in youth perhaps you are admitting to a feeling that this has never really gone away, and that this is materially a real problem for you.
**ABOVE LEFT** The excitement and intensity of your first romance can never be matched. If you dream of young love perhaps it reflects a dissatisfaction with your love life.
**ABOVE FAR LEFT** Dreaming of the wilder side of youth culture might mean that you are yearning for a more exciting element in your life, whatever your age.

### DREAM OF YOUTH

"In my dream I had dyed my hair red and wore a biker's jacket, and I was behaving like a teenager again. Not that I dyed my hair when I was a teenager, but in my dream it made me feel young again. Since I passed forty I've got it into my head that I must be wild, rebellious and wacky to recapture my youth and ward off middle age and all the implications of sedateness that that time of life has. I think I'm also a little jealous of my own teenage children and the fun they seem to have."

# THE MIDDLE YEARS

THE PREOCCUPATIONS OF OUR MIDDLE YEARS TEND TO BE MORE PRAGMATIC THAN THOSE OF OUR ADOLESCENCE — WORK, PARTNERS, CHILDREN AND PROPERTY ARE LIKELY TO DOMINATE OUR THOUGHTS. IT IS ALSO A TIME WHEN WE COME INTO OUR OWN AS ADULTS — BECOMING ESTABLISHED IN VARIOUS WAYS, TAKING ON RESPONSIBILITIES AND MAKING DECISIONS AND JUDGEMENTS BASED ON EXPERIENCE RATHER THAN CONJECTURE. AT THE SAME TIME, WE MAY REGRET THE LOSS OF YOUTHFUL FREEDOM AND STRENGTH OR FEAR THE APPROACH OF OLD AGE. WHATEVER AGE WE ARE THERE WILL BE HAPPIER TIMES, WORSE TIMES, AND WE WILL LOOK BACK WITH REGRET OR FONDNESS. IN OUR DREAMS THIS MAY BE INTENSIFIED.

### THE MATERIAL WORLD

As adults we often define ourselves by the job we have or the work we do, and others also judge us and position us in the social hierarchy accordingly. Our self-esteem may be bolstered or dented by the status of our job, or by not having any work. Changing careers can be a difficult time as we adjust our self-image, perhaps getting used to being on the bottom rung of a different career ladder.

Work also brings money, and with it the many benefits and encumbrances of the material world. In particular, buying our first property is a material milestone, with the implications of commitment to staying put and to being able to finance the purchase for years to come. Living in our own home also gives us the opportunity to express our personal style in the type of home we buy and in how we furnish it.

Our relationship with material things may be an aesthetic statement, and it may be about making life easier or more enjoyable, but it is often also about status and power.

Dreaming of acquiring something may be wish fulfilment around a particular object, or it could be that you want a change of lifestyle which that object represents. If it is higher social standing you are after, this could be related to your sense of self-worth rather than external issues. We also become attached to things and worry about losing them, or about being tied down by our possessions, and this may manifest itself in our dreams.

### SETTLING DOWN

As well as becoming materially established and leaving youth behind, we may start actively looking for a partner, someone with whom we might settle down and perhaps start a family. But while some people feel their lives will be meaningless or unbearably insecure without these things, the idea of "settling down" may fill others with horror and they may prefer the kind of freedom that is only possible without such ties. Such preferences will influence how you read dreams in which these aspects of adulthood are significant. Dreams of 'settling down' may be a form of wish fulfilment, or a way of trying out a different lifestyle. In a less literal sense though, they could indicate a sense of being settled

**BELOW** All of our rites of passage will become food for our dreams but probably none will be more intense than our first real love, as we move in together, set up home and start to plan a family.

in yourself and knowing what you want – even if your lifestyle doesn't seem to reflect this – or a desire for stability.

## MIDDLE AGE

The stereotype of middle age that we may use symbolically in our dreams is likely to be one of settled routine and staidness. However, it can also be a time of great change and readjustment as roles alter, and these aspects may figure in a person's dreams at this time. After years of striving to establish ourselves, we may feel at a loss as to how to proceed once this is achieved. The midlife crisis that many people go through is prompted by the vision of life developing into routine. Dreams can hint at other possibilities or make us aware of exactly what is bothering us about our circumstances.

## EXPERIENCE

Whatever path your life takes, the experience you gain on the way can give you maturity and insight, and it may be this aspect of adulthood that is being reflected in your dreams rather than specific rites of passage.

Although our physical form and strength gradually declines over the years, we may feel increasingly confident in ourselves and in what we do. We may come to have authority and power over others and take on increasing responsibilities. Our dreams can be a useful vehicle for coming to terms with this, and with the relationship they put us in towards others, and how we learn to handle them.

**ABOVE** We put our mark on our home as soon as we move in and we may well dream about it as we adapt to the newness of it all.
**LEFT** Dreaming of moving house might be indicative of some other kind of change in our life that we need to cope with.
**BELOW** Dreams of children could indicate a readiness to take on the major responsibilities of being a parent.

# AGEING

WE ARE GETTING OLDER ALL THE TIME, AND GRADUALLY THE FEAR OF WHAT THIS MEANS FOR US AND OF WHAT COMES NEXT BEGINS TO PERMEATE OUR UNCONSCIOUS AND WORK ON OUR IMAGINATION. WE KNOW OR FEAR THE HORRORS OF THE FIRST GREY HAIRS, OF WRINKLES AND AN EXPANDING WAISTLINE. WE ARE AWARE THAT WE MIGHT BECOME INFIRM OR ILL, OR LOSE OUR MENTAL FACULTIES WHEN WE GROW OLD. BUT THESE FEARS CAN ALSO BE BALANCED BY THE WISDOM THAT A LIFETIME'S EXPERIENCE MAY HAVE BROUGHT US, AND OLD AGE CAN BE A TIME WHEN WE ALLOW OURSELVES TO ATTAIN A LEVEL OF PEACE AND CONTEMPLATION.

We dream of ageing for several reasons. It may be that we are worried about it, about losing our youthful looks and our physical strength and ability. It could also be that we are coming to terms with ageing, content with what we have seen and done so far in our lives and looking forward to the prospect of a comfortable and interesting retirement. A dream of old age may also be a metaphor for times past, and serve as a kind of nostalgia trip.

### FEARS OF AGEING

We all react to the fear of growing old in different ways. We may face up to it, but often this is too painful and we choose instead to deny the unpleasant realities of old age, or to suppress them by ignoring them or laughing them off. We try to reverse the ageing process by going for cosmetic surgery, dyeing our hair, applying anti-ageing creams, and wearing youthful clothes.

Our unconscious is not easily deceived though, and will deal with our fears in our dreams if we don't do so in our waking lives. It knows that we are terrified at the prospect of our lives ending and our bodies decaying, that we are afraid to confront the possibility that when we reach old age and drop the frantic activity of our younger years, we will discover that it has all been meaningless.

Dreams in which we see ourselves getting older, or already old, can be quite shocking, and act as a wake-up call for us to pay more attention to what we are doing with our lives, to make us realise that time is passing. Sometimes these dreams mask a concern about our health, and may be taken as a cautionary note to make sure we remain as fit and active as we ought to. Recurring dreams about ageing may indicate an ongoing concern, and if you have them it is important to get to the bottom of what is bothering you.

### RETIRING

Even if you are still fit and active, retiring from the working world can be the first step in starting to acknowledge that old age is not far off. You may dream about retirement in a literal way if you are approaching it in your own life, or if your partner or parents are soon to retire. This will provide you with a way to

**BELOW RIGHT** As time passes we can start to feel edgy, as if there are things to do that we need to concentrate on.
**BELOW** How we feel about our health will be shadowed in our dreams – if we are healthy while asleep it is pretty much how we will feel when we are awake.

## A DREAM OF AGEING

"I was looking in a mirror and while I watched I saw my own teeth fall out and my hair turn white. The whole ageing process was immensely speeded up. I know I am getting older, but this dream really shocked me and made me feel that I wanted to hang on to my youth at all costs. But it also made me realize that I really have to enjoy what I've got because time goes so fast and I won't have it for long. And as it all slips away I have to keep reminding myself to enjoy each and every moment."

**LEFT** As we get older we do get more experienced, better equipped to be successful. If our dreams reflect this we can be reassured about how we fit in to the world around us.

explore possible anxieties you have around this transition.

How you see retirement will depend to a considerable extent on how well you are prepared for it, both financially and emotionally. It can be difficult to adjust to the lack of structure and activity, the loss of status, the lack of contact with your colleagues, and the sheer weight of idle time that you now have. But you may equally see it as a time to reap the benefits of your hard work, to enjoy a leisurely life or turn your hand to hobbies or other interests you have not had time for before.

### WITHDRAWAL

Whatever your age, your dreams may also use retirement or old age as a metaphor for withdrawing – especially from society or from an overly active lifestyle. Indeed old age is for many a time when our contact with the outside world lessens as our ability or desire to get out decreases and our friends and siblings die. It can be a lonely time, and it may be this that your dream is trying to draw to your attention – either your own fear of becoming isolated, or guilt at not paying enough attention to an elderly relative.

### WISDOM

Our stereotypes of old age are not all negative though, and while the elderly are often marginalized in Western society, we may find the archetypal figure of the wise old man or woman appearing in our dreams as a source of advice or understanding; we may even be that figure ourselves.

Grandparents or other familiar old faces may also crop up in our dreams as symbols of stability and continuity, allowing us to feel grounded and supported in our family, and giving us perspective on our lives.

**BELOW FAR LEFT** To dream of old or worn-out objects might point to something in our life that we feel needs to be rejuvenated.
**BELOW LEFT** Dreaming of possible loneliness in old age might reflect the way you feel about your life currently rather than a fear of the future.
**BELOW** But even when there is no hope of living forever we can rest assured that there is new life even in our dreams.

# DEATH

WE ALL KNOW THAT SOONER OR LATER, DEATH WILL COME TO US, HOPEFULLY NOT PREMATURELY, BUT AS THE INEVITABLE AND INESCAPABLE LAST STAGE IN THE CYCLE OF LIFE. HOWEVER MUCH WE TRY TO AVOID THINKING ABOUT OUR OWN DEATH, OR THAT OF OUR LOVED ONES, OUR UNCONSCIOUS WILL AT SOME STAGE START TO ADDRESS THE ISSUE AND TRY TO PREPARE US FOR IT. THERE ARE MANY ISSUES ASSOCIATED WITH DEATH THAT MIGHT FEATURE IN OUR DREAMS: LOSS, LONELINESS OR RELEASE FOR EXAMPLE, AND WHETHER OR NOT THERE IS LIFE AFTER DEATH MIGHT BE ANOTHER THEME THAT WE MAY TRY TO SPECULATE ON AND EXPLORE IN OUR DREAMS.

## COMING TO TERMS WITH MORTALITY

Dreams of funerals or graveyards, grief and mourning, dead bodies or skeletons may be quite literally about death and dying, and often show that we view this process in a negative light. If we are worried about death and dying then dreams of death probably happen to make us do something to try to come to terms with our own mortality. But if we dream of people celebrating, being happy, remembering the dead person with pride and love, then perhaps we have made some progress in coming to terms with it. This doesn't necessarily mean we have to look forward to it, but merely that it holds no power over us to frighten us, and that we are as prepared as we can be for this event.

## A LOVED ONE'S DEATH

Dreams about others dying may indicate a worry that they will die or leave us. Who we dream about may be telling us who we most fear will leave us, but it could also be that rather than a literal death, the dream represents some figurative termination of a quality that you particularly value (or dislike) in that person.

## IMAGES OF DEATH

History has given us many morbid death images which our society seems to have taken eagerly on board – vaults and misty graveyards, mourners dressed in black, skeletons and gravediggers, crows, the Grim Reaper, and countless images of hell. People down the ages seem to have enjoyed frightening and torturing themselves with such images, and in your dreams they could point to disturbance and fear around death. Dreaming of being buried – especially being buried alive – may have nothing to do with death but rather a feeling of having the life squeezed out of you, of being stifled in some way.

But death is not always disturbing – it can be very undramatic, even mundane, or very peaceful and part of the natural order. A graveyard in your dream may be a beautiful, calm place where you spend time remembering people you loved.

## LIFE AFTER DEATH

Death is our biggest rite of passage, the one that takes us out of this existence and on into the next – whatever that might be. If we do believe that death is merely a transition into the next life, our unconscious may choose to show us images of change, of journeys and rebirth – which may indicate that it knows that death is not final but is indeed merely a symptom of great transformation. These dreams may be suggesting radical change or the need for such change, and not actual physical death.

How we dream about death reflects not only our views of the process but also our views of what we think happens to us afterwards. We may dream of heaven or hell as if we know what they are like, though such imagery is generally based on

**BELOW** Even if we never consciously think about our mortality it will be a source of worry to us on a deep level. We might also dream of death as a way of focusing on worries that we have of being separated from others.

**LEFT** Images of death don't have to be negative. They can also generate a feeling of ultimate peace and tranquillity that we may feel we need.

**BELOW** The religious trappings of death might suggest an awful state of nothingness, or inspire awe and acceptance. It depends on how we view death.

countless images that have been handed down to us by others. Such dreams may indicate some kind of self-judgement, seeking reward for good behaviour or fearing punishment for bad.

Whatever else it may involve, death means separation from the body, so may reveal a wish for release from ill health. It could also mean that we are coming to terms with our preoccupations with the body, or, less literally, the material world.

**ABOVE** Standard images of death in our dreams might actually be about some other kind of rite of passage, and perhaps something quite mundane in comparison.

**LEFT** Whatever religion we follow will give us plenty of imagery to fuel our dreams and visions of death and the afterworld.
**RIGHT** Dreaming of someone's death might mean you are reflecting on the passing of a relationship, or a phase of your friendship together.

## DREAM OF DEATH

"I was in a foreign country like Egypt, being buried alive. I could feel the sand filling my mouth and my body sinking deeper and deeper into the ground. I felt I was suffocating. Just then someone uncovered my face with a spade and I could breathe. They said, 'look – some bones!' and I realized I had been dead for a long time.

I think the whole dream was about an inability to change. I felt it meant that I had to look at what was important to me, and get rid of a lot of things in my life so that I was not so stuck and held back by my possessions and rigid attitudes. I think there was also a fear that it might actually be too late to change."

# MIND, BODY AND SPIRIT

Our emotional and physical experiences, together with the things we are told or learn throughout our lives, give us a framework for our beliefs, which we try, often unsuccessfully, to use to keep us safe in times of trouble and crisis. With experience we have the opportunity to develop an understanding of our limitations, to grow and change, learn and expand. Some say that through such experiences our "soul" also learns and grows; when we have learnt all we need to, we move on. At times these lessons are enjoyable, but often we learn best through adversity. We incorporate our experiences, our hopes and our fears into our dreams. It is here that our unconscious tries to come to terms with guilt or with the heartache of grief; explores our sexuality and faces our mortality; and endeavours to answer some of the great questions of our existence.

# EMOTIONS

OUR EMOTIONS COVER A VAST RANGE OF EXPERIENCES, FROM ANGER AND JEALOUSY THROUGH BOREDOM AND SADNESS TO LOVE AND HAPPINESS. WHILE WE ARE ONLY TOO GLAD TO HAVE THE POSITIVE EMOTIONS, OTHERS ARE UNCOMFORTABLE AND WE MAY TRY TO PUSH THEM AWAY. BUT WE CAN'T ALWAYS CONTROL THEM, AND THEY CAN WELL UP AND OVERWHELM US, TAKING US BY SURPRISE. IN OUR DREAMS WE EXPERIENCE THE FULL RANGE OF OUR EMOTIONS, OFTEN MORE INTENSELY THAN IN OUR WAKING LIVES, AND THEY MAY HELP US COME TO GRIPS WITH THE REALLY DIFFICULT ONES.

## BURIED EMOTIONS

We often hide or lose track of our emotions because we want to appear mature or civilized or in control. At times strong emotions threaten to take us over and then we may be afraid of seeming weak or vulnerable, or of doing something that we will later regret, or simply of wasting time that we think we should be spending on something else. We develop coping mechanisms to make sure that our feelings don't show, and some people are so successful at this that they lose touch with their feelings. They may also divert attention from one emotion and express it as another that may seem more socially acceptable – for instance, men who have been brought up to believe that "boys don't cry" may express sadness as anger, and conversely many women who have had their anger curbed by social or parental disapproval may cry when angry.

When we control or divert our emotions we may delude ourselves into feeling stronger, braver, wiser, or in some other way more acceptable, but there is often a price to pay for being cut off in this way. We need to feel and express our true our emotions if we are to be well-rounded and complete human beings, to find a balance between heart and mind. Our dreams can help us to do this by unlocking unacknowledged feelings.

## FEELINGS IN DREAMS

It is always worth looking at the feelings that come up in a dream. Usually they are consistent with what you would imagine you should be feeling in the context of the dream, but sometimes the feelings and the plot may be puzzlingly at odds. Events may occur in your dream precisely to provoke a response that you will take note of, to make you think about what is really going on inside you. Sometimes this can be hard – if you always play the role of the kind and loving mother, for instance, a dream in

*Dreaming permits each and every one of us to be quietly and safely insane every night of our lives.*

WILLIAM DEMENT

which you sit reading a book impassively while your children are tormented will be really shocking and hard to come to terms with, but it could be a reality check on your ability to be the saint all the time, and may bring to your attention your frustrations or the fact that your own needs are not being met.

EMOTIONAL POINTERS

In some dreams the emotional content will be the take-home message rather than any events or images, and it may even be that the only thing you remember about the dream is that it was terrifying, or that in it you were extremely anxious about running out of time.

If you are not ready to deal with emotions square on, though, your mind may produce symbols to stand in for these feelings. Virtually all of your dream images can be read symbolically, or are present in your dream because they provoke some strong emotion or train of thought. Some are fairly obvious – for example a heart may stand for romantic love – while others are less clear but nevertheless widely accepted – such as the notion that water in all its many forms represents our emotions. Many of the symbols we use to represent emotions are discussed more fully elsewhere.

The main thing is to look at the context of the symbol and your response to it in order to be able to access the emotional content. Once you understand what emotions are being brought to the surface and how they come across in your dream, you will probably have a clearer idea of how to deal with them in a useful and positive way.

**ABOVE** Expressing strong emotions can have a knock-on effect in our dealings with others.
**ABOVE LEFT** Dream imagery is often bizarre. Feeling tied-up in knots is frustrating and can make you feel like screaming.
**ABOVE FAR LEFT** Emotions that are held back or suppressed in your waking life may surface later in your dreams.

**LEFT** To dream of a macho man may suggest that it is hard for you to own your feelings as you like to appear "cool".
**FAR LEFT** The context of our dreams is important. A mother with her baby will mean different things for each of us, depending on our circumstances.

# LOSS AND GRIEF

WHEN DEATH ENTERS OUR LIVES IT OFTEN COMES AS A COMPLETE SHOCK, AND WE ARE LEFT BEWILDERED, LOST, ANGRY AND CONFUSED. ADDED TO THE PAIN ARE FEELINGS OF REGRET AND GUILT, THE SENSE OF "IF ONLY I'D KNOWN", "IF ONLY I'D BEEN ABLE TO SAY ALL THE THINGS I WANTED TO", OR "I DIDN'T GET A CHANCE TO SAY GOODBYE". BUT IT ISN'T JUST DEATH THAT GENERATES FEELINGS OF LOSS. DIVORCE, REDUNDANCY AND EVEN THE LOSS OF PRIZED POSSESSIONS CAN BRING THEIR OWN SUDDEN SHOCKS TO OUR LIFE. HOW WE COPE CAN AFFECT HOW MUCH FINDS ITS WAY INTO OUR DREAMS, AND IT IS HERE THAT WE WILL TRY TO COME TO TERMS WITH THIS LOSS IF WE ARE NOT FACING UP TO IT IN OUR WAKING LIFE.

## GRIEVING

The word "bereaved" is from an Old English word *bereafian*, which means "to plunder". And that is the feeling we have when we have lost someone or something close to us. We feel plundered, we feel that someone or something precious has been carried off without our permission or knowledge.

The experience of bereavement is not only triggered by a person's death, but other significant life events, such as divorce, separation and redundancy. The loss of such things as our health or our youth – or even our personal possessions – also have associations with grief and loss, and may affect us quite deeply.

Whatever the reason for our grief, we may try to work it out in our dreams. A lot of people are shocked and surprised if grieving continues in their dreams when they think they have "got over it", but the stronger the emotional tie, the longer the process is likely to go on. After someone you were close to has died, they may return to your dreams from time to time for the rest of your life.

**ABOVE** Although we may chide ourselves for being silly, the loss of a precious possession is likely to stir up our emotions. If you dream of your lost treasure, consider what it symbolizes for you.

## FUNERALS

A funeral is an official ending. It gives us a chance to say "goodbye" and to mourn our loss. In some cultures, open displays of crying and even wailing are perfectly natural at funerals, and grieving can be expected to last, and be marked with cermonies, for months. In western society we are expected to "pull ourselves together" or "put on a brave face" and get on with our lives as quickly as possible, and far too little time or emotional energy is given to grieving. Yet if we have not fully come to terms with someone's death, they will in a sense, haunt us. Once there has been a proper grieving process, our dreams will by and large return to normal.

**BELOW** It is very common when someone close to us dies that they continue to appear in our dreams – for months, or even years afterwards. This may be to help us work out aspects of our relationship with that person.

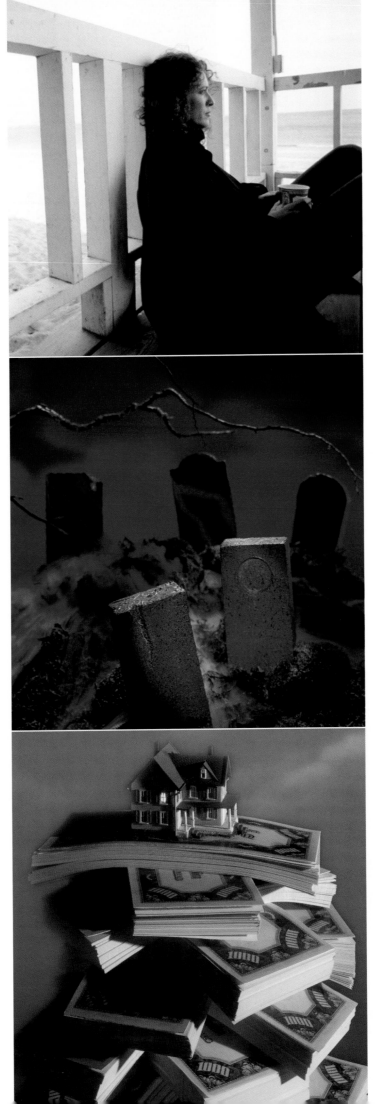

## WORKING IT OUT

In our dreams the person or object we have lost may appear in glorious technicolour. They may seem perfectly normal and present, just as they were in life, and on waking we may feel the shock and sadness all over again when we realize it was "just a dream". This process is essential to our unconscious even if it is difficult and confusing for us. To our unconscious it is a way of working out what has happened and laying the ghost to rest. It also gives us the opportunity to say things that we feel were left unsaid, or to replay events in our unconscious mind so that we can be with our loved one once more. It is a hard and sometimes wrenching process but essential if we are to be able to get on with our lives and become as whole and as healed as possible.

## DREAMS OF LOSS

Losing things in a dream may indicate that you need to mourn a loss or achieve closure on some aspect of your life. It may be something physical, such as a valuable object, or it could be more abstract, such as the loss of freedom, or of a particular phase in your life that has ended – for instance the transition from being single to being married. Even something frivolous, like having your hair cut, can be traumatic if it represents a loss of identity,

In all these cases there is a period of adjustment as you come to terms with losing something that is integral to your self-expression, or that reminds you of someone you love.

**LEFT** There is no easy way to mourn, but spending quiet time alone each day in reflection can help you come to terms with your loss.
**MIDDLE LEFT** A graveyard appearing in your dreams could be a reminder to lay the past to rest and move on with your life.
**BOTTOM LEFT** Piles of money in a dream may represent concerns with material security. What do you fear to lose?

### GRIEF DREAM

"The year that my grandmother died I saw her in my dreams every night for months. Every morning when I woke up, I was convinced she was still alive and would run into my parents' room to tell them the good news; every morning they had to tell me she was dead. I felt the shock anew each time. It was terrible and sad, and for a good while I was frightened to go to sleep at night because I didn't want to face the shock in the morning. I even left notes to myself by my bed saying 'Granny is dead'. Each morning I woke grieving the loss. I think it helped. I feel that I can talk about her now and remember her with warmth and love."

# FALLING IN LOVE

MORE SONGS, POEMS AND LETTERS HAVE BEEN WRITTEN ABOUT LOVE THAN ANY OTHER SUBJECT, AND IT IS ONLY NATURAL THAT SUCH AN IMPORTANT EMOTION SHOULD FIGURE SO LARGELY IN OUR DREAMS. WE ALL NEED TO LOVE AND BE LOVED, AND WHEN WE FALL IN LOVE WE LITERALLY CAN'T STOP DAYDREAMING ABOUT OUR CHOSEN ONE, SO IT IS COMPLETELY UNDERSTANDABLE THAT THIS CARRIES ON INTO OUR SLEEPING WORLDS TOO. FALLING IN LOVE AND HOLDING THE STEADY LOVE OF A REAL PERSON ARE TWO DIFFERENT THINGS, BUT BOTH REPRESENT OR CONTAIN POWERFUL EMOTIONS, AND MAY DOMINATE OUR DREAMS FROM TIME TO TIME.

In our dreams our partner may take on a new dimension – not who they really are but who we think they are, or who we would like them to be. They may be wilder, fiercer, bossier, kinder, more or less loving, but their essence remains the same. Our unconscious may amplify an aspect of their character to draw our attention to some particular point of view so we can adjust our relationship accordingly, or in order to flag up characteristics that we don't want to see.

### FIRST LOVE
For teenagers, falling in love is often a painful experience. Our first love affair can be very formative, as all our future relationships may be built on the lessons we learn in those first few soulful gazes or fumbling embraces. Likewise, that first ever love affair will probably feature prominently in our teen dreams.

It is also quite natural, especially at this young age, to fall in love with someone who is unattainable – someone we adore from afar, or who is forbidden – perhaps because they are too old for us, or are already in a partnership. This person is likely to appear in our dreams, which may have a sexual or erotic bias. Such dreams can be very realistic and make us feel confused and embarrassed, particularly when we meet the person in daily life.

### ROMANCE
A kind of scene-setting for love, romance usually features more prominently at the beginning of a relationship when our feelings are based more in fantasy than in the reality of the person on whom we have focused our attentions. At this stage it functions as wish fulfilment – we want everything to be wonderful and so we put all our effort into impressing the other person and making them feel special. We also want to be made to feel special ourselves. Romance provides a smoke screen, a context and loose set of rules and rituals in the framework of which we can get to know the other person, but it may also serve to distract us from who they really are.

The symbols and activities that we associate with romance – anything heart-shaped, candlelit dinners, sunsets on the beach, love poetry and so on – are many and wide-ranging, so dreaming of these things, whether they

**BELOW RIGHT** When we are in love, it can feel as if we are floating on air and our dreams may have a romantic feel to them. **BELOW** Falling in love is an exciting experience and it is most likely that our lover will keep on appearing in our dreams.

**RIGHT** Dreams of falling in love with someone in a very physical way might reflect something that you feel is lacking in your love life, or might recall the intense feelings that are associated with first love.

involve a particular person or not, may point to a wish for romance in our lives or the possibility that it is on the horizon. Men in particular may find themselves feeling particularly vulnerable if they show their softer side, so a romantic dream may have more to do with getting in touch with vulnerability and owning your feelings than with any kind of actual partnership.

Whether the romantic dream scenario will hold together coherently or is flawed in some way may also be taken as a hint as to how you should be approaching love and relationships. Ask yourself whether you are looking for a person to have a real relationship with or merely someone who will make you feel better by distracting you from areas of dissatisfaction in your life.

## THE FOOD OF LOVE

Love and food go together in many ways, so you could consider whether food images in your dreams are linked to love. For many people food and drink are an intrinsic part of the rituals of romance and courtship, and

are also the subject of fetishes. Your unconscious may make reference to expressions such as "all-consuming passion" when it dreams of eating, to suggest the nature of how you relate to a lover, and perhaps to warn you not to become too obsessive.

### DREAM OF LOVE

"I was madly in love with my girlfriend's mother and dreamed of her every night for months. Every morning I would walk my girlfriend to school. Her mother would see her off, and I would barely be able to talk to her. In fact I only really went out with the daughter so I could see the mother every morning. The dreams were all quite erotic, although we never made love either in my dream or in real life. There was no way I could ever have had a relationship with her in reality for lots of different reasons, so this was my substitute."

**BELOW LEFT** Red roses and champagne are popular symbols of romance.
**BELOW FAR LEFT** Our dreams may dwell on the physical intimacy we share with our lover. This may be the actual reality or else represent some kind of wish fulfilment.
**BELOW** Almost everyone can remember their first kiss and what it was like to fall in love for the first time. Teenage love is an emotional roller-coaster where feelings are experienced intensely.

# SEX

THE MASTER OF THE EROTIC DREAM IS UNDOUBTEDLY FREUD, WHO HELD THAT MUCH OF WHAT WE DREAM, EVEN IF IT
SEEMS TO HAVE ABSOLUTELY NOTHING TO DO WITH SEX, SYMBOLIZES SUPPRESSED SEXUAL DESIRES. IN THE FREUDIAN
MODEL, A SNAKE, LADDER, KNIFE, STAIRCASE, CANDLE OR PEN REPRESENT THE PENIS, AND CAVES, BOXES, TUNNELS OR DARK
ROOMS ARE THE VAGINA. BUT WHILE IT IS POSSIBLE THAT SUCH OBJECTS MAY ACT AS SYMBOLS IN THIS WAY, THEY ARE NOT
NECESSARILY DOING SO IN EVERY CASE, AND AS PREVIOUSLY DISCUSSED, SYMBOLS WILL HAVE DIFFERENT MEANINGS FOR
DIFFERENT PEOPLE. WE MAY ALSO WORK WITH OUR SEXUALITY DIRECTLY THROUGH OVERTLY EROTIC DREAMS.

**ABOVE** Erotic and stylized images may appear in our dreams, but only you will understand how they relate to you.
**ABOVE RIGHT** The kinds of things you dream about might be symbolically, or overtly sexual.
**ABOVE FAR RIGHT** For both men and women, snakes are a traditional symbol of sexual power and energy. Are you comfortable with your sexuality?

Many dreams contain symbolism that only you will understand. Certain things may have become associated with sex for you by dint of your experiences – for example, if there was music playing the first time you made love, the same tune may always trigger the memory of your first sexual experience.

### SEXUAL FANTASIES

Two common sexual fantasies are of having sex in a public place and having sex with a stranger. Such dreams will tend to have different meanings for men and women because their basic sexual needs and responses differ.

Dreaming of making love in a crowded stadium, for instance, may reflect the tendency of men to boast about sex, or a woman's desire to be less inhibited. In this kind of dream a woman may be showing a need to be cheered on or encouraged by others to express her sexuality in a full and satisfying way, or she may enjoy the fact that she is capable of doing so and wants to let the world know about it.

If the dream is of having sex in a lift or on public transport, it may highlight the fun and thrilling aspect to sex, and remind us how it feels to do something "naughty". Such a dream may bring into question your attitude to rules and social behaviour and may show a desire to break a taboo.

For men, the biological imperative to spread their seed widely is met with confusingly divergent attitudes in society – on the one hand it is frowned on as infidelity and on the other it is prized as prowess. So dreams of sex with a stranger may reveal a yearning for just this model of

People don't fall in love with what's right in front of them. People want the dream – what they can't have. The more unattainable, the more attractive.
XANDER

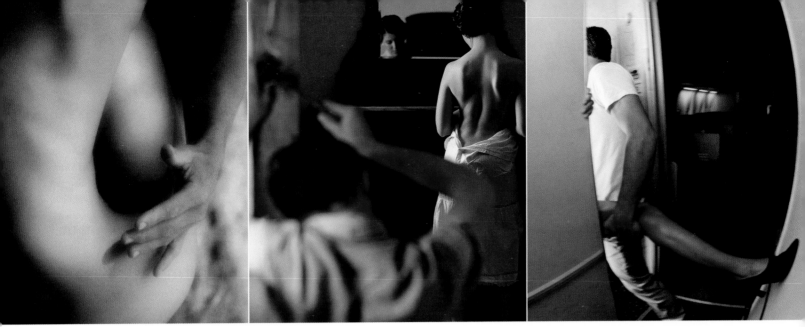

behaviour, either to escape social restrictions and enjoy the taste of forbidden fruit, or to reassure the man of his virility.

## WISH FULFILMENT

Your sexual desires and urges do not simply go away if you are on your own, and you will probably find other ways to express them. The more cut off you are from a healthy sex life, the more likely it is that sex will appear in your dreams as a substitute for the real thing. If there is no-one special in your life you may dream of sex with a stranger, or perhaps you have met someone you desire and can't wait to be intimate with in real life. Even if you have a relationship, you may be expressing your desire for something better if your present situation is unsatisfactory. Whatever the case, these dreams are usually healthy explorations of possibilities or expressions of our needs, and we can use them as a guide to how we are feeling.

## SEXUAL PROBLEMS

We may have erotic dreams that help us deal with our sexual difficulties. Our problems could be quite obvious – for example frustration at not having a sexual partner – or your unconscious might be drawing to your attention something you haven't even admitted to yourself yet. Even if you feel unable to talk about a problem, you will still need to process it and try to overcome it or come to terms with it, and your dreams can provide a useful framework for doing just this.

## DISCOVERING OUR SEXUALITY

Adolescence is a time of sexual discovery and exploration, but our need to understand ourselves as sexual beings doesn't end here. Throughout our lives we may use our dreams to help work out particular aspects of sexuality of which we are unsure, or to release sexual urges that may be

buried under taboo, or that we have not had the opportunity to express. We may dream of fetishes, or have homosexual fantasies, and in so doing uncover sexual impulses that are real for us, or play with ideas that we are curious about but don't want to act out in real life. Acting out the role of the opposite sex may give us an understanding of how our own sexuality may be experienced by our partner. Many people are self-conscious about their bodies, and it can be liberating to have dreams in which they can enjoy sex. Our erotic dreams can enable us to discover and fulfil our sexuality in a positive way.

**ABOVE** Our sexual fantasies will often be played out in our dreams. Having sex on a train is a fairly common fantasy.
**ABOVE LEFT** Talking about sexual problems is a sensitive area, so we may dream about them to help us work them out.
**ABOVE FAR LEFT** Our dreams can provide a "safe space" where we can allow and explore sexual feelings.

**BELOW** It may be easier to enjoy "perfect" sex in our dreams than in our actual relationships. This could be because our inhibitions don't get in the way and our partner seems to know exactly how to give us pleasure. Sharing intimate dreams with your partner can help build trust.

## IMPOTENCE DREAM

"I was in a fencing tournament, and my opponent was my boss. I had already donned my mask and jacket, but while my boss was ready and waiting with his sabre raised, I couldn't find mine anywhere.

I had been unable to have an erection for some time, but this dream made me realize that it was the stress of work that was making me impotent."

# PAIN AND ILLNESS

WHEN WE ARE ASLEEP ANY PAIN OR DISEASE WE HAVE IN OUR BODY OR MIND WILL FILTER THROUGH INTO OUR DREAMS AND BE EXPRESSED EITHER DIRECTLY OR METAPHORICALLY. CONVERSELY, EMOTIONAL DISTRESS WE MAY BE EXPERIENCING IN OUR LIVES MAY MANIFEST IN A DREAM AS PHYSICAL PAIN OR INJURY. DOCTORS AND OTHER MEDICAL STAFF THAT APPEAR IN OUR DREAMS MAY BE THERE TO HELP OR HINDER OUR PROGRESS TO HEALTH, WHILE DREAMING OF BEING IN HOSPITAL COULD BE SEEN AS AN ACKNOWLEDGEMENT OF THE SERIOUSNESS OF A CONDITION. DREAMING OF PAIN AND ILLNESS MAY ALSO BE A METAPHOR FOR SOMETHING ELSE IN YOUR LIFE, AN EMOTIONAL AILMENT FOR EXAMPLE.

**RIGHT** If we are suffering from pain in real life, then it wouldn't be a surprise if our dream reflected this. If we go to bed with a headache the pain might filter through into our sleep, so we dream of it.

## DREAM OF ILL HEALTH

"In my dream I was ill and the doctor was applying leeches. These black slimy things were literally sucking the lifeblood out of me. I woke up feeling quite nauseous. The dream prompted me to look at my new relationship: although my new partner seemed a loving and caring person, as a doctor ought to be, I felt she was using me financially. The blood in the dream was money, and I was letting my partner bleed me dry."

### PAIN

In India there is a widespread belief that dreaming about pain in any part of your body indicates that something is wrong with that part; even if a doctor finds nothing wrong it is taken as a sign that this is where pain will get to you sooner or later. But dreams are seldom prophetic, so dreaming of pain doesn't necessarily mean that an injury is going to befall you, although it is possible that your body is trying to tell you that you are ill. If you dream of pain, note what sort of pain you experience and where it is located, and consider what it could be telling you. Also look at what you do about the pain in your dream.

If dreams of pain crop up often, pay special attention to them as they are almost certainly highlighting an area of some importance to your unconscious and may well be your mind's way of expressing emotional rather than physical pain. How we respond to painful or frightening experiences can have major repercussions – they may lead to growth and wisdom, but they can also cause us to retreat to a space that seems safe but is actually stultifying, and prevent us from growing into new awareness.

### INJURIES AND ILLNESS

Your body is often symbolic of the self, so any illness or injury that affects your body in your dream is one that affects you as a person. Bruises and cuts may be symbolic of emotional bumps and scrapes, cancers of emotional malignancy, festering wounds of problems that are getting worse, blindness of not seeing or not wanting to look at something.

The fear of being seriously ill is common and we may act it out while we sleep. But the health problems in our dreams are often not life-threatening. Colds, diarrhoea, spots, rashes and warts, for instance, may be uncomfortable, embarrassing or irritating rather than painful, and suggest such discomforts in your life. You may resent being ill, perhaps being too busy to make the time or effort to look after your body. What you feel in your dream about your illness may well be what you are feeling in waking life, and your dream is a way of getting this feeling out into the open.

### THE MEDICAL WORLD

If you are given medication in your dream, it is important to note how you respond to receiving it. It may seem like a gift of health, or a poison in disguise; if you don't know what it is then it may bring up control or trust issues for you. Take note of the form the medicine comes in, as well as who gives it to you, and what your relationship is to that person. Receiving an anaesthetic could suggest an emotional numbness or a kind of unconsciousness in your waking life, while surgery may indicate that drastic action is needed around some problem, or that

**ABOVE** How we view pain and illness – and how we would cope with being confined to bed – can be reflected in our dreams.

**BELOW** If we have real underlying fear of needles or even doctors, then our dreams may well reflect this.

**ABOVE** If we are taking medication that we don't really understand, or which may have side effects that we feel ill-prepared for, it will worry us in our dreams.

someone is already taking it for you. Many people may be involved in our dream illness – doctors and nurses, hospital porters and ambulance staff, to name a few. What role do these people have in your dream? Do they take charge, or are they bystanders? If medical personnel are not actually helping you, you may feel let down, and it could be useful to see if this is reflecting something you are experiencing in your life. Depending on your relationship to such figures in your own life, they may well represent the wish to be looked after, to hand over responsibility for your wellbeing to someone who you think is better qualified than you.

A dream that takes place in a hospital may suggest more significant problems in your life or more serious concerns with illness. As an environment a hospital may be alien and frightening, and one in which you have to relinquish much of your control. Many people fear that they will never leave a hospital alive, so it may also indicate that you are facing up to your mortality.

**RIGHT** Dreaming of a cold might not be a simple reflection of our physical state in real life. It might be a metaphor for something.

**BELOW** Medical tools can seem intimidating and invasive. If we dream of these perhaps they are symbolic of something in our lives that we feel threatened by.

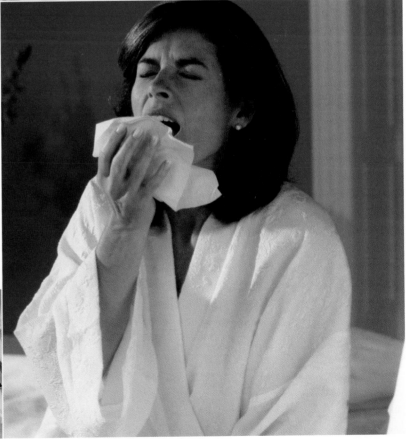

# Engaging with People

Of all the elements we are likely to encounter in our dreams it is people that will feature most often. At times in our waking life we respond to people strongly, falling passionately in love or running into conflict, and without them we can become lonely. Usually when a person appears in a dream their significance is unique and relevant in the context of that dream alone, although if you have a series of dreams on the same theme they might become representative of something particular – some aspect of ourselves, or an archetypal figure. Besides the characters that we meet in our dreams there is always you, the observer or participant.

Many of the activities that fill our lives revolve around people. We keep busy for many reasons – sociability, fun or fitness, out of curiosity or necessity – and in our dreams we can continue to explore, to do things we can't do in real life, or to work through issues that are troubling us in our day-to-day lives.

# FAMILY

THE MEMBERS OF OUR FAMILY ARE POTENTIALLY THE CLOSEST PEOPLE TO US. THEY ARE WITH US FROM BIRTH, WE GROW UP WITH THEM, WE KNOW THEM INTIMATELY AND, HOPEFULLY, LOVE THEM DEARLY. WE SPEND A LOT OF TIME WITH OUR FAMILY, AND THIS CAN CREATE BOTH A WONDERFUL CLOSENESS AND TREMENDOUS STRESS. THERE CAN BE MORE CONFLICT BETWEEN FAMILY MEMBERS THAN ANY OTHER RELATIONSHIP. AT SOME TIMES IN OUR LIFE THE BONDS CAN BE STRETCHED TO BREAKING POINT, AND AT OTHERS THERE IS A DISTANCE THAT YOU FEEL RECONCILED TO BUT WHICH IN FACT IS SUBCONSCIOUSLY BOTHERING YOU. IT IS HARDLY SURPRISING THAT THE FAMILY FEATURES FREQUENTLY IN OUR DREAMS.

**ABOVE** The concept of family, and the individuals within it, is a powerful force and will figure large in our dreams. Our parents will be the most influential aspect for most of us.

Family members are irreplaceable – while friends and acquaintances may come and go, if we lose a parent or grandparent, child or sibling, or if we fall out with them irrevocably, their role can never be taken by someone else. Thus when we do get into conflict situations with them there is a lot at stake. If we are unwilling or unable to resolve issues effectively, they almost inevitably surface in our dreams.

The family can be seen as a microcosm of society, and in it we learn to understand social roles and behaviours, and establish core norms and values.

Our responses to authority, power, love, companionship and many other aspects of human behaviour and social structures will be learnt in the family and taken with us into society. Because of this, dreaming of a family member might often be pointing towards a characteristic rather than a dream about that person. For example, if you felt that your father was a forbidding and authoritarian element in your childhood, in your dream his presence might actually be a reference to a real-life bullying boss you are having difficulty with at work.

## PARENTS

Our parents are probably the most influential people in our lives. We are heavily dependent on them during our early years, and they are an important source of information about the world. We also learn from them a vast array of attitudes and behaviours that may help us to integrate into society or that may be dysfunctional and present us with constant difficulties.

Our relationship with our parents evolves through childhood and changes during our adult years as we mature, and as they grow old and perhaps dependent. In dreams of our parents we are often trying to

work through unresolved childhood issues and how they continue to affect us as adults. For instance, a child that is often punished for something they haven't done may carry unjustified feelings of guilt with them for the rest of their lives. On the other hand the appearance of your parents in your dream may suggest that you are feeling a need to be loved and looked after if your parents are loving and nurturing people.

## CHILDREN

Many parents expend a lot of energy on worrying about their children. They may take these worries to be bed with them, exaggerating them in their dreams, as they play out worst-case scenarios as a way of anticipating and preparing for unexpected or difficult situations. It is also quite possible that you are unconsciously aware of some difficulty with your child, and your unconscious is trying to bring this to your attention.

Dreaming about our own children after they have grown up might be an attempt to go back and change something we did, to put it to rights, and in so doing to absolve our feelings of guilt about the mistakes we made as a parent. If we can see what aspect of our parenting is

**ABOVE** Position and hierarchy within the family group might still affect us even when we've moved away from home.

**RIGHT** It is said we never really recover from our childhood and our dreams may well reflect and support this view.

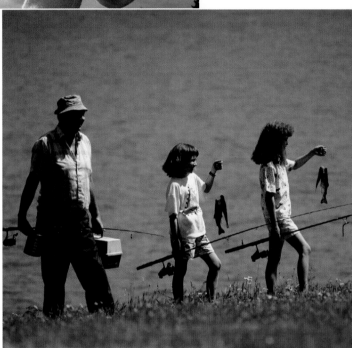

disquieting us, we can to try to make amends. We can also relive the joy of our own childhood through our children, updating and perhaps improving on the experiences that we had ourselves. Our children can show us how our childhood might have been, and how we can get in touch with the child within us, giving us the opportunity to recapture the freedom and innocence of our early years. Much will depend on the nature of your own childhood and on how you relate to your children.

BROTHERS AND SISTERS

Sibling relationships are particularly complex because we may feel some ambivalence around our brothers and sisters. On the one hand they are our constant companions during childhood – we share our experiences, we play games and have jokes with each other, we have the same family situation, and so are often in a position to understand and empathize with each other more than anyone else. For a younger child, older siblings can be invaluable role models and teachers as well.

**LEFT** If our childhood was happy then we will find any dreams of it will also be happy – and we can just enjoy them.

**BELOW** If on the other hand our childhood was less than safe, or we still have unresolved fears about it, our dreams may also make us feel unsafe.

However, sibling rivalry should never be underestimated – the first-born may always at some level resent the loss of parental attention that the birth of younger siblings inevitably brings, and constant comparisons by parents and teachers can be irksome, depriving a child of their individuality and potentially bringing a sense of inadequacy.

Dreams of siblings can underscore these feelings and allow us to address buried resentments, perhaps by being more assertive. Your brother or sister may have qualities that you wish to bring out in yourself, and their presence in your dream may be an attempt to do this.

# FRIENDS

THE FRIENDSHIPS WE HAVE OCCUR AT MANY LEVELS, FROM SUPERFICIAL ACQUAINTANCES TO LIFELONG COMPANIONS. CIRCUMSTANTIAL FRIENDSHIPS — SUCH AS THE COLLEAGUES WE LIKE AND WITH WHOM WE MAY OCCASIONALLY HAVE A CHAT, OR THE PEOPLE WE MEET AT NIGHT SCHOOL — MAY DEVELOP, BUT BASICALLY THEY ARE ON THE OUTSIDE OF OUR NETWORK. AT THE OTHER END OF THE SPECTRUM ARE THE PEOPLE WHO ARE OUR CLOSEST COMPANIONS, PEOPLE WE REALLY CONNECT WITH ON A DEEP LEVEL, OR WITH WHOM WE HAVE SO MUCH SHARED HISTORY THAT OUR DIFFERENCES BECOME IRRELEVANT. DREAMS OF FRIENDS MAY BE OF EITHER SORT, AND WILL HAVE SIMILARLY DIFFERENT LEVELS.

We relate to our friends on different levels, sharing deeply personal things with them and relying on them in difficult times or simply having a good time and a laugh with each other. We may have a lot in common with them, or be completely at odds with them in many ways but still value their companionship. Because our relationships with our friends are so diverse, they can mean many things to us when they appear in our dreams.

## FRIENDS IN OUR DREAMS

We choose our friends, responding to aspects of their personality or shared experiences that we can relate to, and because of this they may sometimes be closer to us than our relatives. Friends become all the more important if your family is not loving and supportive, and can in some cases provide a kind of substitute family. But we also befriend people with whom we share common activities or interests, and this may be the focus of the relationship rather than any deeply shared personal connection with them.

We may dream of friends for many reasons — out of love or guilt, or in order to resolve conflict issues. If the friend you dream of is associated with an activity such as a sport or hobby, then it could be some aspect of the activity rather than the qualities of that person that you are investigating. With closer friends though, we often dream of them because they have a particular quality on which we need to focus our attention, perhaps to understand it, adopt it ourselves, or reject it.

> ### DREAM OF A FRIEND
> "I hadn't seen my friend Paul for a long time. He'd been abroad teaching and I guess I missed him. I dreamt that he was back and we were on his motorbike together. He turned to me to say something and didn't see there was a lorry coming towards us. We crashed and I woke up. I was concerned at the time because I hadn't heard from him in such a long time and I think I was worrying that something might have happened to him. I didn't know if anyone would think to let me know. On another level it could have been that I was worrying about our friendship having 'died'."

**BELOW RIGHT** We all need friends and companions to be a healthy part of society. We might take it for granted in our waking lives, but celebrate it in our dreams, however bizarrely.
**BELOW** A friendship dream doesn't have to be particularly profound, but might simply highlight the importance of a friend's presence in your life.

## FRIENDS OR STRANGERS?

Sometimes in our dreams our friends will be transformed into unfamiliar people – so much so that we are not sure whether or not they are still the same person that we know and love. Such transformations draw our attention to the differences – so for example, if a friend who is always bouncy and jovial appears in your dream in tears, this may be a sign that you have lost touch with the positive things in life, that you need to reconnect with what makes you happy and perhaps with the people that you really enjoy being with.

## LOSING A FRIEND

Such transformations may also be our unconscious mind's way of working out how we feel about relationships. Friendships are often fragile and changeable, and can easily evaporate if we don't take care of them or if our circumstances change or we develop in different ways.

Having friends can make us feel valued, and the loss of a friendship can be a heavy blow. If we do lose contact it might be no more than an accident but it still hurts, and we still feel the loss. Dreams may be a way of coming to terms with such losses, or of bringing determination to putting a friendship back on track.

**LEFT** A good social life is an essential part of a happy and wholesome life; it emphasizes the positive. Just as close one-to-one friendships are vital, so are groups of friends where a different dynamic exists.

**BELOW LEFT** We may feel the loss of friends long after they have grown away, and remember them in our dreams.
**BELOW** In childhood we begin to establish friendships that may last us a lifetime.

Let us learn to dream, gentlemen, and then we may perhaps find the truth.

F. A. KEKULÉ

# LOVERS

FINDING AND RELATING TO A LOVER IS ONE OF THE BIG PREOCCUPATIONS OF ADULTHOOD. IF WE DON'T HAVE A LOVER WE PROBABLY WANT ONE, AND IF WE DO, WE MAY DREAM OF THEM TO REINFORCE HOW WONDERFUL IT IS TO BE IN LOVE, OR TO WORK THROUGH THE CONFLICT ISSUES THAT INEVITABLY CROP UP FROM TIME TO TIME. WE MAY DREAM NOT ONLY OF OUR CURRENT PARTNER, BUT ALSO OF PAST LOVES, OR OF PEOPLE WE ARE ATTRACTED TO BUT WHO ARE UNAVAILABLE; WE MAY EVEN HAVE FANTASIES ABOUT COMPLETELY UNATTAINABLE LOVE OBJECTS. IF WE STIFLE OUR LOVE FANTASIES OR AVOID LOOKING AT DIFFICULT RELATIONSHIP ISSUES CONSCIOUSLY, THIS MAY WELL SURFACE IN OUR DREAMS.

## PAST LOVERS

It is quite common to dream of past lovers. It may mean that you are hankering after being with them again, but often it is simply your unconscious mind's way of cataloguing and storing away experiences and memories. Often it is important that you process why a relationship ended so that you don't make the same mistakes again with the next person. You may need to regain a level of self-esteem after a damaging or abusive relationship, and realize that it is alright to be just who you are.

Whatever it is you need to work through, dreams give you the opportunity to do so.

**BELOW** Our notions of what makes a romantic situation are often conditioned by our culture, and the standard ideals may surface in our dreams as our mind replays the images we have absorbed.

## PRESENT LOVERS

Just as we dream about our friends and family on a fairly regular basis, so too do we dream of our present partner. There are many reasons for this. It can be our unconscious mind's way of reassuring ourselves that we are still loved. Even playing with notions of being unfaithful or out of love, or being cruel, hurtful, or distant may be our unconscious mind's way of checking that things are in reality alright, or of experimenting with ideas or situations without us having to try anything out for real.

Unpleasant dreams about a lover may also hint at a certain dissatisfaction in a relationship, and give you an opportunity to see how it might be to behave differently from the way you do in real life.

## POTENTIAL LOVERS

Our unconscious likes to keep an open mind on what is around us. This may be unsettling if you are in a good relationship, but it is also normal and natural. Just because we dream about people we fancy doesn't mean we would do anything about it in our waking life or even that we want to. It may be just a way of experimenting with the idea without having to go there. It may also mean that unhappiness in your relationship is prompting you to see a way to finding a more satisfactory partner.

## FANTASY LOVERS

The most common fantasy lovers in our dreams are real people whom we might, in an ideal world, make a play for, but with whom a relationship is at best extremely unlikely. These might be people in the public eye, like pop stars or actors, or people with whom it would be too risky to have an actual relationship, such as a boss or married person.

When we are asleep there is no limit to our imagination, and occasionally the lovers of our dreams may be really bizarre and

**RIGHT** Dreaming of having an affair might reflect a desire you have for the unknown.
**MIDDLE RIGHT** Dreaming of your love life could be a way of working through the everyday concerns of any relationship.
**BOTTOM RIGHT** Dreams of a romantic new affair can simply be highly enjoyable escapism.

completely unobtainable. We may also dream of breaking taboos, and have sexual dreams involving incest, or animals, for instance. Many people might be shocked by having such fantasies, and for some they may be an indication of disturbed psychological states, in which case professional help may be needed. For the most part though, our unconscious likes to slip the leash occasionally and dream of things we would simply never do – it does not mean that we would want to act these out in reality. Our dreams are a way of approaching taboos in safety, experimenting or letting off sexual steam. The meaning will depend on who we are – it could be that we are reacting to social restrictions and trying to find greater freedom of expression; in fact breaking taboos in dreams may be a liberating experience.

If you are the kind of person who worries what others think of you this may be disturbing. In our dream we may need to deal with others being judgemental, or even with our own self-condemnation, if we take unusual or inappropriate lovers. But a taboo lover may also be a companion on your journey to self-fulfilment and have qualities that you don't find elsewhere.

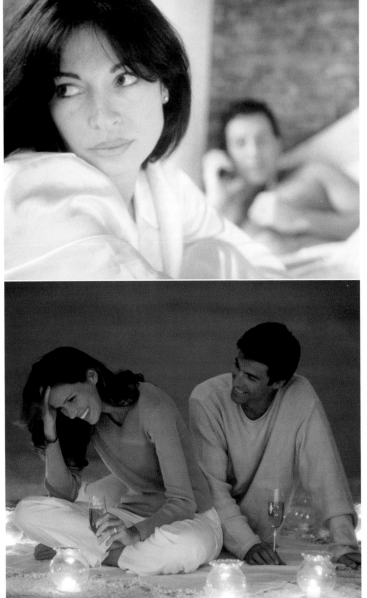

### DREAM OF LOVERS

"I had about half a dozen dreams about my boss, who I rather fancied. They were never exactly the same, but they always involved being physically intimate, and always one or other of us was a reluctant partner in this intimacy, usually because we were afraid of discovery.

I think that this dream was my way of attaining something that in reality would never be possible. I think that the reluctance was to do with my fear that my own partner would find out that I was attracted to someone else, as well as with the fact that my boss was in reality very happily married. "

# PEOPLE IN OUR LIVES

IN GOING ABOUT THE DAY-TO-DAY BUSINESS OF OUR LIVES, WE ENGAGE WITH COUNTLESS PEOPLE. OUR ENCOUNTERS WITH THEM MAY BE INSIGNIFICANT OR TRIVIAL — THE FELLOW PASSENGERS YOU SIT BESIDE IN SILENCE DURING A TRAIN JOURNEY AND NEVER SEE AGAIN, THE CHECKOUT OPERATOR IN AN UNEVENTFUL VISIT TO THE SUPERMARKET — OR THEY COULD BE MORE INVOLVED, SUCH AS THE RELATIONSHIPS THAT DEVELOP WITH COLLEAGUES OR NEIGHBOURS. WE EVEN HAVE A RELATIONSHIP OF SORTS WITH FAMOUS PEOPLE WHOSE FACES ARE FAMILIAR AND WHOSE LIVES WE MIGHT READ ABOUT, BUT WHO WE MAY NEVER MEET.

**RIGHT** Whoever we are intimidated by in our everyday waking life is likely to "visit" us in our dreams in a similar way. If this happens repeatedly you might want to work with why this person affects you so deeply.

Any of these people could appear as characters in our dreams, whether they are playing supporting roles or taking the lead, and although at times they may simply be a necessary part of the scenery, like extras in a film, they will often appear in our dreams for a reason. Notice what role they play, as well as how you behave towards each other in the dream and how you feel during and after the interaction.

### FAMILIAR FACES

In going about the routine of our lives, we get to know many faces in the places we frequent – neighbours, the people who work in the local shops or bank, the people we work and socialise with and countless others. When such people appear in a dream,

try to establish whether it is their role that seems important or their personal qualities. For instance, a neighbour may have to do with having your privacy and personal space invaded, or it may be reminding you that there are friendly people about who are always willing to help you. Dreaming of your boss is quite likely to be about issues of power, authority, status and so on, but it may be that the formal relationship you have with each other is secondary to particular personality traits that you feel he or she exhibits.

### IN THE PUBLIC GAZE

Royalty and politicians, media celebrities, and others who have made it into the public arena may all feature in our dream

world. As we only know them from a distance, it will be the qualities they present to the outside world – their public face – that we probably focus on. This may be simply the fact that they have achieved fame and fortune or infamy, that they have reached the pinnacle of success on their chosen path, or it may be more specifically about what it is that they have done, or how they have gone about getting what they want. We may want their success to rub off on us, to use them as a role model, or to engage with them and turn the one-way relationship into a more personal one.

### STRANGERS

What does it mean, though, if the people we encounter in our dreams are not familiar faces, but apparently arbitrary individuals? Realistically, strangers are likely to appear in our dreams as often as they do in real life, but if we do engage with them or something about them grabs our attention particularly, it may be worth looking at whether they have a particular significance to us. It may indeed be the very fact that we don't know them that is salient – we may feel uncertain or wary of them, they may behave in unpredictable or mysterious or dangerous ways, or they may be

**ABOVE** We might all fear crowds, especially if they are made up of strangers, but being part of a mass gathering can also be quite exhilarating.

**BELOW** If you dream of people who are famous in real life you are probably dreaming of what they represent to you. Alternatively, maybe there is something about fame itself that intrigues and attracts you?

**ABOVE** You have to look at what qualities each person brings to your dream to understand them and their impact on your life.

people we are attracted to and want to get to know. Look at the kind of interaction you have in the dream and how you feel about the contact you have with them. Obviously, a stranger chasing you with a loaded gun will bring up quite different feelings from one who shows you the way when you are lost.

In particular, see what qualities are dominant in your dream, as a stranger could present some aspect of yourself that you have yet to bring to awareness. Also look at whether the person seems to conform to any stereotypes – the tall, dark and handsome stranger who may be the lover of your dreams, or the wise old man or woman who can be your guide or angel.

Strangers who are obviously foreigners or people of different races may bring issues of difference or prejudice to the fore, and whether the person is a man, woman or child could be drawing your attention to your own personal masculine, feminine or childlike qualities that may be useful for you to focus on right now.

**RIGHT** Fear of getting to know people may figure in our dreams and we may seek ways to get round this in our waking life.

**BELOW** Work colleagues might not be our best friends but we spend a disproportionate amount of time with them, and this dominance in our lives might be reflected in our dreams.

# GATHERINGS

**ABOVE** If you dream about a party at which you feel out of place and lonely, then analyse why this might be so. What kind of party was it? Who was there? What made you feel peripheral?
**ABOVE RIGHT** A gathering of lots of people in a dream can act as an indicator of how we think we fit into society.

WE GATHER BECAUSE WE ARE SOCIAL BEINGS. WE ALL BELONG TO COMMUNITIES OF VARIOUS DESCRIPTIONS – FAMILY, NEIGHBOURHOOD, WORKPLACE, NATION – AND SHARE RESOURCES, INFORMATION AND COLLECTIVE EXPERIENCES WITH EACH OTHER. WE GET TOGETHER AS A FAMILY, WE MEET COLLEAGUES TO DISCUSS BUSINESS, AND WE JOIN THOUSANDS OF STRANGERS IN PUBLIC FOR A CONCERT OR TO CELEBRATE A NATIONAL EVENT. THE GATHERINGS OF OUR DREAMS REFLECT THIS DIVERSITY, AND THEY ALSO EXPRESS HOW WE FEEL IN THE CONTEXT OF SOCIAL GROUPINGS.

## HARMONY
Gatherings where people understand and support each other, and want to be together, can give a tremendous sense of belonging, and help you to feel safe, supported and sustained. If you have been struggling with such issues, dreaming of such a gathering may show that some

aspect of your personal sense of community is now being satisfied in some way.

Harmonious gatherings can also be an expression of general consensus on society's norms and values. Looking in on them from the outside, though, or being excluded from them, could indicate a rejection of these norms, or that you still have some kind of unresolved social issues – isolation, a lack of confidence about your role in your community or workplace, or uncertainty about how accepted you are by the people you value.

Unfortunately, gatherings can also be fraught with discord. Antagonism, dominance or bullying are all too present in our society and you may be using the gathering in your dream as a

metaphor for these. If this is the case, look for any signs of resolution, and also see who is present and what their dominant characteristics are. If you are involved in the dream rather than an onlooker, see what role you are playing.

## ROLES
The characters in your dream gathering are probably playing particular roles, perhaps in some kind of hierarchy, or at least contributing to the group identity. They may be people you know or complete strangers – leaders and followers, teachers, diplomats trying to keep the peace and finding solutions to problems, jokers defusing situations with their humour, and the black sheep, pulling in a different direction and at odds

---

### A DREAM OF REJECTION

"I was looking through a window into an expensive restaurant. All my friends were gathered together, eating and drinking and having a good time. I became very distressed at not being amongst them. Were they talking about me? Had I not been invited? Had I lost the invitation or been turned away? I banged on the window but no one could hear me. In the dream I became anxious that this was all an elaborate joke; they were pretending to ignore me, and wanted to hurt me.

I had just split up with my partner, who had been quite hurtful. I was feeling insecure and shut out, and my self-esteem had taken a blow."

with everyone. Gatherings may also speak to us of individuality, whether suppressed or given freedom. See what your own role is within the group, how others perceive you, and how you respond to that role as well as to the goals or beliefs of the group.

## FORMALITY
Some people like the informality of an unstructured gathering, with its sense of companionship, freedom and youthful energy, while others prefer the more formal circumstances of an organized event. Formality can give us the safety of structure if we understand and feel comfortable with it, but it can also be intimidating if we don't feel we belong.

## CROWDS
Being in a large crowd, such as at a major sports match or a New Year celebration, can be an exhilarating experience as the happy, excited mood of the people rubs off on you. But it can also be immensely stressful – even downright scary if the

crowd becomes a mob. Your relationship with the crowd in your dream is important in understanding what it means – does it give you a sense of belonging or community, a unity of purpose, a celebration, or is it threatening, in which case you may panic at the thought of getting crushed, or feel that you need to escape and be alone?

Try to relate this to your everyday life – crowd dreams could be telling you something about the amount and type of contact you are having in relation to your needs as an individual, or

about your relationship with conventions and the mass of opinions. If you tend to need time alone to recharge your batteries and aren't getting this, you may be expressing a need to get away from people for a while. Conversely you may be feeling isolated, and need people around you to make you feel human again. A crowd dream where you can't escape or where the attention of the crowd is focused entirely on you may indicate that you feel pressure to conform rather than taking your own direction in life.

**ABOVE** Really big crowds can be scary – but that is true in waking life as much as dreams and we shouldn't read too much into such fears.
**ABOVE LEFT** In a social gathering we may feel "small", which might represent that this is how we feel about ourselves in real life.

**BELOW** Any crowd scene can represent how we feel about being part of a group. Do you blend in or are you singled out in some way as being other than the norm? Does this please or daunt you? Do you want to conform or rebel?

# CELEBRATIONS AND CEREMONIES

CELEBRATIONS CAN TAKE MANY FORMS — FROM SPONTANEOUSLY OPENING A BOTTLE OF CHAMPAGNE WITH A FEW FRIENDS, TO THE FESTIVITIES AND RITUALS OF A RELIGIOUS HOLIDAY OR A FORMAL AND HIGHLY REHEARSED NATIONAL CEREMONY. WHEN WE DREAM OF SUCH CELEBRATIONS THEY ARE LIKELY TO BE EVENTS IN WHICH WE ARE PERSONALLY INVOLVED, ALTHOUGH THE GRAND CEREMONIES OF CELEBRITIES AND LEADERS — A ROYAL WEDDING, THE FUNERAL OF A STATESMAN, OR AN INAUGURATION — MAY FEATURE TOO. OUR DREAMS MIGHT ALSO FEATURE THE SYMBOLS OF THESE CEREMONIES RATHER THAN THE GATHERINGS: A WEDDING RING, AN ELABORATE CAKE, BALLOONS OR STREAMERS MIGHT MAKE AN APPEARANCE.

**ABOVE** We all like to celebrate and we enjoy having our friends around us to help us party. Our dreams are no different and are to be enjoyed.
**ABOVE RIGHT** There are a lot of cycles in our life that need to be marked as a rite of passage. You might dream of the symbols that are linked with an event rather than the event itself.

## ANTICIPATING AN EVENT

In the build-up to a major life event such as a wedding or the birth of a child, the excitement and apprehension can spill over into our dreams. In dreaming of the event our unconscious attempts to work out the fears we have around it – saying the wrong thing, forgetting something crucial, or making a fool of ourselves in some way. With weddings in particular, we are publicly entering into a social contract and may be anxious about having made the right

decision. Perhaps we are even responsible for the administration of such events, in which case it might be sheer nerves that makes us dream about them. On the positive side, such dreams give you a chance to rehearse and familiarize yourself with the event, and to anticipate things that could go wrong.

## CEREMONY AS SYMBOL

Dreams of ceremonies are not necessarily about real events though. If the dream seems to spring out of nowhere we should view the ceremony as a symbol –

probably for the achievement or event that it is designed to mark, or for the feelings that the prospect of such an event evokes. So a 21st birthday party may mean that we are maturing in some way, or feeling the increased freedoms or the responsibilities of adulthood, while a wedding could be prompting us to ask ourselves about our relationship – perhaps about how committed we feel – or if we are single, to explore what kind of person we would like to settle down with.

The exact purpose or structure of the celebration may be less important than the feelings that it brings up in you, and it is worth asking yourself if you fear such events or anticipate them happily. Maybe you want to be the centre of attention but have difficulty reconciling this with being shy or modest, or perhaps you find it stressful making speeches or playing the host or hostess – roles that also put you firmly in the spotlight.

If in your waking life you are being caught up in routine and yearn to be more spontaneous, your dream celebrations could give you the opportunity to let your hair down. If you think this is true then try and create a time where you can do it for real, and live the dream.

## THE PARAPHERNALIA OF CELEBRATIONS

More subtle indications or symbols of ceremonies may be present in your dream – a wedding ring standing in for the unity and commitment of marriage, a coffin for the death of a loved one, a crown or sceptre for a coronation, balloons for a festive occasion.

Clothes are an important part of many traditional ceremonies, and if in your dream the clothes are wrong for the occasion, you should look at what makes them so – wearing casual clothes to a formal occasion, for instance, may indicate your resistance to the event, or a feeling that you are not ready for it.

Gift-giving can be fraught with difficulty and evoke a strong emotional response. Look at what the gift is and how appropriate it is, the spirit in which it is given and received, who the recipient and giver are, and, if many presents are changing hands, whether they are comparable or unfairly distributed. Gifts can represent our talents and opportunities, so receiving them or being disappointed by them may hint at how you feel about broader issues in your life.

**RIGHT** A dream that involves a dramatic or epic celebration on a large scale might indicate that you are fretting about a real-life one you are involved with, or might be highlighting a desire you feel to live a little wildly for a time, and forget about your usual routines. **MIDDLE RIGHT** By letting off steam we can release a lot of the tension that such events may induce. **BOTTOM RIGHT** A symbol of celebration, such as popping corks, might be a sign or expression of happiness.

## RITUAL

Many ceremonies are highly ritualized. Their stylised and formulaic nature means that everyone has a role and knows how to behave. Some rituals are extremely taxing, such as some complex and physically exacting initiation rites, which are a test of stamina, physical prowess and ultimately, of whether the initiate is ready for his or her new role.

In dreams we may try to resolve issues around a role we need to play, and so our unconscious will replay this and try to analyse our response to it. Rituals are often able to give us the comfort of predictability, but they may also be markers of change. Look at whether you are a creature of habit or if you enjoy change, and consider why change features in your dream.

## DREAM WEDDING

"I was getting married and all the invitations had been sent out, but in my dream I was trying to post them and they kept turning into scorpions in my hand. The harder I tried to post them the more they fought back and tried to sting me. It was quite terrifying. Although I really wanted to get married, I had had to invite a whole bunch of people that I didn't know – my fiancé's relatives and a lot of my mother's friends and distant relations – and this was where the problem lay. I didn't want them to be there on my big day, and the dream was my way of resisting having to invite them."

# SEPARATION

WHETHER IN OUR DREAMS OR IN WAKING LIFE, SEPARATION ALWAYS IMPLIES CHANGES IN OUR LIVES, LETTING GO AND STARTING ANEW. WE MAY TYPICALLY THINK OF PARTING FROM LOVED ONES, BUT THE IDEA CAN EQUALLY BE APPLIED TO LEAVING HOME, ENDING A JOB, GOING ON A JOURNEY, OR A PHASE IN LIFE DRAWING TO A CLOSE. WE MAY HAVE SADNESS AROUND THE SEPARATION AND THE LOSS OF THE LOVED AND THE FAMILIAR, BUT MANY A SEPARATION WILL INSTEAD BRING HAPPINESS, RELIEF OR EXCITEMENT AS WE LOOK AHEAD. DREAMS OF SEPARATION WILL REFLECT ALL THESE ISSUES DIRECTLY, AND CAN ALSO PINPOINT ANXIETIES WE ARE FEELING THAT AREN'T NECESSARILY OBVIOUSLY LINKED TO SEPARATION ANXIETY.

**BELOW LEFT** Separation leads to an emotion that goes very deep indeed; we may carry over such deeply held scars all of our life.
**BELOW RIGHT** Our dreams may reflect such feelings of separation and loneliness, and may need addressing when we are awake in order to find the source, and hopefully alleviate the pain.

## PARTING FROM OUR LOVED ONES

It is inevitable that we will at some stage be separated from people we love. As well as coping with the loss, we are afraid of being lonely and having to become self-reliant when perhaps we lack the confidence to do so, and we may give vent to these fears in our dreams. The loss of a long-term relationship is likely to affect us particularly strongly as we grow increasingly dependent on the person whose life is intimately involved with our own, although for some it may come as a relief or a blessing, a way to flourish. Either way we may use dream time to come to terms with the changes and the feelings they bring up.

## LEAVING HOME

When leaving our family and home, even temporarily, we have to discover our independence, perhaps for the very first time, we need to stand on our own two feet without the support we are used to. While being a valuable and important voyage of discovery, this may also be hard to deal with.

Students often report disturbed dreams during their first year away from home. These dreams are often about their childhood, as if by dreaming it they can recapture some of the security they felt then, and are possibly missing now. Leaving the past behind in this way provides an opportunity to discover yourself as an adult, without parental constraints, and you may well use your dreams to engage with new issues and lifestyles as much as to separate from and lay to rest your childhood.

## DIVORCE

Going through divorce is almost always a traumatic experience, and if you are experiencing this process your dreams will probably reflect your distress. Conflict and haggling over possessions may be scary and worrying, especially if you stand to lose a lot in the divorce. You may feel guilty about having caused your marriage to fall apart, or about not having put in enough effort to make it work – or you may blame your partner for exactly the same things. You may even be angry with yourself for having wasted time in the relationship. Coming to terms with our own role in a divorce is part of the long painful process to a new normality, to achieving independence for ourselves.

For many people the worst part is having to be separated from children – both the loss of their presence and guilt at abandoning them. The partner with custody may feel anxiety around having to look after them unaided. How you feel about these issues will affect the quality and content of your dreams.

Divorce is also a traumatic time for children, as they get caught in the cross-fire between the adults involved, and have immensely strong feelings that they are often not able to express or deal with fully. They may feel responsible for the split, abandoned by the parent that leaves, and in some cases fearful and unsettled around the other changes that are happening at the same time, especially if these are not explained fully to them. Children are more prone to nightmares than adults, and may be particularly affected by them at these kinds of stressful times.

## MOVING ON

Long-term separation requires a major adjustment, even if there are positive spin-offs. Moving on may mean coming to terms with past issues and letting go of them, and the new start in life could provide the chance to gain or regain our freedom and sense of self. Dreams that involve objects strongly associated with your past, such as favourite childhood toys or gifts given to you by your partner, may well be showing you what you need to let go of.

**LEFT** Dreaming of going away somewhere, perhaps alone, might point to feelings of separation anxiety that you are trying to subdue. It might also point to a desire to get away and move on.

## SEPARATION ANXIETY

At the age of around seven or eight months, a baby starts to show signs of having a strong attachment to its primary carer, and distress when separated from that person, especially when upset or ill.

At first the infant may protest by crying, but can be comforted by another. If the separation is prolonged, the child may despair, seeming calmer but becoming apathetic, no longer looking for its carer and trying to comfort itself by thumb-sucking or rocking. In the most extreme cases of separation anxiety the infant becomes detached and unresponsive, and will even ignore the return of the caregiver.

These very human reactions we have to separation might be at their most acute when we are young, but they can carry on to adulthood, and can perhaps be as traumatic and damaging. Dreams may well bring up these issues, and if you dream of them often, perhaps you need to examine where your anxieties come from.

**ABOVE** When it is time to move on from an unhappy relationship, the grief of separation can be hard to bear, for all concerned, even if we know it's the best course of action. If a separation you were involved with happened long ago, but is still part of your emotional baggage, you may well deal with it in dreams.

# PERFORMANCE

WHEN WE THINK OF PERFORMANCE WE PROBABLY HAVE SOME KIND OF DRAMATIC PRODUCTION IN MIND. BUT THERE IS A SENSE IN WHICH WE ARE ALL ACTORS PLAYING MANY DIFFERENT ROLES, WITH LIFE ITSELF AS A STAGED PERFORMANCE. OUR DREAMS MAY SHOW US THE STYLIZED AND PUBLIC ASPECTS OF OUR LIVES AS MUCH AS OUR PRIVATE INNER WORLDS, AND DREAMS IN WHICH PERFORMANCE FEATURES COULD WELL BE GIVING US IMPORTANT INFORMATION ABOUT THE TYPES OF ROLES WE ARE ACCUSTOMED TO PLAYING IN DAILY LIFE.

### THE WORLD OF STAGE AND SCREEN

Theatrical or film productions are artificial and stylized portrayals of reality. The breakdown of a play into acts and scenes gives it a structure and predictability lacking in normal life; scenery and props are usually pared down to the essentials and actors may speak in a noticeably dramatic way for emphasis, showing and saying only what is essential to get the story or the message across. Films contain a different type of artifice, tricking us into believing that what we see is real by virtue of their detail, or abandoning any pretence at reality altogether in special effects or animation.

When theatre and film appear in our dreams, there are several aspects we need to look at.

Having a dream that features a stage or screen performance can be something of a conundrum – the entertainment is often a fictional scenario played out within the fantasy of the dream, and it can be difficult to tell where one fantasy ends and the other begins. The performers are dream characters one step further removed from reality than usual – what is being highlighted is that they are in a sense not real people even in the dream reality; they are in role, they are not what they seem. Their exaggerated movements and speech may be stressing things that we particularly need to notice. Such exaggerations, together with the fact that the actors are presenting a persona or donning a mask, may also be trying to express how ill at ease

we feel in ourselves, in that we are choosing to project an image rather than being authentic. They may also allow us to take on roles that we ordinarily cannot or will not assume – being a king or tyrant, a jester or fool, a child or even a fantasy figure.

Mime figures may be there to underscore our inability to be heard, although their exaggerated body movements could be telling us that we are more in touch with expressing ourselves physically than verbally.

### PERFORMING FOR AN AUDIENCE

Asking yourself how the audience responds could give you insight into why your unconscious is using the performing metaphor. Do they like the performance, or are they chatting among themselves, heckling or walking out? Is the performance an audition? We are constantly being assessed in our daily lives, measured against standards that may be beyond our control, and rewarded in our jobs for "performing" well. It is tempting to measure our self-worth in the light of such standards, and we will work hard towards getting a positive response. In our dreams we may be looking for this response, or may fear being challenged by others when we put ourselves forward. If the audience is ignoring you though, this could be saying something about you not getting a message across or not being noticed. If they are laughing or you are performing badly, it can reveal a fear of failure.

In a dream performance you may forget your lines – losing the thread of why you are performing, or perhaps feeling anxious or over-challenged. It may be that you are being required to say something that goes against the grain, and are having difficulty internalizing it.

## CIRCUSES AND CARNIVALS

There is something intriguing about circuses and carnivals. We relish the glitz and glamour, and get an adrenalin rush from watching the daring feats of the high wire. Running away to join the circus is a classic example of escapism, and dreaming of such performances may point to a lack of adventure in our lives – we desire to be part of the show, to become a travelling player and see the world. If you do dream of a circus, look at which roles or acts dominate – the ringmaster,

lion-tamer, trapeze artist tightrope-walker, or clown, may provide clues to the issues you are trying to address.

## BEING FAMOUS

In our dreams we may dream that we are playing to a packed house, that we are feted as a superstar. This may be because we desire the fame and fortune that stardom brings, or it could represent a desire for attention or recognition of our talents, or a need to be praised just for being who we are. It could also indicate something we long to achieve.

**ABOVE** Appearing naked in front of a laughing audience is a classic nightmare scenario. Such a dream may be about performance anxiety.
**ABOVE LEFT** If you have a performance dream, notice if you are a solo player or part of the chorus. Which role suits you best and what does this mean for you?

Be not afeard; the isle is full of noises,
Sounds and sweet airs, that give delight
    and hurt not.
Sometimes a thousand twangling instruments
Will hum about mine ears, and sometime voices
That, if I then had waked after long sleep,
Will make me sleep again: and then, in dreaming,
The clouds me thought would open and
    show riches
Ready to drop upon me that, when I waked,
I cried to dream again.

WILLIAM SHAKESPEARE, THE TEMPEST

# CREATIVITY

EXPRESSING OUR CREATIVITY IS A VITAL PART OF THE HUMAN EXPERIENCE AND WE DO THIS IN A MULTITUDE OF WAYS, BOTH ABSTRACT AND LITERAL, THROUGH MEDIA SUCH AS MUSIC, PAINTING, HANDIWORK, POETRY, THEATRE AND DANCE. WE MAY ENGAGE IN THESE PURELY FOR OUR OWN ENJOYMENT OR FOR THE BENEFIT OF OTHERS, FOR AESTHETIC PLEASURE, PERSONAL DEVELOPMENT OR SPIRITUAL REASONS. EVEN PEOPLE WHO REGARD THEMSELVES AS LACKING IN TALENT CAN ENJOY GETTING THEIR HANDS DIRTY, SINGING IN THE SHOWER OR BOPPING TO A CATCHY TUNE. AND WE ALL SHOW TO THE WORLD ASPECTS OF OUR PERSONALITY AND OUR SENSE OF AESTHETICS IN THE CLOTHES WE WEAR AND THE WAY WE DECORATE OUR HOMES.

**ABOVE** In our dreams there are no restraints on our creativity. We may be able to express ourselves in ways that are not usually available to us.
**ABOVE RIGHT** The music in our dreams can be warm and inviting or strident and discordant. It may also tell us something about how we express our creativity.

Creative expression may be about entertainment, telling a story or giving a message, but often what we are doing is simply giving an outlet to a mood, or exploring abstract concepts of sound, colour, form or texture.

## VISUAL ARTS

In graphic art we are interpreting the world around us and creating a new version that does not exist in reality. In our dreams the reality of an artwork is twice removed from that of our waking life – once by being a graphical representation (on canvas or paper) and again by being a fabrication of our unconscious. The artist may rearrange objects, distort them or place a special focus on particular features. In

your dream image, distorted perspective may be an indication of too much emphasis being placed on something. Being out of focus may point to confusion, obscurity or a lack of clarity, while depth or detail in a painting can show an awareness of complexity in your life.

In creating an artwork, there is a significance or value in the subject matter, which is probably key to interpreting your dream. In photography in particular, we may be wanting to take a snapshot of life, to preserve or record something; this may suggest a yearning to hang on to things, to remember, or perhaps to dwell in the past.

In craftwork we add a practical element to creative expression, so

if you dream of handcrafted items, you need to look at their function as much as their visual appearance. The presence of such objects may suggest individuality, or a strong personal touch in your environment.

## MUSIC

Harmony and discord in music can signpost the same moods in your life – showing whether or not you are at one with your surroundings, your lifestyle, or the people with whom you have regular contact.

Music may be soulful, fun, energetic or restful, romantic or mathematically precise, abstract or lyrical, and these qualities may reflect your moods and feelings. Likewise, different instruments may evoke particular responses in you, or have symbolic value – playing a loud instrument such as a trumpet may enable you to be heard, while drums are used to keep in time or set the pace, and have military associations.

Orchestras, bands and choirs are useful symbols for group behaviour and co-ordination. Depending on the type of group, it may be important to blend in with the crowd, or to let your contribution stand out. Being a soloist or conductor in a dream may be about needing to "go it alone" in some venture, or take responsibility in some way that places you in a spotlight. As a soloist you may feel exposed, but you will also feel the security of having a backing group supporting and adding value to your solo performance.

Practice makes perfect – but going over something again and again can be tedious and stifle your self-expression. In your dreams it may be telling you that you are stuck in a rut or being prevented from doing other things that may be more worthwhile or enjoyable. On the positive side, though, practising is about getting things right; see how the mood of the dream ties in with your life.

## CLOTHES AND DÉCOR

The way we dress and decorate our homes says a lot about our personal style – aesthetics, attitudes toward comfort, functionality, culture, prestige and so on. In our dreams and our waking lives alike, we may use colours and styles of dress in a variety of ways; to attract

attention or to blend in, to impress others, to express our sexuality, or to act as camouflage. Our notions of what clothing is appropriate may be quite vague, but appearances count, and we are often judged by them.

**BELOW** When dreaming of creative pursuits, notice whether the participants enjoy what they are doing or if they are doing it to please someone else. What does the dream say about your creativity?

**LEFT** An artist is able to interpret the world and create something original. Each night in our dreams we all become artists as we draw on our experiences to create and recreate countless images of ourselves.

# COMMUNICATION

HUMANS ARE SOPHISTICATED COMMUNICATORS. WE HAVE EVOLVED NUMEROUS COMPLEX LANGUAGES THAT WE CAN USE TO EXPRESS THE MOST DETAILED NUANCES OF OUR FEELINGS AND EXPERIENCES. WE HAVE DEVELOPED INGENIOUS SYSTEMS OF RECORDING INFORMATION AND TRANSMITTING IT ACROSS TIME AND DISTANCE. WE ALSO COMMUNICATE WITHOUT WORDS – BODY LANGUAGE AND TONE OF VOICE SOMETIMES GIVING MORE INFORMATION THAN WHAT WE UTTER. DESPITE THIS, OR PERHAPS BECAUSE OF THE COMPLEXITY OF OUR AVAILABLE COMMUNICATION CHANNELS, WE ARE OFTEN FRUSTRATED BY MISCOMMUNICATION, A LACK OF INFORMATION, OR BY CONFUSION OVER MIXED MESSAGES.

In trying to decipher our dreams of communication, we need to pay attention to what is being said, who is saying it and in what way, as well as to what is happening at the same time. Are people shouting or whispering? Are they looking at us? Do we understand them? Is what they say compatible with what they are doing? Also consider whether the communication is happening face to face or at a distance.

**BELOW** Shouting in a dream can indicate that you need to speak up for yourself. Does it feel as though no one is listening to you, or that in order to make yourself heard you have to raise your voice?

## SPEAKING WITH A PURPOSE

To give information and express our feelings and opinions are probably the most important reasons we communicate. But we also speak and write to change or manipulate others – to persuade them round to our point of view, by preaching or dictating to them or by using our expressions to intimidate them. We may feel uncomfortable with silence, and feel we need to fill the void with chatter to hide or deny our insecurity. And of course we talk for the pleasure of it – to make or maintain contact, or to entertain.

Get a feel for the purpose of the communication in the dream and relate it to how others speak to you in real life, as well as how you use communication yourself.

If your communication is not straightforward in the dream, try to understand why this is – perhaps you don't trust that others will accept you or agree with you if you say what you mean. If this is the case, it could be worth looking at your beliefs and checking if they are still true for you so that you can feel more confident in them or dispense with them.

## LANGUAGE

We often use our dreams to try to decipher situations we don't understand, and may use language as a metaphor for our confusion – indistinct speech, riddles or foreign tongues, for example. There may be clues in the dream to why we are not communicating effectively or

---

### COMMUNICATION DREAM

"I was at a noisy party where everyone was talking at the same time. I couldn't understand what anyone was saying – but I realized I could understand what they were thinking. They were thinking really rude thoughts, criticising each other's clothes, making personal comments. But their words were all jumbled as they came out. I was too embarrassed to say anything and I wanted to run out. I was afraid that someone else could understand my own thoughts – namely, that they were all animals. I woke up feeling completely lost and disoriented.

I am quite perceptive about what is going on with others, but don't always trust my intuitions and get confused by lies and subterfuge. I have also always had a problem saying what I mean and this dream was showing me my fears and frustrations around this – often I just keep quiet when I am angry with someone and really feel like being very rude. "

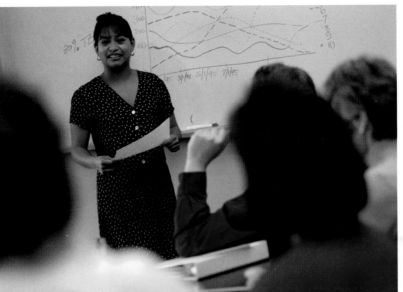

**BELOW** What would a child shouting mean in your dreams? Could it be that you are afraid to say what you think for fear of being judged as childish or rude? Or perhaps you have a child who is struggling to be heard?

**LEFT** We adapt the way we communicate to fit with the situation. Talking to our work colleagues is different from talking to close friends or family. How you communicate tells you a lot about how you relate to other people.

**RIGHT** Pay attention to body language and subtle signals as well as what is being said. Looking away while someone is talking to you could mean many different things.

understanding others, and it could be useful to see if you are in contact with people in your daily life who are hard to fathom, or who are not what they seem.

### SELF-EXPRESSION

In our dreams, we may be involved in the communication process or perhaps we are onlookers seeing others interact. Watching ourselves talking can be very revealing. Are we at ease talking? Or do we find it difficult in the dream? Are we happy with what we are saying or are the words stilted and awkward? If we can't see ourselves but we are still part of the dream how do we interpret what people are saying to us? The whole secret to good

**RIGHT** Children love to whisper and share their secrets. Is there something private that you would like to say to someone? What is holding you back?

or accurate dream interpretation is asking questions: why are we saying this? Who are we talking to? What is their response?

### SHOUTING

We cry out to make others hear, or express intensity. It is not uncommon, especially among children, to dream of shouting at the top of your voice but barely a whisper comes out. This is almost certainly to do with feeling you are not heard, that your voice doesn't count.

*The meaning of every dream is the fulfilment of a wish.*

SIGMUND FREUD

# ENERGY AND POWER

ENERGY TAKES A MULTITUDE OF FORMS, AND IN OUR DREAMS WE ENCOUNTER IT IN THE CATACLYSMIC ERUPTIONS OF NATURE — VOLCANOES, LIGHTNING, EARTHQUAKES — AS MUCH AS IN OURSELVES. THOUGH WE CAN EXPRESS OUR ENERGY POSITIVELY THROUGH DANCE, SPORT AND VERY MANY OTHER ACTIVITIES, IT IS OFTEN CHANNELLED INTO AGGRESSION AND VIOLENCE. LEARNING HOW TO CHANNEL VIOLENT, AGGRESSIVE ENERGY CAN BE A LIFELONG STRUGGLE AND WE MAY NEVER FEEL TOTALLY CONFIDENT THAT WE HAVE IT UNDER OUR CONTROL. THE TRICK IS TO ALLOW THE FEELINGS WITHOUT ACTING THEM OUT. IF WE SUPPRESS THEM AND TURN THEM IN OURSELVES, WE WILL DO OURSELVES HARM.

**ABOVE** The universe is born out of energy and our powerful responses may be much more natural than we think. To dream of nature's forces may mean that you have personal power issues to work out. How do others see you?

## VIOLENT ORIGINS

Stars are born out of cosmic explosions on an unimaginable scale. Fiery forces deep within our own planet erupt as volcanoes so destructive that they can engulf entire cities and set up far-reaching tidal waves. Our entire universe was created in violent energy reactions, and continues to evolve and be transformed in this way. Even our own birth is an energetic and sometimes violent moment, a dramatic experience for mother and child alike, and the baby's first gasp of breath is a struggle.

It is not surprising, then, that we may be troubled when such images occur in our dreams. It is as though we are struggling with the violence inherent in our existence, and trying to reconcile this with the passivity and control that are in many ways esteemed in our society.

## VIOLENCE CURTAILED

The struggle with energy and violence is so instinctive that it permeates our unconscious, but there are precious few socially sanctioned outlets for this in our normal waking lives. Being civilized, controlled, elegant, and sophisticated are prized at the expense of emotional expression. We still have the same instinctive

reactions and negative emotions as our primitive forebears, but the "fight or flight" response is often not appropriate in our modern world. We are not allowed to be violent, no matter how incensed we are, and if we do become violent or if we have temper tantrums, we are punished, and we may feel overwhelmed, frightened and guilty at the very thought of it.

We need these dreams as safety valves for our unexpressed violence, anger and frustration, and to give us an opportunity to find alternative ways of dealing with the world so that these feelings don't well up in the first place. Sometimes our unconscious presents us with dreams of energy or violence in its raw and awesome state in order to forge a safe link between our calm outer persona and our turbulent inner self, between our civilized, rational exterior and the anger and passions that many of us tend to bottle up. In this way, having violent dreams can be a healthy experience.

The more elaborate, complex and impenetrable the mask of sophistication a person wears, the bigger the gap between feeling and response. Conversely, the more instinctual and expressive the person, the less likely they are to be troubled by such dreams, as they have already found ways of venting their energy safely in waking life.

## ATTACK AND DEFENCE

If violence is a real part of your life, you may be constantly in fear and on your guard against being attacked. The trauma of even a single attack may linger for years. It can prompt feelings of anger and violence, and you may want to act these out on particular individuals. However, the feelings may be unfocused and you are simply searching for a target for them. But if you are powerless to act on your feelings in real life, you may well have these encounters in your dreams instead. You can also actively use your dreams to deal with violence in a positive way – it can be beneficial to replay the scene of an attack in your dreams in such a way that you successfully defend yourself. This can give you the strength and feeling of self-worth you need to move on.

The physical attacks of your dreams can be metaphors for many other ways in which you might be attacked. Perhaps your ideas or actions have been harshly criticized and you take this personally, or you have to bear the brunt of someone else's anger, even when you haven't deserved it. In these cases it is useful to look at the role you play – are you aggressive, taunting, or an innocent bystander, a victim of circumstances? How you respond to an attack is also important, and your dream could give you clues as to how to deal with aggression in others.

**LEFT** We may think ourselves cool and calm, yet our dreams may show what is bubbling beneath the surface, like a volcano waiting to erupt.
**MIDDLE LEFT** The tighter the grip on our natural responses, the more likely we are to "blow up".
**BOTTOM LEFT** Cosmic explosions are what sets the universe in motion. Powerful, violent energy is part of life – we can use this force to create or to destroy – it's up to us.

## ENERGY DREAM

"I could see worlds in collision, entire galaxies erupting in fireballs and glorious colourful explosions. It was staggering, mind-blowing, and I could see how the world was made out of conflagration. It seems strange that such violent destruction can result in so much beauty.

I think that my dream was trying to tell me that I had to put more energy, more passion, into making things happen, that I had to get rid of the apathy that was holding me back."

# LIVING IN THE WORLD

From the moment of our birth until we die we build up a wealth of experiences through our interactions with the "world out there". These experiences shape who we are and guide our behaviour. How we feel, how we express ourselves, how we react with the world and the people in it, combine to produce a unique experience for each of us. Often we peg our self-worth on external factors, such as our level of wealth, or our achievements or social status, and we expend a great deal of time and energy trying to gain more of these things. Our aspirations become preoccupations and we try to work out aspects of these things in our dreams. In comparing ourselves with others, we may set ourselves up for competition and conflict. But sometimes the world delivers experiences over which we have little or no control – change is part of life and accidents can happen – and our dreams can help us adjust and warn us of potential trouble.

# AMBITIONS AND GOALS

WE ALL HAVE OUR AMBITIONS AND GOALS, HOPES AND DESIRES, AND ENJOY THE SATISFACTION OF SUCCESS WHEN WE FULFIL THEM OR DISAPPOINTMENT WHEN WE CANNOT. BUT IF WE GET TO A POINT AT WHICH WE ARE CONSUMED BY UNFULFILLED AMBITIONS, OUR UNCONSCIOUS WILL TRY TO WORK WITH THEM IN OUR DREAMS, TO SEE A WAY FORWARD OR TO ACCEPT SOMETHING DIFFERENT FOR US. IF WE FAIL TO ACHIEVE SOMETHING THAT IS REALLY IMPORTANT FOR US OR TURN OUR BACK ON A BURNING AMBITION, OUR UNCONSCIOUS WILL PRODUCE DREAMS THAT MAKE US FOCUS ON THAT GOAL AND FIND A WAY TO MAKE US SUCCEED.

### REACH FOR THE SKY

We don't have to put a limit on our hopes and aspirations. If we aim for something in our dreams that we have no hope of actually achieving, it may not matter that our ambitions are unrealistic. Such fantasies can be liberating – they give us scope to stretch our self-imposed limitations, and to make possible things that might otherwise seem far-fetched.

**BELOW** A lock and key is a powerful symbol. Do you have an unfulfilled ambition locked away inside of you, and if so, what is the key to realizing it? Perhaps the key is just out of reach, or maybe it doesn't quite fit the lock.

If an ambition remains out of reach because we have aimed too high, however, it can cause distress. It may leave us feeling that we will never achieve what we want and make us feel like giving up. In which case we may need to take a closer look at it, at the symbolic value of what we are failing to achieve. In asking questions about a dream symbol we may find out why we are being so unrealistic and aiming too high. We can gain more insight into what makes us set ourselves up for failure and find ways to set ourselves more realistic targets.

### STUMBLING BLOCKS

There may well be valid reasons for not achieving an ambition – perhaps deep down inside you know that achieving it may not be as beneficial as you might like. For example, you may have been offered a fantastic job that will mean moving abroad, but because it offers you things you really want you may well be blinded to the attendant

**BELOW** To dream that you are doing a tedious, repetitive task may suggest that your goals are set too low. Perhaps it's time to get your ideas in order, rather like the bottles on the assembly line, and review your ambitions.

disadvantages or dangers – your family doesn't want to go, your parents would miss you, the company is not as stable as you want to believe, or your expertise isn't up to a high-powered job.

These unconscious realizations may manifest themselves as something stopping us in our dreams. This could be a locked door or a fence that stops us going along a certain path. A guard is another common symbol; this is usually someone impassive, anonymous and immovable who bars our way. If we don't find a way past the obstacles in our dream, then perhaps we ought to reconsider our ambition. But if we do manage to get through, this may give us a clue as to what our best course of action should be. We can relate it to our waking lives and find a way of achieving our goals and ambitions. On the other hand it may show us that although achieving our goal is possible, it is going to be very difficult, so perhaps it would be better to scale back or drop what it is that we are after.

## SYMBOLIC IMAGERY

Literal images of goals and targets may appear in our dream to symbolize our personal ambitions. Games involving scoring goals, or aiming accurately for a small target, such as golf or darts, can show us how focused we are and whether or not our ambitions are fixed or keep changing. As well as looking at the nature of the

goal, notice whether the game in your dream is a team effort, and if so who is helping or opposing you, or whether you are solely responsible in some way.

## THE SCALE OF OUR AMBITIONS

Remember that our goals may be anything from major lifelong ambitions to relatively trivial targets, such as tidying up a messy cupboard, so if the dream does appear obviously to be about goals or ambitions but you are unable to see immediately what it could be referring to, think laterally about the nature of what you might be trying to process. Even small goals may take on greater significance than they deserve if they link into personal hang-ups – if your mother was always pestering you to tidy your room when you were a child, for instance, you may feel obsessed, angry or resistant about tidying up. Being goal oriented may also mean that you will tend to turn ordinary activities into goals, into something you can check off a list, rather than just being a regular part of daily life.

**RIGHT** Some ambitions are not easy to achieve but require great skill and tenacity if we are to make it to the top.
**MIDDLE RIGHT** A dream could suggest that achieving your goal will require total commitment, just like an athlete preparing to race.
**BOTTOM RIGHT** Our dreams may tell us to take control and put ourselves forward, rather than sitting in the background waiting to be asked.

Dreams are a dress rehearsal for life. ALFRED ADLER

# ACHIEVEMENT AND SUCCESS

FROM THE MOMENT WE TAKE OUR FIRST BREATH, WE ARE DRIVEN TO ACHIEVE. FOR INFANTS, LEARNING TO EAT, CRAWL, STAND UP, WALK AND SPEAK IS A MATTER OF SURVIVAL, AND OUR NATURAL INSTINCT TO ACHIEVE THESE THINGS IS SUPPORTED BY PARENTAL ENCOURAGEMENT. AS WE GROW UP, OUR ACHIEVEMENTS BECOME MORE COMPLEX AND THE WAY WE MEASURE SUCCESS CHANGES. AT SCHOOL AND COLLEGE WE ARE ENCOURAGED TO SUCCEED ACADEMICALLY AND WHEN WE ENTER THE WORLD OF WORK, ACHIEVEMENT IS LINKED WITH JOB SATISFACTION. OUR DREAMS CAN SHOW US WHERE WE FEEL PROUD OF OUR ACHIEVEMENTS AND POINT TO AREAS WHERE WE FEEL DISSATISFIED AND UNFULFILLED.

## MAKING IT

You may dream of winning an award or prize of some sort to mark your achievement. Or perhaps someone claps you on the back and says "well done". You may dream that you score a goal or play the winning hand or captain your favourite team, or that you suddenly have acquired a new skill, such as being able to play the violin. Maybe you have suddenly become famous and are signing autographs and giving

**BELOW** What would a running child mean in your dreams? Are you still that racing child eager for success or do you have some growing up to do before you make it?

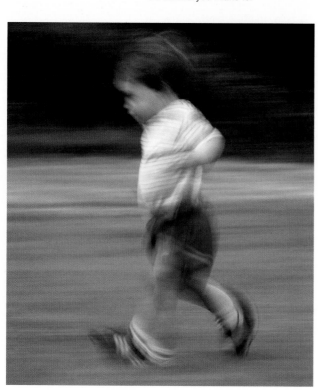

press conferences. Your dream may even give you a halo, a set of wings, a new power such as flying or walking on water. Such dreams could suggest that you are proud of your achievements. Alternatively, they may point up a glaring mis-match between your dream self and your actual experience. Perhaps you need to define what "making it" would mean for you and find an arena in which to express yourself.

## SUCCESS IN OTHERS

In your dream, it may even be someone else and not you who is successful. Consider how you feel towards this person. You may feel warm and supportive and full of encouragement or you may feel jealous and competitive. But it is also worth bearing in mind that the other people in our dreams may also actually be displacements of ourselves.

Dreaming of someone else's success could be as close as we can get to admitting our own success, to being told we've done well and to knowing that we're alright. If you know the person who is successful in your dream, try to understand what they represent to you, and see what it is about their character or what they are doing that makes things go well. This may show you how you can be more successful.

## TEAM EFFORT

Sometimes we dream of the success of a group – our favourite football team winning the cup or scoring lots of goals, a country finally negotiating peace after being at war for many years, or the company we work for expanding so we get that pay rise we wanted. In this kind of scenario, the group effort may be key to understanding the meaning of your dream – perhaps it is a hint not to try to do everything yourself if you want to achieve your goals, or to enable you to place some trust in the people who may help you on your way.

## ACKNOWLEDGEMENT

Part of our drive for success is rooted in our desire to be acknowledged, and to be noticed and admired. Dreams of parents, friends and partners watching and cheering you on may demonstrate that you feel valued as a person, while being feted by the public, such as being cheered by a crowd or carried on their shoulders, may show a desire for public recognition. Perhaps you would like the world to see and acknowledge your status and everything that you have achieved. Prizes and medals may indicate that you need a constant reminder of your successes, and

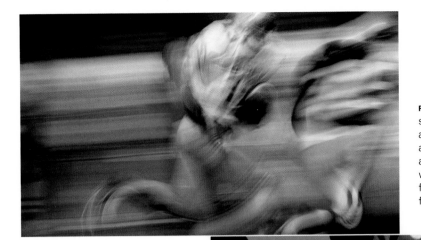

**RIGHT** A silver cup is a symbol that most of us associate with successful achievement. Seeing it in a dream may mean we would like to win a prize for something that we feel proud of doing.

**ABOVE** How does it feel to be successful? Life's peak moments can pass us by in a blur because we are so caught up with speed and wanting to win.

that you are not able to rely on your own awareness of your abilities to realize what you are worth. The appearance of any of these things does, however, mean that you know within yourself that you are worthwhile and that you deserve some level of recognition.

**LEFT** College graduation is typically marked by fun and celebration in honour of our achievements. For many people this moment represents the fulfilment of a childhood wish.

## DREAM OF SUCCESS

"I was riding in a limousine along a street lined with cheering fans; as it was a convertible, they could get really close. I looked really cool and well dressed. All these people were cheering and whistling as if I had done something really amazing. I didn't know what I had done, but it felt really good! When I woke up I thought it would be cool to be recognized like that, and since then I've been sending demos off to radio stations and record companies. I don't know if I'll get anywhere, but it feels worthwhile – if I have any moments of doubt I just have to remember that dream to spur me on. I can't wait for it to be real, to be cheered by real fans."

**RIGHT** When can we say we have finally reached the summit? Even in our dreams it may be difficult to plot such an exact moment, although there are times in everyone's life when we should feel proud of ourselves. When did you last feel on top of the world?

**BELOW** It is not always easy to measure our achievements and we may feel the need for some kind of external validation, such as more money or a certificate, to increase our self-esteem.

# JOBS AND WORK

WE SPEND A LOT OF TIME AT WORK, AND EARNING A LIVING IN A SATISFYING WAY IS ONE OF LIFE'S GREATEST CHALLENGES. IT IS ONLY NATURAL FOR WORK TO OCCUPY AN IMPORTANT PART OF OUR DREAM LIFE. BUT WORK IN A DREAM IS NOT ALWAYS ABOUT AN ACTIVITY THAT WE DO — WE ENCOUNTER PEOPLE WHO ARE OPERATING IN THEIR WORK ROLES ALL THE TIME, AND OUR COLLEAGUES MAY ALSO FIGURE PROMINENTLY. ENJOYING OUR WORK MAY BE REFLECTED IN POSITIVE, HAPPY DREAMS ABOUT IT, OR DREAMS IN WHICH WE GRAPPLE WITH INTERESTING REAL-LIFE PROBLEMS THAT WE CAN'T BEAR TO LET GO OF EVEN IN OUR SLEEP. SOMETIMES STRESS AND ANXIETY RELATED TO WORK WILL ALSO SURFACE.

**ABOVE** When work seems like drudgery, it could be time to review your career options.
**ABOVE RIGHT** Your dreams may reflect what it is you really want to do with your life.
**ABOVE FAR RIGHT** You might dream about the work of others rather than yourself. Is this a reflection of someone in your life who has authority over you? Is the authority justified or does it worry and frustrate you?

## WORK AND EMOTIONS
Unfortunately, for many people work means stress, boredom, frustration, unhappiness, and anger; we may feel unchallenged or abused or taken for granted, and our dreams may well reflect such feelings. We may say or do something extreme in the work environment of our dream, and wake worrying that we might act out such stuff in real life. But the point of these dreams may in fact be to address just that possibility – to let off steam in the safety of our dreams so that we don't cause a scene at work.

Work dreams may seem fairly realistic, but at other times our unconscious will create a memorable scenario to draw our attention to what is bothering us.

Dreaming of work might also be symbolic of more general issues, such as survival or money, how to rise to a challenge or deal with pressure, feelings of inadequacy, subservience or anger and a myriad other experiences.

## PEOPLE AT WORK
We do not always dream about our own jobs, however. As in our daily lives, we are constantly in contact with or seeing images of others as they go about their work, from shopkeepers to bank managers, newsreaders to teachers, factory workers to artists and chefs. We probably hold countless attitudes about those roles – wishing we could be in the other person's shoes, or thanking our lucky stars that we

aren't. We may admire people for their work, thinking that they must be clever or talented or courageous to do what they do, and envy the satisfaction or prestige or fame that goes with their wonderful-looking jobs. Or perhaps we hate the idea of the tedium or lack of status of a particular job, the confinement of an office or the uncertainty of contract work.

Engaging with strangers in our dreams may often be in the context of their occupation, and our attitude to that occupation. Teachers, bosses and policemen, for instance, tend to be authority figures, and your experiences in real life will be crucial in forming your attitude to such figures. As a child, did you have teachers who picked on you, inflicted corporal punishment or made you feel stupid? Or did they inspire you, understand and encourage you, satisfy and nurture your curiosity or give you a love of reading?

People at work can symbolize many different things. To dream of a cleaner, for instance, may indicate you need to get your house in order and to "clean up", while an accountant might suggest that you take stock of your affairs and get organized. An artist on the other hand may suggest that you need to relax your attitudes and think laterally or engage more with your intuitive, creative side.

### COLLEAGUES

We spend much of our waking lives with colleagues, so it is not surprising if we dream about them. Often their function in our dreams will be similar to that of friends, in that they will appear because they have particular characteristics that we need to address. But in many cases their role will be more important – bosses in particular may bring up important issues relating to authority, power and status.

**RIGHT** Some workplaces are big and imposing. Dreaming that you are in such a building can make you feel small and insignificant, especially if you are alone.
**MIDDLE RIGHT** Sometimes it feels as though you are just going round and round and not getting anywhere. Your dream may be showing you that progress does not always follow a straight line.
**BOTTOM RIGHT** Repetitive work is not necessarily boring. Your dream may be a reminder to take a pride in all your endeavours and know that every job has its part to play.

### WORKPLACES AND RESOURCES

If you find in your dream that you are unable to do things because the equipment you have for doing your job is inadequate or the work environment is unpleasant, it could be saying something general about your material wellbeing or your ability to get things done.

Do you feel that you get what you want out of life, or that there are constantly obstacles to what you want to do? Our physical environment can have a major impact on our emotional state, so it is worth noting how you feel about the workplace of your dream as much as what you are doing or the people you are with.

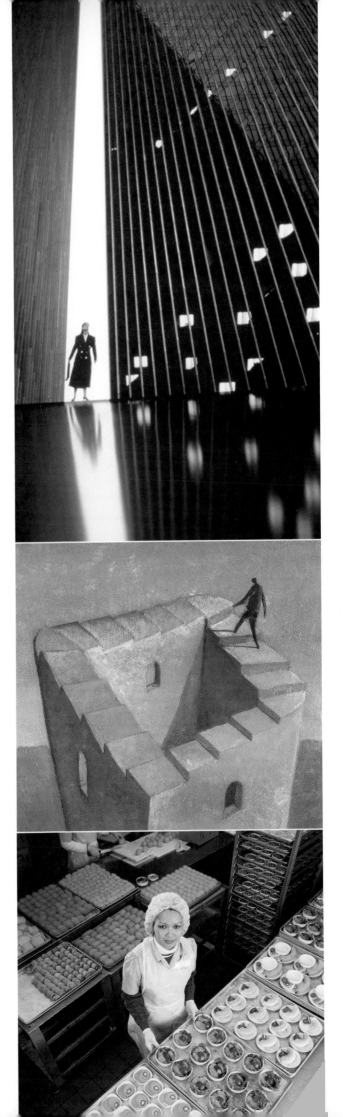

### WORK DREAM

"I was due to go on my first business trip, to the headquarters of a major bank. In my dream I arrived at their imposing building and went up in the lift. The doors opened directly into the boardroom, which contained a massive table surrounded by middle-aged men in suits. As they looked up I realized to my horror that, although I was wearing a smart black jacket and smart black shoes, I was also wearing a frilly, homemade nightdress.

This dream was clearly to do with not feeling confident in myself or comfortable in the imposing and masculine setting of the bank. I was afraid that I couldn't pull off the meeting successfully, that I would somehow make a serious gaffe, be intimidated or not be taken seriously."

# SPORTS AND GAMES

FUN, PHYSICAL WELLBEING AND A SENSE OF ACHIEVEMENT ARE JUST SOME OF THE REASONS WE TAKE PART IN SPORTS AND GAMES. THEY ALSO PROVIDE A WAY OF ENGAGING WITH OTHER PEOPLE IN A VERY ACTIVE WAY, AS BOTH TEAM MEMBERS AND OPPONENTS, AS WELL AS HELPING US RELEASE STRESS AND CHANNEL OUR AGGRESSIVE IMPULSES. FOR ARMCHAIR SPORTSMEN OR TEAM SUPPORTERS AT SPORTS FIXTURES, THERE IS THE EXCITEMENT AND CAMARADERIE OF WATCHING A FAVOURITE TEAM OR FAVOURITE SPORT IN ACTION. WITH THESE DREAMS, WE NEED TO ASK OURSELVES ABOUT THE SPORT WE ARE ENGAGED IN, HOW WE PLAY, AND OUR MOTIVATIONS AND FEELINGS, AS WELL AS WHAT ACTUALLY HAPPENS.

**BELOW** What sport are you pursuing in your dream? Is it something that you normally do?
**BELOW RIGHT** What are the items of equipment associated with a game or sport? Perhaps these have a significance in your dream.
**BELOW FAR RIGHT** Dreams of running a race may raise issues of winning and losing in your life.

## GAMES PEOPLE PLAY

The various forms of sporting and leisure activities represent many qualities. For instance, a violent rugby match may have more to do with aggression and teamwork than the leisurely, non-contact style of a round of golf, while an intellectually absorbing chess game is mainly concerned with strategy and has almost nothing to do with physicality. There are also many games that we play simply for fun, such as beach volleyball or the role-playing games of a child's make-believe world where the rules are made up as they go along.

## SUBLIMATION OF AGGRESSION

For many people, sports and games provide a much-needed way of working through aggression and frustration. The positive effects of strenuous physical activity on the emotions are well documented, and in some sports, hitting or kicking a ball can be a great substitute for doing the same to someone who has made you very angry! By analysing how we feel and how we are behaving and reacting to others in our dream, we can try to uncover the real cause of our aggressive feelings and work through them or lay them to rest.

## OPPONENTS

Who are you playing with and against in your dream? Your opponents may be real people, they may represent abstract qualities – luck, fate, challenges, opposition – or they may be an aspect of yourself that you are at odds with.

Often opponents will be people with whom we are having some kind of power struggle or conflict. Who wins is often a vital question, as it could indicate what is actually happening in an important relationship, what you wish for or what you fear. Look at how seriously you take the game – you may want simply to put your opponent in their place, to hurt them badly, or even to eliminate them altogether.

## TEAMS

Being part of a team gives a great sense of belonging, going beyond our individual needs to unite in a common goal. Teams give us a place, a role, a bond with others. They show us who our friends are and how much we rely on others to achieve our goals. Sports teams can also be a

**RIGHT** Dreams of top sports people are fairly common. Such dreams may represent a wish-fulfilment, an ambition to be the "best" at something, or to be famous and admired. What could this mean for you?

metaphor for other social groups in our lives, such as the family or work team, and looking at how they pull together and the roles people play may be significant in relation to these units.

## COMPETITION AND RESULTS

Competition is an all-pervasive feature of our society, and the games we play are often about proving who is best, who has the greatest talent, skill or intellectual ability. For many people, getting ahead gives a feeling of self-worth that they may otherwise be not capable of feeling. Winning or losing a dream game could be crucial to how you see yourself – your confidence or assertiveness, what your role is in relation to your opponent or your team, or how you view your skills and talents. If you have a relationship

where you are constantly racking up points against each other, this may show up in your dreams as a competition of some sort.

## PLAYING THE GAME

Cheating or rule-breaking may hint at an unfair situation in your life, or one in which someone is being underhand with you. Rules may be about social restrictions, so check whether you know what the rules of the game are, and whether it is you or someone else who is breaking them.

### COMPETITIVE DREAM

"I was playing chess against my father, using life-sized pieces. Although we laughed and joked as we played, I knew we were playing for big stakes and this created an underlying seriousness, a feeling of menace that affected my game. Behind the laughter I was in crisis: I wanted to win so badly it hurt, and I wanted to hurt him, even kill him, by winning. This was a very powerful dream and it made me realize that I had a lot to work out about my relationship with my father. We have always been competitive, and he is also very pushy, expecting me to do well, earn well, and drive myself as hard as he does. I've always felt I have a lot to live up to and although I don't like it, I've always done what he wants. In this dream I realized that I didn't have to be dominated by him forever, but that I would need to be more assertive for that to happen."

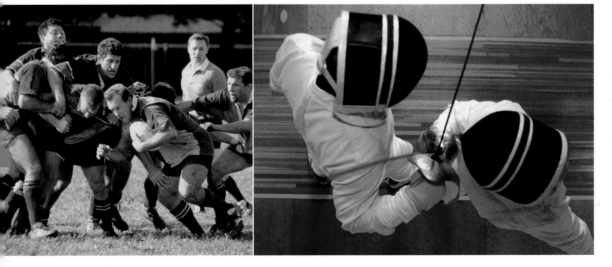

**LEFT** Every sport has its own set of rules and we need to understand them before we can enjoy the game. Are you a player or a spectator in your dream?
**FAR LEFT** Very physical team sports can be a good way of letting off steam. Being part of a team in your dream is a sign of belonging, or wanting to belong.

# MONEY

What does money represent to you? When it comes to working with our dreams the answer to this is crucial. Most people will acknowledge that they want it, and almost certainly that they need it, but beyond that our responses can differ markedly from person to person. Perhaps you see it as a means to an end, or an end in itself; maybe you think that it represents freedom and can liberate people, or you might see it as an enslaver. Our own and others' attitudes to money in real life will inevitably be reflected in our dreams; how much there is, where it came from and what we do with it will also be significant.

### ASSOCIATIONS

Money is generally said to point to opportunity and reward or power. Some associate it with relationships, so in this way receiving it is linked to the birth of a child, finding it could suggest benefiting from a prosperous marriage, and wasting or losing it may mean that you are wasting your love on someone unworthy.

Using a Freudian model, hoarding money implies anal fixation. Money can also be used to represent resources in general. Bear in mind that it could be denoting riches in terms of time, energy, knowledge, love and so on, rather than material or monetary wealth. Consider your relationship with these other resources too and think about how rich or poor you feel.

Some of these money associations may make sense to you and help you to understand what your dream is really about. If not, you will need to dig a bit deeper, and really try to understand what money means to you on a much more personal basis, and thus what it symbolizes in your dream.

**BELOW** Think about what money may symbolize to you. Love? Security? Status? Freedom? Success? It is important to understand your own reactions before you interpret your dreams on the subject.

### WHAT MONEY CAN BUY

It is what we can have and do with money – as well as what is unavailable to us if we don't have it – that gives it much of its value. We may feel that it gives us the freedom to have the things we want, including leisure time and opportunities to see and do things that aren't free. But having acquired wealth, we may feel burdened by our possessions and afraid of losing them, and we may also feel trapped by the need to carry on generating it.

Dreams of money may be simple wish fulfilment, or we may find they show us how to get it, the frustrations of not having it, or the fear of being suddenly deprived of it. But we can also use money dreams as a more general symbol for greed and materialism, opportunity, the loss of something we value, or even of being trapped.

### STATUS AND POWER

Money can convey power and status. We can add to this the idea that money is a reward, so having or not having it differentiates us further and makes us feel more or less worthwhile as people. These issues may well bother us, keying in to our inherent sense of self-worth, and dreams of money – especially in relation to a salary or wage – can be about this idea of our value, of how much we are being appreciated.

## GIVE AND TAKE

If you are hoarding or counting money in your dream, you may be afraid that it will run out or be feeling insecure; similarly putting it in the bank may be to do with security,. Holding on to money can also represent holding on to ideas, rather than putting them into action. If you are giving money away, do you do so with a spirit of generosity, or because you simply want to get rid of it? Spending or giving money freely can imply a certain faith or trust in things working out, that your own needs will always be met, and this can be tremendously reassuring if you normally worry about such matters.

Owing or being owed money in a dream could be a worry about literally being burdened by debt. Looked at in a broader sense though, ask yourself if you are concerned about being indebted to someone in a more general way – perhaps they have done you a favour or you feel guilty about asking for help. You may also feel taken advantage of.

## TYPES OF MONEY

The form the money takes in your dreams may hold another layer of significance. Cash is readily available, and whether it comes in the shape of coins or notes may indicate how much you value whatever it represents to you. An IOU or cheque may signify indebtedness, delayed gratification or uncertainty around whether you will be repaid; gift vouchers may suggest generosity, but may also hint that whatever they represent has some specific value or limitation placed on it. If you dream of foreign money it could be that you are unsure of the value of something.

### MONEY DREAM

"I was being asked to pay admission to the cinema. I had brought a single coin in my pocket, but couldn't find it anywhere – it had slipped through a hole. A terrible grief washed over me. I couldn't understand why it should pain me so much – it was only a trip to the cinema after all.

This dream was about having given up a successful career in film-making to devote myself to my family. My children were growing up and needed me less and less, and I was aware that in the meantime my precious career seemed lost. Although I didn't regret having had children, I was experiencing pain at having let my career slip through my fingers."

# AUTHORITY AND DISCIPLINE

WHEN WE ARE CHILDREN OUR PARENTS AND TEACHERS TELL US WHAT WE CAN AND CAN'T DO. OFTEN THE AIM OF THIS IS TO TEACH US SOCIAL NORMS OR PREVENT US FROM HURTING OURSELVES. BUT MUCH OF THE AUTHORITY THAT ADULTS WIELD OVER CHILDREN IS TO DO WITH THEIR OWN INTERESTS – PROTECTING THEIR BELONGINGS, THEIR NEEDS, THEIR FEELINGS. AS ADULTS WE MIGHT ASSOCIATE PUNISHMENT WITH AN ELEMENT OF UNFAIRNESS AND IMPOSITION, OR WE MIGHT SEE IT AS SOMETHING WE DESERVE MORE OF. AUTHORITY FIGURES MIGHT BE SEEN AS UNJUST AND REPRESSIVE, BUT WE MAY ALSO PRODUCE THEM IN OUR DREAMS AS A SYMBOL OF SECURITY, OR OF WISDOM AND GUIDANCE.

In punishing a child the stated aim may be to teach the child what is safe or dangerous, right and wrong, and acceptable or unacceptable, but from time to time, punishment may be meted out that has nothing to do with a child having done something "bad", but rather with an adult venting frustration or simply being a bully, and this can be frightening and perplexing.

### INNER DISCIPLINE

When we grow up our attitude to authority and punishment can be quite complex, so we may use dream time to unravel how we feel, especially if we come up against problematic authority figures, moral dilemmas or confusion in our daily lives. As adults, there usually isn't the same sort of immediate authority

figure standing over us like when we were children. Hopefully we will have developed an innate sense of what is right and wrong; we have a greater understanding of the consequences of our actions and are able to exercise our own judgement and discretion. Laws and the fear of punishment keep most of us in check where our self-discipline or morality may otherwise slip.

Over the course of our lives, our unconscious takes note of the countless rules and injunctions laid down in our early years by parents, teachers and prefects; as we grow older we become aware of other authority figures and bodies of law, and we notice how others respond to these as well. We also develop subtle ways of avoiding punishment and guilt. If we are acting in a way our

unconscious thinks doesn't suit our own interests, it will let us know through the symbolism of our dreams by creating a figure who can tell us how to behave.

### PUNISHMENT

Our experience of punishment and how we respond to it is also a personal one. Being given detention at school may have been immensely shameful and humiliating for one person, but for another merely irritating or even a fairly normal occurrence. Indeed for some, being punished by "the establishment" establishes "street cred". In some societies beating a child for a wrongdoing may be considered a normal – even essential – part of their growing up, whereas in others it is anathema, and thought to be damaging. So to understand what

**BELOW RIGHT** As children we soon learn who is in charge and this may be reflected in our dreams. Who was the dominant authority figure when you were growing up?
**BELOW** How we respond to authority in any of its smallest forms is very revealing. Even a red traffic light can trigger issues around sticking to or breaking the rules.

**RIGHT** Laws and the fear of being punished keep most of us in check. This can make us feel that we are under surveillance or living in a police state, and may show up in our dreams. Who is watching you?

punishment means in your dreams may mean coming to terms with how you view it in real life. Does it make you feel angry, guilty, submissive or humiliated, or does withstanding it give you strength? Did you feel you deserved it? If you are meting it out, look hard at what you were feeling and who you are punishing. Note what the punishment is, how severe it is, and if you feel it is deserved. Also try to discover why it is being meted out, and what it achieves.

### REBELLING

What if you don't want to be told what to do, or you believe that an authority figure is wrong or evil, or you feel that someone is acting in an authoritarian way towards you but shouldn't? If your boss tells you to forge a signature or your partner dominates or controls your

relationship, you may well feel resentful but unable to be assertive or to inject a reasonable balance. If you can't deal with the matter in an adult way, you may represent the dominant person in your dreams as a teacher or parent. Your powerlessness may reduce you to a small child or even animal, or your resentment may manifest in your dreams as a symbolic rebellion or mutiny.

### AUTHORITY FIGURES

The area of our lives in which we are having difficulties, together with our upbringing, social standing, beliefs and cultural background, will determine who the authority figure in our dream will be. It may be a police officer if we are in danger of breaking

the law, or a priest if religious or moral principles are at stake. For others it might be a judge, lawyer, traffic warden, headteacher, monarch, even a god. Each of these represents something different, and we need to look at what they mean to us to find out what their presence in our dream means.

> ### AUTHORITY DREAM
>
> "In my dream I couldn't find my car keys, and realized my wife had hidden them. I asked her for them back but she said no, it wasn't my turn to drive the car. She told me to go and stand in the corner for being naughty, that I'd asked for the keys before she had told me to. I stood in the corner and she was standing behind me flicking my ears and telling me I had been naughty and deserved to be punished. I felt like a small boy and was really seething inside but I couldn't do anything. In real life my wife is in control, and I guess I hate this."

**BELOW LEFT** Sometimes we may wonder who is pulling the strings. Our dreams can show us who is running the show and what we can do to take more charge of our lives.
**BELOW** It is easy for an adult to overpower a child when he wants to assert his authority. This can create a fear of authority, which we carry as adults.

# Wars and Battle

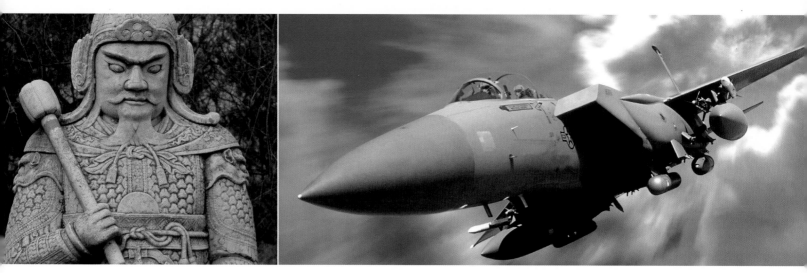

**ABOVE** Many societies recognize warrior values such as strength and courage. When a warrior appears in your dreams it may mean that you need to develop such qualities.
**ABOVE RIGHT** If images of war haunt our dreams we may feel very shocked or disturbed. But being in conflict is something that can happen in personal relationships or you may be fighting with yourself.

ALTHOUGH NOT MANY OF US WILL HAVE ACTIVELY PARTICIPATED IN ARMED COMBAT, THERE IS ALWAYS A WAR BEING FOUGHT IN SOME PART OF THE WORLD THAT WE ARE AWARE OF AND PERHAPS CONCERNED ABOUT. ACTS OF INTERNATIONAL TERRORISM UNSETTLE US AND MAKE US ANXIOUS FOR OUR SAFETY, OR PERHAPS WE LIVE IN A NEIGHBOURHOOD BESET BY GANG CONFLICT. OUR FEARS OF DEATH AND DESTRUCTION, INJURY, INVASION, INSECURITY, HELPLESSNESS, SORROW, PAIN AND LOSS RISE TO THE SURFACE, AND IN TIMES OF WAR OUR DREAMS CAN BECOME EVEN MORE VIVID.

## THE ENEMY

Dreams of war don't necessarily reflect the belligerent or defensive attitude of a nation – they are quite likely to be more to do with acting out our own private battles. Our dreams reflect why we are under attack or what we are fighting for.

Identifying the enemy and understanding what they symbolize is crucial in analysing such a dream, as is the matter of which party is the aggressor. If the war represents a power struggle or a fight over scarce resources, it is also important to understand who has the upper hand. Are you retaliating for something that has already happened, or defending yourself against an ongoing attack? Perhaps you feel invaded by a particular person or circumstance in your life, and you have to defend your "territory", or someone is bullying or abusing you and you are too frightened to fight back in real life.

It may even be that you are simply recognizing the need to be more assertive, or that you are not being taken notice of and realize that spectacular action is required in order to get through.

## ALLIES AND FIGHTING STRENGTH

We also need to ask questions about our own side – whether we are fighting alone or have allies, and if so how organized and how strong they are, and what kind of tactics they use. Our own attitude and that of the people around us is important. We may feel passionately that there is a lot at stake, and that this is a war worth waging, but equally the war could be something we are forced to participate in against our will; for a pacifist, it may be complete anathema. If others seem keen, but we are not, then this could indicate some disharmony with the people we do things with in a team of some kind. A formally organized army may well bring up feelings around authority and discipline,

## DREAM OF WAR

"I was a soldier stalking an unseen enemy, a sort of sniper in a ruined city. I followed every move of the enemy, but knew that although I was the hunter I was going to get killed. Sure enough, as I turned a corner this faceless soldier let me have it. I was blown away.

For me this was about acting aggressively because this is expected of me as a man. As a sniper I may have seemed to have the advantage, but actually I was just hiding because I was afraid that I would eventually meet my match, and didn't know when or where that might happen, or who it might be."

leadership and obedience. Being armed could signify being ready for the fight – either feeling aggressive or being prepared.

If you are not evenly matched against your opponents, though, and using bows and arrows against an enemy with firepower, you will feel the disadvantage keenly. Depending on the exact nature of the dream, actually using arms may signify either being in control of a situation or having lost it.

## THE SETTING

On land, on the sea or in the air, in a jungle or a desert, or even in the streets of a city – the terrain will suggest the underlying mood of the conflict. Particularly note whether you have a clear view, and if you know where you are going, as these can indicate some clarity on the issues over which you are at war.

## PERSONAL BATTLES

War in a dream is often a metaphor for the personal battles and struggles of our everyday lives. If in your dream you are

being invaded, try to feel whether there is something or someone who is invading your space. If you are waging war in your dreams, then look at conflict situations in your waking life, and whether people you have a lot of contact with are being aggressive or overbearing.

**BELOW** War is also about its after-effects, and the devastation that follows in its wake.

If you are defeated or outmanoeuvred in your dream, see whether you are feeling defeated or manipulated over a real issue. Also note what you are feeling in the dream – fear, anger, sadness, confusion or rebellion may all play a part and relate to events in your life. If you can identify these situations and feelings you are more likely to be able to take appropriate action.

**ABOVE** In our dreams, the landscape in which the conflict takes place may give us a clue as to what the dream is about.
**ABOVE LEFT** There are many ways of symbolizing victory. What would it look like in your dreams?
**ABOVE FAR LEFT** The battle for resources is one of the reasons we humans go to war.

# TROUBLE AHEAD

OUR DREAMS OFTEN DROP HINTS ABOUT HOW THE FUTURE MAY UNFOLD. ALTHOUGH THERE ARE OCCASIONS WHEN PEOPLE HAVE HAD DREAMS THAT SEEMED TO PREDICT SPECIFIC EVENTS, MORE USUALLY THE INFORMATION IN OUR DREAMS IS OUR UNCONSCIOUS MIND'S WAY OF TRYING TO ALERT OUR ATTENTION TO THINGS THAT MAY HAPPEN IF WE CARRY ON DOING WHAT WE'RE DOING, RATHER THAN PREDICTING THAT SOMETHING IS DEFINITELY GOING TO HAPPEN. SYMBOLS OF WARNINGS IN OUR DREAMS MAY BE AS SIMPLE AS THE WARNINGS WE RECEIVE IN DAILY LIFE. SUCH DREAMS CAN BE TRICKY TO INTERPRET AS IT MAY NOT BE CLEAR WHAT THE SYMBOLS RELATE TO.

## WARNINGS

In general, the modern Western view is that our dreams exist primarily as a means of communication between our unconscious and conscious selves. Other cultures, however, have believed that our dreams can tell us of impending trouble and have used the information as a basis for their subsequent actions. There is plenty of anecdotal evidence to support this view. Famously, the American president Abraham Lincoln dreamed of his own death, which to the great interest of dream analysts ever since, he left an account of.

Unfortunately Lincoln did not heed the warning the dream contained, and met with an early demise. Still, we have no proof that it was not mere coincidence, or evidence of what must be a common fear among those with a high political profile. While dramatic dreams such as Lincoln's are the ones that seize our imagination, part of our fascination with predictive dreams lies in how we are able to foresee such an event, and what, if anything, we should do about it. If we were to alter our behaviour to protect ourselves from the possibility that every negative dreamt experience will come true, our lives would be blighted by paranoia and become an impossible nightmare.

## READING THE CLUES

Our dream warnings may be less clear than a scenario of impending death, though. More typically, the warnings we receive in dreams will be of conditions or future events of which we are already aware but are trying to ignore, or that we could foresee if we took the trouble or the courage to notice the signs. Our lives are filled with stimuli, so it is not always possible to notice everything consciously, but these dreams allow us to become aware of the fact that we are not seeing or hearing something that we need to. In fact our unconscious may remind us of this by literally making us blind or deaf in our dreams, or by giving vivid or exaggerated pictures – either symbolic or literal – of our situation.

## DANGER SIGNS

In real life, dangers are often helpfully signposted using fairly universal symbols. Traffic signs warn of hazards on the road, the

### LINCOLN'S DREAM

It is easy with hindsight to interpret a dream as a precognition. These are the words of Abraham Lincoln as he recounted his dream in which he had foreseen his own death at the hand of an assassin.

"There seemed to be a death-like stillness about me. I heard subdued sobs, as if many people were weeping. I feel that I left my bed and walked downstairs. I went from room to room. No living person was in sight, but the same mournful sounds of distress met me as I passed along. I kept on until I arrived at the East Room, where I met with a sickening surprise. Before me was a catafalque, on which rested a corpse wrapped in funeral vestments. Around it were guards and a throng of mourners, many weeping pitifully. 'Who is dead in the White House?' I demanded of one of the soldiers. 'The President,' was his answer. 'He was killed by an assassin.'"

stylized image of the skull and crossbones is used to signify poison and other similar dangers, while "keep out" signs warn you that you are about to trespass on private property. If such symbols appear in your dreams, you can take them as an indication of some danger or difficulty you are headed for, given your present circumstances or actions.

An alarm fitted to your house or car may point to feelings of insecurity or vulnerability, either around your physical being or possessions, or around your sense of self. You may feel that you need to protect yourself from attack, or from losing things that are significant. If the alarm is ringing, there may be more of a sense of urgency in these feelings, as though you are already in danger, it is important to take such a clear warning seriously.

## DECODING A SITUATION

Sometimes the benefit of heeding a warning lies in the process of working out what it is about. The next step is to actively take on board the significance and

implications of a situation, and in such cases our unconscious may present us with more obscure signs. If we can decode them, we will understand how to adjust our lives. For instance, you may dream of a realistic situation in your present life getting out of control. From this you may conclude that you need to make some adjustments about how you relate to the people in that situation; or that your life is going too fast and you must slow down; or that you need to take control of this aspect of your life.

## RECURRING DREAMS

If you repeatedly dream of something that worries you, take whatever action you feel necessary to set your mind at rest. It doesn't mean that your dreams are foretelling things that will definitely go wrong, they are merely drawing your attention to a possible problem.

Recurring dreams can be an attempt by our unconscious to point out when we are ignoring danger; the dream may be repeated over and over again until we do something about it.

**ABOVE** Sometimes the mood or atmosphere in a dream can make us feel uneasy and could be a warning of trouble ahead. **ABOVE LEFT** Warning dreams are not easy to interpret. It may not be clear whether the warning is of an event about to happen or is a metaphor for personal issues.

**BELOW** When life is not going our way it is easy to feel a victim. Perhaps your dream is about improving your own circumstances. Maybe you need to take more control and stop blaming the "hand of fate"?

# DANGERS

**ABOVE** As a society, we grapple with issues of safety and danger and it is likely our concerns will surface in our dreams. Walking alone late at night is a potentially dangerous situation.
**ABOVE RIGHT** If we are attacked in our dreams it may indicate that we feel under attack in everyday life and may need to find a way of dealing with it.

EVERY NOW AND AGAIN OUR DREAMS SEEM TO COME TO US SPECIFICALLY TO TELL US OF DANGER, USING METAPHORS FOR WHATEVER DIFFICULTIES OUR UNCONSCIOUS BELIEVES WE MIGHT BE IN. WHEN PLANE CRASHES, NATURAL DISASTERS, OR ACCIDENTS IN THE HOME FIGURE IN OUR DREAM NARRATIVE THEY MAY SIGNAL SPECIFIC PROBLEMS IN OUR LIVES THAT COULD LEAD US INTO TROUBLED TIMES. THEY MAY BE TELLING YOU ABOUT SPECIFIC FEARS THAT HAVE ARISEN BECAUSE OF THE SUPPOSED DANGERS THEY MAY PRESENT, OR TIE IN TO EVENTS THAT HAVE ALREADY OCCURRED IN YOUR LIFE AND WHICH YOU ARE AFRAID MIGHT HAPPEN AGAIN. THEY MAY EVEN BE COMPLETELY IRRATIONAL.

### DANGEROUS PEOPLE

Threatening behaviour by other people is a common sign of social or emotional trouble. We might dream of being attacked – an intruder with a knife, a crazed lunatic rushing at us out of nowhere, someone grabbing us from behind. The attack may represent a personal threat rather than a physical one, for example if you have a bullying or critical boss or a domineering partner. Such scenarios may well be warnings, indications that our unconscious actively believes we are under attack or being overwhelmed by someone, and it is best to take notice of what such dreams are telling us.

### NATURAL DISASTERS

In some dreams we might be threatened by dramatic events of nature – lightning, avalanche, storm, flood, earthquake, meteor strike – and again we should take note of these dreams. They have a symbolic intent, to warn us that we may feel insecure, out of control and at the mercy of fate, or overwhelmed. Different types of disaster are likely to place emphasis on different aspects of our being – for instance flooding can relate to the emotions, fire to passion or anger, an avalanche or earthquake to the stability of our lives – although the details will vary from person to person. All are disruptive, but in their upheaval they may also suggest a purging of some central aspect of our lives, sweeping away all that has gone before so that we can start afresh.

### DANGER IN THE HOME

The dangers of our dreams can be minor domestic mishaps like getting an electric shock from a faulty plug, losing or breaking something we value, or the kitchen being flooded due to a blocked drain. Such dreams could be warnings of real dangers

## DREAM OF DANGER

"I was walking along a dark, rural lane. It had been raining and the trees were dripping black water. Suddenly I felt myself grabbed from behind and thrown to the ground. I remember, in my dream, worrying more about my coat getting wet than about what was to happen to me. I felt I knew the person who had attacked me, even though I couldn't see his face. He stood over me in a very threatening attitude with his fists clenched. This dream seemed so real that I didn't feel I could ignore it, and I spent ages trying to work out who my attacker was. I came to the conclusion that he represented a colleague I worked very closely with but had never really trusted. I had a quick look at his work later that day and found he had been taking my ideas and passing them off as his, and I had been literally 'in the dark' about his behaviour for some time."

that could actually occur in our waking lives. We may have seen but ignored the signs of an "accident waiting to happen" – a frayed wire, a blocked drain – and this is our unconscious mind's way of bringing these defects to our notice and making sure that more serious mishaps don't happen. But they may also be symbolic rather than literal – pointing to discord in the home or fears around a multitude of issues to do with loss or damage or danger.

A more calamitous event, such as the house falling down, could indicate difficulties around your security, stability or domestic situation, while a dream of being trapped in a house on fire may be a powerful metaphor for how you feel about some central aspect of your life.

## EMOTIONAL OUTCOMES

The accident or disaster in your dream may be intended as a catalyst for some behaviour or emotion rather than a sign of danger. For instance, you may have feelings of guilt or blame around some completely different scenario in your life where things are not working out – maybe you need to express these feelings and work with them. Or you may be contemplating failure, especially of something that you see as being very important – perhaps your plans or dreams for the future are going awry and the life journey you had envisaged for yourself is being abruptly curtailed. But in every disaster a hero emerges, and it could be that you are seeking to take on this role – to gain recognition for strength or bravery, or love.

**ABOVE** Our unconscious is infinitely creative in the way it produces its dream images. Being in a precarious situation is highlighted by this image. It may indicate things slipping out of control.

**LEFT** In dreams, as in waking life, danger can come at us from any direction and from where we least expect it.

# CHANGE AND IMPERMANENCE

WHEN THINGS ARE GOING WELL IT IS FAIRLY NATURAL TO WANT THEM TO LAST THAT WAY FOREVER. BUT CHANGE IS ACTUALLY ONE OF THE FEW CERTAINTIES WE HAVE IN LIFE AND OUR DREAMS OFTEN DROP HINTS ABOUT HOW THE FUTURE MAY UNFOLD. WHATEVER OUR SITUATION IS NOW, IT IS SURE TO BE DIFFERENT SOON. WE MIGHT BE ENERGIZED BY THIS PROSPECT AND FIND IT EXCITING, OR WE MAY FIND IT THREATENING AND SCARY. WE MAY EVEN REFUSE TO BELIEVE IT COULD BE TRUE. BUT NO MATTER WHAT OUR ATTITUDE, THERE IS NO GETTING AWAY FROM THE FACT THAT CHANGE IS A NATURAL AND INEVITABLE PART OF LIFE AND OUR SUBCONSCIOUS MIND WILL BE DEALING WITH IT IN OUR DREAMS.

### CONSTANT CHANGE

There is a story of a king who asked his advisers to come up with a saying that would be true for all time, no matter what situation we find ourselves in. The advisers thought long and hard but were defeated, so the king turned to a Buddhist monk who said, "This too shall pass." This was the phrase the king had been looking for.

This story illustrates the point that change is inevitable. The changes we experience may be more or less noticeable at different points in our lives.

Some, such as having a baby, getting married or divorced, or leaving school, will be major and will alter the course of our lives and the roles we play. Other changes will be more subtle and may have more to do with our inner world – our feelings and perceptions change over time and affect the way we relate to others.

### RESPONDING TO CHANGE

Some changes are self-generated, and we have some control over them. We are able to decide what happens and when. But often change is out of our control and can take us on a journey that we didn't intend. These sorts of changes, such as losing a partner or a job redundancy, may be scary as we have to adjust to an unknown that is not of our choosing. Changes that are forced on us can be useful and welcome or they can provide setbacks – whether we resist or "go with the flow" will make a huge difference as to how well we cope.

How we respond to change is reflected in our dreams. If we cope well, then change may be symbolized by something that is fluid or flowing, such as a running brook or clouds moving across an open sky. If the change is dramatic or important, then an image of transformation, like that of a caterpillar turning into a butterfly, or a chicken hatching from an egg, may appear. If we are finding it difficult to cope with change, then the symbolism may be more intimidating, such as dreaming that our teeth are falling out. Our unconscious will always provide the clues about what is happening.

### TRANSITION

As we move through life, we leave behind the behaviours and attitudes of one phase to move into something new: when one door closes another opens. Such

**BELOW** Our dreams will reflect how we view change and how we adjust to the unknown. Do we hanker for the past, or are we able to move with the times? Consider what an image like this steam train could mean in your dreams.

times of transition are not always easy. We may find it hard to adjust to losing our youth for instance, or when we discover that our thoughts and feelings are outdated. Like a bird learning to fly, we have to find new ways of coping with life as we settle into each different phase.

At such times, our dreams may be filled with images of running away, travelling or exploring; in such activities we may be searching for the energy of more youthful pursuits; trying to escape from the narrowing of focus that often goes with the ageing process; or, in a more positive light, we may be discovering the value of our present lives and looking forward to some kind of transition.

### TRANSFORMATION

Some dream images can be frustratingly fluid. In a second our surroundings may have transformed, through the shapes and colours of objects, the size or layout of a room, or a person's character. We are more flexible than we imagine, and often it is a matter of courage or imagination to see how wonderful change can be. On the other hand, we may use our dreams to confront or justify our fears of change and difference, or of uncertainty about the stability of a situation. Transformation in our dreams can guide us in how to make positive changes in our lives and overcome our resistance to things being different.

**RIGHT** Whether we find change easy or difficult will depend to some extent on our attitude. Our dreams may show us scenes from nature to remind us that every ending also contains the seeds of a new beginning.

**ABOVE** All change is a metamorphosis of one sort or another – things changing from what they were to what they will become. Some of these changes will feel weird or unsettling in our dreams.
**ABOVE LEFT** Change lies hidden beneath the surface of what we can already see, and is something of a mystery.

### DREAM OF CHANGE

"I was chasing mice, trying to get them back into their cage, but each time I caught one it suddenly rotted in my hand. I was panicking and running everywhere trying to keep these mice in. I wanted to scream at them 'Stay in the cage or you'll go to pieces'.
My children were leaving home, and it was very unsettling; I didn't know what to do with myself and I felt left behind. Each mouse in the dream was a child. I wanted them to stay in the cage with me. If I have to stay why shouldn't they have to as well? I also worried about how they would cope in the big wide world and wanted to stop them from leaving, but I suppose in my heart I knew that this was a change they needed to make whatever I felt about it ."

# MOVEMENT, MACHINES AND STRUCTURES

Our dreams are often signals of change and progress, and movement, machinery and structures can be connected with these things. We all use machinery of one kind or another. It enables us to effect changes, and mould our environment to our needs and taste. Technology means that both the machinery and the things we can do with it are constantly evolving. This evolution may be challenging and exciting, but for many it is stressful and bewildering. It is easy to feel lost as if in a maze of new ideas. Alternatively we seek security in the structures we create – the comfort and safety of our homes or other buildings. Sometimes we don't know whether we are coming or going and we may try to escape from it all by flying or running away, or going on a journey. Indeed movement, whether of ourselves or of things in our surroundings, can signify change and show us how at ease we are with ourselves and our environment.

# MAZES AND BEING LOST

**ABOVE** A maze is a kind of puzzle that is designed to get us lost and it can be fun to find ourselves going round in circles. See what being in a maze means for you.
**ABOVE RIGHT** Any dream about getting lost has been given to help us find a way out of a confusing situation in our waking life. It would be foolish to overlook the opportunity.

BEING LOST IN OUR DREAMS MAY BE AS SIMPLE AS FEELING LOST IN OUR WAKING LIFE. CERTAINLY THE SYMBOLIC VALUE OF MAZES AND LABYRINTHS IN OUR DREAMS IS ABOUT BEING LOST. WE MAY BE LOST THROUGH PHYSICAL DISORIENTATION, CONFUSION OR MISUNDERSTANDING, LOSS OR LONELINESS OR THROUGH OTHER DIFFICULTIES. THE THEME OF BEING LOST COULD ALSO POINT TO A MORE COMPLEX ISSUE, HOWEVER, AND IT IS BEST NOT TO JUMP TO QUICK AND EASY CONCLUSIONS, BUT TAKE SOME TIME TO WORK OUT THE DETAILS OF THE DREAM AND WHAT THEY MIGHT MEAN.

Mazes and labyrinths both consist of a network of pathways, but while a maze is designed to get you lost, a labyrinth has a definite goal at its heart. There may be a whole system of forked paths and dead ends but they are there to steer you towards the centre, to stop you retracing your steps and finding your way out.

A maze will often take you round in circles before spitting you out where you first began. It isn't designed to take you inward and indeed may deliberately keep you from the centre.

### BEING LOST

When we dream of mazes and labyrinths, what is important is finding out why we are lost, what it is that we are turning away from. We all encounter difficulties and fears from time to time, but while some of us get on with trying to work them out, others feel unable to address them immediately and prefer to set them aside until they feel strong or clear-headed enough to do so. For the latter, this may manifest as dreams in which we are lost or misled, where we can't find our way out of a situation or to a place of safety. We struggle in the maze, held captive by our confusion. The reason we are being given the dream is not necessarily to spur us on – although that may be part of it – but rather to give us some insight into how to get out simply and easily. The dream is like a map written in code, and we can

### DREAM OF BEING LOST

"I was underground, caving in a series of potholes with a friend. He had the map but it fell into a pool of deep water. We were lost and the light from our helmet torches began to fade. We were standing in a cave with many exits. We were concerned that there were underground lakes we would fall into so we felt we had to go up. Suddenly a bat flew out of nowhere and disappeared up one of the shafts. We knew which way we had to go: the bat had shown us the way.

Later on I realized that I was feeling bad about my job. I had wanted to study biology but had done accounts because it seemed a more practical career choice. I guess the bat was telling me to start again, to be true to myself. Once I did this the whole of my life seemed to improve."

study our dream to see if we were helped through the dream maze by something or someone. This may be someone we know or a stranger; it may be some sort of angelic being or even an animal, wild or domestic.

## THE CONFUSION OF CHOICE

Mazes and labyrinths often involve making a series of choices. If we make the right decisions we get to where we want to be, achieving a goal or clarity. If we make the wrong choices we remain lost, or land up where we began. It can be hard to remain clear-headed in such a situation, and if we are confused, making choices becomes a difficult process, and one in which we may easily make mistakes. The dream may well be helping us to make the choice based on intuition or on information that hasn't been accessible to our conscious mind.

The fact that we are in a maze in our dreams may even simply be warning us that some aspect of our lives is more complicated

than we thought, and that we should pay attention to the complexity of the choices we have to make. In your dream, look at the nature of your decision-making process – whether it is impulsive or random, or calm and rational, based on carefully weighed up factors. Notice whether it is

effective, and whether you are alone in the maze, and if not, does your companion help you or distract or mislead you? The answer to these questions may reveal the extent to which you can rely on others in your decision-making, how much trust you feel, or whether you want and are able to "go it alone".

**ABOVE** The symbolism of the stylized maze is a very powerful one, and one that your dream self will love to explore.
**ABOVE LEFT** Notice your surroundings in your dream. Are you where you want to be?
**ABOVE FAR LEFT** When we get our wires crossed, things get confusing. Our dreams may show us how to untangle the obstacles.

**LEFT** Are you lost and alone in your dream or is there someone who can lend you a helping hand? See if you can relate this to your life. Do you tend to struggle on alone because you find it hard to ask for support?

# EXITS AND ENTRANCES

PHYSICALLY, AN ENTRANCE AND AN EXIT ARE SIMPLY TWO SIDES OF THE SAME OPENING, WHETHER IT IS A DOORWAY OR SOME OTHER KIND OF OPENING. ALTHOUGH THEY ARE PHYSICALLY IDENTICAL, WHAT DIFFERENTIATES ONE FROM THE OTHER IS YOUR VIEWPOINT AND WHICH WAY YOU PASS THROUGH. DOORWAYS MIGHT ALSO SYMBOLIZE A WHOLE VARIETY OF DIFFERENT THINGS IN YOUR LIFE; AN ENTRANCE OR AN EXIT MIGHT REPRESENT AN ESCAPE FROM A PROBLEM OR AN UNPLEASANT CIRCUMSTANCE, OR IT MIGHT BE A TEMPTATION TO ESCAPE FROM RESPONSIBILITY AND REALITY. WHEN YOU DREAM OF PORTALS YOUR INTERPRETATION WILL DEPEND ON THE CIRCUMSTANCES AROUND YOU.

**BELOW** Every exit is also an entrance and vice versa – it depends on which way we look at it. **BELOW RIGHT** Dreams about exits and entrances may be trying to tell us something about the transitions that are going on in our waking life.

Freud would no doubt have attributed some sexual meaning to exits and entrances, while others suggest, for instance, that doors opening outward indicate a need to express yourself more and those opening inward a need to explore some aspect of your inner being. Each of these interpretations may fit in some circumstances, depending on the context in which the door appears in the dream and on your own circumstances. But even if they do fit, it is also important to find out more about the dream and how and why the doorway features – the kind of

entrance, whether it is you or someone else who is opening the door, and whether you are going in or out, for instance. It may be a small doorway, a huge gateway, or a cleft in a mountainside, and you should take note of the kind of structure it is part of as this may also be significant.

## TRANSITIONS

An entrance or exit marks a transition from one space to another – spaces that may be similar, such as two rooms in a house, or quite different from each other, like an interior space and a garden. This could suggest

being at some kind of threshold or making an adjustment in your life, so look at how the transition works in your dream. Perhaps you make a grand entrance to the applause of a crowd, or you have to squeeze through, or maybe you slip between one dream scene and another without really noticing how you do so. These scenarios may all say something about how comfortable you are with the transition, whether or not you look forward to it, and how easy or difficult it is.

Every time you move from one space to another you are making an entrance and an exit at the same time, so it is worth looking at which aspect of the movement draws your attention – leaving or arriving, getting out of a place or going in. Sometimes you may be poised on the threshold itself, in a sort of limbo. How you feel about the space you are leaving behind as well as the one you are entering may also give important clues about the meaning of the transition — say, whether you have any regrets, or are relieved to be moving on. Whether or not you can retrace your steps will have a bearing on how easy it is to make your entrance or exit.

Transitions in your life may be physical ones, such as moving house, starting a new job, or going to live in a new country. But the entrances and exits in your dream can also be about emotional or spiritual thresholds, such as starting a brand new relationship or ending an existing one, or about the transition between consciousness and unconsciousness, or many others.

### CLOSURE

Exits can be about achieving closure, about ending a period in your life or a way of being so that you can move on. You may need to start something afresh or begin a new venture, and it may be important for you to be able to leave behind any "baggage" you may have been carrying.

### EXCLUSION

Sometimes the entrance in your dream is tantalizingly or frustratingly impassable; perhaps it's something that is perfectly visible but just beyond your reach. It may be a locked door, or a skylight up in the roof, or a barred window; if you encounter one of these, ask yourself if there are situations in your life from which you feel barred or excluded. Or perhaps you can see a way forward to something you want but are not sure how to get to it because there are obstacles in the way; if this is the case, see whether there was any

alternative route to the place you were trying to get to in your dream, or someone who could help you unlock the door or reach the skylight. These could suggest alternative ways of achieving what you are after in your waking life.

**ABOVE** Our dreams can show us that we have an opportunity to step out into new terrain.
**ABOVE LEFT** Sometimes the exits and entrances in our dreams are out of reach. We may want to go there, but it is impossible or too dangerous just now.

### EXITS AND ENTRANCES DREAM

"There was a cocktail party going on in a large room that was accessed by a large door off a long corridor. There were lots of people standing around talking, smoking, eating and drinking. I kept walking in and out of this big doorway, I was the only one that was coming and going. Each time I came in I fell over, more and more drunk, and people kept turning round to look at me, but I didn't care. As soon as I went out and was standing in the corridor I was quite sober again.

For me, a cocktail party is the kind of boring, formal, old-fashioned function that older people like my parents would go to. The people at the party were all drinking, but they could handle it while I just got really drunk. But I was deliberately playing the fool each time I came in, perhaps as a way of rebelling against the older people.

I think the dream was actually about the prospect of joining my parents' business. I thought I'd come round to the idea but the dream showed that I haven't really – I actually find the business boring, and I think I'm too young to be getting into something like that! I'd rather find my own way through life, and do the kind of things my friends are doing."

# VEHICLES

IF THE TRAVELS IN OUR DREAMS ARE ABOUT ESCAPING OR ABOUT OUR LIFE JOURNEY, VEHICLES ARE THE MACHINES THAT MOVE US FROM ONE PLACE TO ANOTHER, PROVIDING OUR MEANS OF ESCAPE OR PROGRESS. THE TYPE OF VEHICLE WE CHOOSE TO REPRESENT IN OUR DREAMS MAY GIVE US CLUES TO THE NATURE OF OUR JOURNEY, AND ITS STATE OF REPAIR CAN SHOW US HOW OUR JOURNEY IS PROGRESSING. DIFFERENT KINDS OF FEAR OR UNEASE WILL PROBABLY SURFACE IN YOUR DREAMS; DO YOU HAVE A FEAR OF FLYING OR A TERROR OF BEING LOST AT SEA? PERHAPS EVERYDAY MEANS OF TRANSPORT, SUCH AS BUSES OR TRAINS MAKE YOU FEEL UNEASY, PACKED FULL AS THEY ARE WITH OTHER TRAVELLERS.

## MEANS AND MEDIUM OF TRANSPORT

In looking at the kind of vehicle in which we are travelling in our dreams, it is useful to consider how and where the vehicle usually travels as well as its speed and if we have control over it.

Travelling on the ground may have quite different implications to flying or going by boat, as earth, air and water have their own complex sets of symbolic meanings that also need to be considered. So road travel could indicate groundedness and practicality, while flying may suggest ideas and fancies, and water an emotional journey. Getting airborne could be an allusion to our ideas or plans taking off and coming to fruition.

We also have preferences and feelings around different means of transport – for instance, catching a bus when we are used to travelling in a chauffeur-driven car may have implications of loss of status, of reliance on public services instead of self-sufficiency, of having to wait, of being part of an anonymous crowd instead of having individual attention. Depending on whether or not the journey goes smoothly, the dream may be allaying fears around these issues or confirming your worst nightmares. Meandering down a lane on a bicycle can take a long time, and you may be frustrated at the slow pace or choose to enjoy the countryside as you go; it could also give you a sense of being in control as you can decide your route as well as where you stop. Space travel, by contrast, may suggest exploration of the unknown, and as we hurtle at an incredible speed into the vast emptiness of space, away from everything and everyone that we know and love, we may feel lonely and isolated. We may also use a space ship to represent the pinnacle of technology, change and progress.

Many people are afraid of flying or boats, so dreams of travelling in these may well be bringing to the fore some of the insecurities you may have around not being on terra firma.

## CARS AND DRIVING

As they are such an integral part of our lives, cars often feature in our dreams. We attach meanings to owning or being seen in certain kinds of car, and may use these meanings to represent certain things in our dreams. So a sports car implies power and

**BELOW** There are many types of vehicle. The ones we choose in our dreams can say a lot about us.
**BELOW RIGHT** Dreams of driving a car are quite common. Are you in control or is disaster looming ahead?

success – material, personal and sexual – while a sedan can be associated with families and stability, an off-road vehicle with adventure and exploration, and a truck with carrying a load. The condition of the vehicle may say a lot about how we are in relation to these aspects of our lives, while whether we own it or have borrowed or stolen it could be telling us about whether we feel we deserve them.

## ACCIDENTS AND BREAKDOWNS

Derailment, car crashes or sinking boats are all powerful symbols of things going wrong in our lives, especially if we are involved in the accident, and can be taken as a warning. The scale of the accident can be used as an indicator for the seriousness of the problem – so a scrape in a parking lot may be a gentle warning, but a full passenger plane exploding in mid-air over the sea could be a more urgent message. Unlike accidents, hijackings are deliberate, and may be warning you that someone wants to take over your life or is holding you to ransom.

A vehicle that breaks down may be saying that your life is running into difficulties, or that you need to call a halt to ideas of escape. If this is the case, looking at exactly how it malfunctioned could give you a more precise picture of the area of your life that has broken down. Brake failure could show that you are unable to slow down or stop; running out of power is likely to be about your lack of energy.

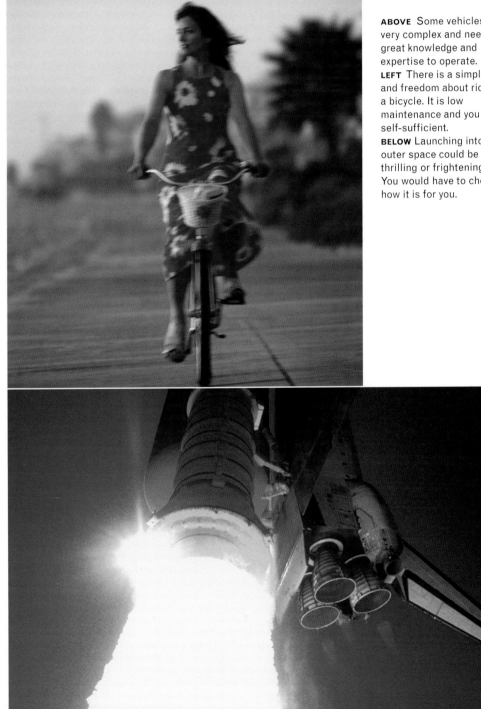

**ABOVE** Some vehicles are very complex and need great knowledge and expertise to operate.
**LEFT** There is a simplicity and freedom about riding a bicycle. It is low maintenance and you are self-sufficient.
**BELOW** Launching into outer space could be thrilling or frightening. You would have to check how it is for you.

# MAGIC AND FANTASY

Magical, mystical people, mythical beasts,
heroes and demons parade through our dreams,
inspired by the fictions and superstitions of our
culture and brought to life by our imagination
as metaphors for our hopes and desires, for the
irrational terrors of our early years, and even for
the tricksters and con artists we meet as we go
about our daily lives. We also use them to
access possibilities beyond the mundane reality
of everyday life, to help us shed the
conventional boundaries that keep our
imagination earthbound, and give us the
courage to bring the seemingly impossible
within our reach.

These dreams can be tremendously
challenging as we can take nothing for granted
in this fantasy reality, removed from the context
of the here and now, and in them we confront
our fears and demons head-on. The underlying
universal truths of the archetypal figures we
sometimes meet allow us to get in touch with
our deeper, instinctive levels of being.

# FANTASTICAL DREAMS

DREAMS IN WHICH LANDSCAPES, CHARACTERS, MOTIFS AND PLOTS ARE FANTASTICAL OR SURREAL ARE AMONG THE MOST DIFFICULT TO INTERPRET AS THEY ARE NOT BASED IN OUR EVERYDAY EXPERIENCES AND WE HAVE NONE OF THE USUAL REFERENCE POINTS TO HELP US. FANTASY DREAMS CAN BE VERY UNSETTLING, SHAKING US OUT OF ROUTINE OR COMPLACENCY. THEY RETURN TO HAUNT OUR WAKING THOUGHTS AND DEMAND THAT WE STRIVE TO UNDERSTAND THEM – SWEEPING THEM UNDER THE CARPET OR IGNORING THEM SIMPLY DOESN'T WORK. THEY MAY LINGER FOR A LONG TIME AND BE QUITE HARD TO PURGE FROM OUR CONSCIOUSNESS.

## FANTASY CHARACTERS

Dreams sometimes feature fantastical creatures – gentle, dreamy unicorns and ferocious dragons, seductive mermaids, fairies and elves, talking animals and a myriad others we may have created with or without the assistance of literature or legend. The creatures of our fantasies are part of our desire for things to be beyond the real world.

These creations may return us to our childhood where monsters lurked under the bed and the line between reality and fantasy was much more indistinct. They may be frightening or disturbing, forcing us to address our fears head-on, but sometimes they are wonderful, joyful creatures that show us new possibilities or have unimaginable love or wisdom. They may have exceptional powers, or take us to places that we can literally only dream of.

Creatures that we fabricate in our own minds, that are not found in myths or in the books we read as children, may have features that we take from several sources and combine into one character as a kind of catch-all for how we want to be or what we are most afraid of. It may be some idealized figure who will empower us, or a demon who threatens to destroy us.

## FANTASY WORLDS

Dreams of fantasy may consist of unusual events or creatures set in surroundings that seem natural or familiar, or they may take place in weird and wonderful settings – a vast cavern that stretches upward as far as the eye can see, or the strange landscape of another planet; we may be floating in nothingness or surrounded by permeable membranes that melt away, leaving us in a new setting. In fantastical environments even the laws of nature may be different – gravity may be stronger or weaker, we may be able to do things we can't normally do, such as flying – and social structures may be incomprehensible. Great battles or forces of good and evil confronting each other directly strip away the mundane detail of our real lives, along with the rules of politics and diplomacy.

The fictitious worlds of literature are as varied as they are fantastical. Some, such as Tolkien's Middle Earth or C.S. Lewis's Narnia, may look like places we could visit, but the creatures that inhabit them and

**BELOW** Our dreams are very close to the hidden, magical world of the unconscious and many dreams have a fairy-tale quality about them.
**BELOW RIGHT** In fantasy dreams, unusual or mythical creatures are the products of a rich and fertile imagination.

key elements of the plot could only be found in fantasy. Alice in Wonderland has an explicitly surreal dream setting, although it has realistic elements alongside its talking animals, mutations, and spatial distortions. Or the infamous world of Harry Potter shows us ordinary boys and girls who are able to slip out of family life into a world where they have magical powers: people walk through walls and play games in mid-air; cars can fly and animals have special powers. Perhaps part of the reason that all these stories are so popular is that they each explore archetypal themes, such as the use of power or the struggle between good and evil.

## TRANSFORMATION

Like the hybrid animals of mythology, fantastical elements may involve the coming together of objects or beings that are normally quite distinct, or the transformation of one thing into another. Material objects may take on unusual properties or space and time may be distorted. These transformations and mutations draw your attention to both the normal and the unusual properties of the objects or creatures, and you should try to reconcile both and notice what it is that is being distorted.

Fantasy dreams may represent all that we find exceptional about the world. They are our unconscious mind's way of being inventive and unconventional and can help us work through some very human issues. Fantastical or magical dreams also remind us that we are much more than logic and reasoning. We are creatures with a powerful imagination and have the ability to devise creative solutions to our problems and answers to some of the big questions about our very existence.

**ABOVE** Art and literature can provide a stimulus for the unconscious in its nightly dream production. Check the landscape of your dreams to see if there is anything you recognize. Is the narrative running as it should or has the story changed?

> I suspect that there are more things in heaven and earth than are dreamed of, or can be dreamed of, in any philosophy.
>
> J. B. S. HALDANE

**LEFT** Children are usually fascinated by magic and fantasy, perhaps because they are much closer to their instinctive feelings than most adults.
**FAR LEFT** The fantasy images we produce in our dreams will have a cultural emphasis. Traditionally, fairies are magical creatures who use their powers to either help or hinder us.

# MYTHS AND LEGENDS

OUR DISTANT ANCESTORS TRIED TO FIND EXPLANATIONS FOR THE MANY PHENOMENA OF NATURE IN THE WORLD AROUND THEM – THE SUN RISING, THE CHANGING SEASONS, AND CYCLES OF LIFE AND DEATH. BECAUSE THEIR KNOWLEDGE WAS LIMITED, THEY DEVISED EXPLANATIONS BASED ON THE EXISTENCE OF SUPERHUMAN BEINGS, GODS AND GODDESSES WHO NOT ONLY OFFERED AN EXPLANATION FOR WHY THINGS WERE THE WAY THEY WERE, BUT ALSO CREATED THE POSSIBILITY OF INFLUENCING NATURE BY MEANS OF SACRIFICES, PRAYERS AND OFFERINGS. OTHER CREATURES PERFORMED SIMILAR ROLES – FIRE-BREATHING DRAGONS, THE PHOENIX RISING FROM THE ASHES, GIANTS AND MERMAIDS.

242

**LEFT** Our dreams are a way of entering the world of myths and legends. By identifying with the characters in our dreams we may learn something about ourselves.

## TIMELESS, UNIVERSAL TALES

In preliterate societies, the most common way of passing on these understandings, values and beliefs was in memorable stories that could be told and retold. Their significance was easy to understand, and the characters, creatures and events that were portrayed had a universal relevance. In this way, stories became part of the cultural vocabulary of any society, and the creatures of myth and legend are deeply embedded in our psyche; in our dreams we use them as signposts to the qualities that they embody, as icons.

## ENTERING THE WORLD OF MYTH

In our dreams we are free to enter mythical worlds. We can don a mask or join a procession, engage with the king or the fool, the warrior priest or the god of winter. We can even become that character – try out its role, take on its greatness.

These dreams put us in touch with our instinctive and intuitive selves – a side of us that may need attention. They may be an emotive plea from our unconscious mind to dance in the moonlight, to worship the corn, to make a sacrifice or an offering. But we are also fragile beings who are subject to all sorts of fears; myths both allay those fears and add to them.

## GODS AND GODDESSES

Mythical figures probably appear in our dreams in much the same way as they did to our ancestors. In our dreams, making an offering to calm a raging god makes sense to us just as it did in real life to our forebears. Our unconscious processes have not changed, although just as our own personal experiences affect how we understand any dream element, our relationship with these figures will be based on how we respond to what they typically represent to us.

We create gods and goddesses so that we can feel safe and protected, so that we can absolve ourselves of responsibility for something; but in their creation we also unleash the terrible aspects of such deities – death and destruction, their capricious nature, their awesome powers. We create them to protect us but we may also come to fear them, and we learn to deal with this dichotomy in dreams of myths. We are shown that the qualities and powers these supernatural beings have in abundance exist within us if we have the courage to acknowledge them.

## HYBRID CREATURES

Myths and legends from around the world and through the ages are filled with creatures that are part animal and part human, or that are a mixture of two or three different creatures, and have an element of danger. Mermaids – half fish and half beautiful woman – have been blamed for many a shipwreck, as they lure sailors on to the rocks, while the sphinx, with the head of a woman and the body of a lion, is notorious for strangling travellers who cannot answer her riddles.

Minotaurs, griffins, satyrs and centaurs join the line-up of hybrid creatures from the realm of myth and legend. All have particular associations from the tales in which they feature, but they also embody qualities of the creatures they comprise. In this way, the sphinx may have qualities of femininity but also

the ferocious, uncompromising strength of a lion, and by virtue of her behaviour in the Greek legend could represent any threatening and somewhat enigmatic character, particularly if associated with knowledge and learning, such as a punitive teacher. In a sense, by dreaming of a hybrid creature we are hedging our bets, or efficiently representing several qualities in a single character, trying to resolve anomalies in our lives.

## PEOPLE

Not all the characters in myth and legend are fantastical. People appear throughout these tales, sometimes in elevated roles as kings and queens, other times as ordinary mortals who are caught up in greater things. Either way, they could be used to illustrate the ideals and extremes of human nature – heroism, bravery, love, power and so on. Such tales also illustrate some timeless human quandaries and problems, such as the tragedy of Oedipus, who unknowingly kills his father and

marries his mother; the agony of the endless task of Sisyphus, who is obliged to push a rock up a hill, only to have it roll down as he has almost reached the brow. By working with these characters in our dreams, we work with the qualities that they embody and the battles that they fight.

**ABOVE** The mythical figures in our dreams usually have something very profound to convey.
**ABOVE LEFT** Hybrid creatures can remind us of the beast within us all.
**ABOVE FAR LEFT** Giant figures may assume the status of gods with the power to create or destroy life.

---

### MYTHICAL DREAM

"In my dream I was walking through a forest. I could hear the birds singing and could feel the warmth of the sun on my skin. A soft breeze was blowing. As I walked, I came to a tiny cottage – it might sound far-fetched but it really did look like a gingerbread house, the kind you read about in fairy-tale stories. The house looked so inviting and I was tired and hot from walking, so I went up to the door and walked inside. I remember walking up a few stairs and going into a bedroom. It wasn't a room I had ever seen before. As I went in, I heard the front door downstairs click shut and the room I was in became shadowy. I started to feel afraid. There was a dark-haired man at the window and he was trying to get into the room. I tried to run away, but my legs wouldn't move. I woke up shouting.

At first it was difficult to revisit this dream or nightmare, but I decided to focus on what the man at the window represented. As I worked with the dream, to my amazement he turned into a golden-haired Apollo kind of figure, a sort of sun-god. I interpreted this to mean that I am afraid of my own power. I see it as something dark or "bad", so I try to run from it, but actually it radiates light."

# ALIENS AND UFOS

WHEN FACED WITH THE UNKNOWN WE OFTEN TRY TO MAKE SENSE OF IT — IN THE FIRST INSTANCE IN TERMS OF WHAT WE ALREADY KNOW WELL, AND THEN PERHAPS IN TERMS OF CONCEPTS FROM THE REALM OF FANTASY OR SPECULATION, OF WHICH WE COULDN'T POSSIBLY HAVE ANY REAL EXPERIENCE. DREAMING OF ALIENS, SPACE SHIPS, FLYING SAUCERS AND SO ON MAY BE OUR WAY OF EXPLAINING AND VISUALIZING THE INEXPLICABLE SITUATIONS OR PHENOMENA THAT WE ARE TRYING TO UNDERSTAND AND COME TO TERMS WITH. WHEN WE HAVE TO FACE THE UNKNOWN WE TRY TO GIVE IT A FACE, A PERSONALITY. THE CREATURES FROM OUTER SPACE SERVE THIS PURPOSE WELL; THEY ARE, BY DEFINITION, ALIEN.

## ALIENS

It is surprising how the aliens in our dreams are often very similar. How much this is due to us all watching the same films, and how much it is the manifestation of a new archetype that has developed in our collective unconscious, is difficult to tell. Indeed both could be true, and it is simply that the film-makers are the ones that give shape in a visual way to the archetype.

## THE ALIEN WITHIN

Everything in a dream comes from within yourself — you create all of it for your own personal consumption, and there is nothing in it that is actually alien.

If you are creating images of aliens then they represent some part of you that feels alienated or frightened of the unknown – or exhilarated by it. Some part of you is acknowledging an aspect of your life that is manifesting as alien or foreign, that has not been incorporated into your self-image, your lifestyle or your personal environment.

Aliens are often represented as scary, unpredictable creatures that seem bent on threatening our existence and invading our planet. In this way they provide an easy metaphor for situations in our own lives where we feel threatened or invaded by something or someone over

which we have little or no control. It is also significant that we have little understanding of these creatures – we cannot comprehend or anticipate their motives or intentions, and we often have no way of communicating with them. They are unknown and unknowable, and consequently we have no idea of the scale of the threat. Dreaming of aliens is often our way of working through situations that make us feel anxious – perhaps confronting head-on the source of our anxiety and allowing us to try out ways of dealing with it.

Many people feel that they do not fit into society; they feel

**BELOW RIGHT** Some of the most mysterious phenomena on Earth have been connected with aliens from outer space.
**BELOW** When it comes to dreams of aliens and UFOs, there does seem to be some form of universal symbolism that we all understand.

different from most other people they meet, and an encounter with aliens may be a positive, life-affirming experience. Being abducted by aliens may show a yearning for an alternative society where they feel they belong, or it could be an expression of belief in the existence of a society where they are valued.

## SPACE TRAVEL

If aliens use UFOs as their vehicle for accessing or invading us, flying saucers, space ships and rockets might well also offer a dramatic avenue of escape for us. It may be that we actually want to break out of our limited world, and such craft offer us a way of literally reaching for the stars, exploring the unknown, having adventures not normally possible in real life. Seeing Earth receding into the distance may help us to stand back and see our world in perspective, in the context of the vastness of space.

**ABOVE** The concept of UFOs is fascinating. In our dreams they could represent a dramatic way of leaving the everyday world behind.
**LEFT** To dream the aliens are landing may mean that we should be prepared to encounter something new or strange in our lives.
**BELOW** When we break out in our dreams we may be trying to break out in our waking life. Spiralling weightless in the galaxy could suggest a spiritual, enlightening experience.

## SPACE DREAM

"The sky was full of glowing space ships, full of smoking beings. We were firing guns and bullets at the space ships and the aliens were falling down dead everywhere, bleeping as they died. But there were more of them than I could count and they didn't all die – some were landing. Then I woke up."

This was the dream of a six-year-old child who was worried about starting in a new class at school. In his dream the aliens represented the threatening situation he was having to face and his lack of control over it.

# PROPHECY

**ABOVE** Some people have dreamt about plane crashes and other disasters before they have happened, but prophetic dreams are actually quite rare.
**ABOVE RIGHT** What looks like a prophetic dream may have a metaphorical meaning: are you living on a knife edge?

WE USUALLY FIND PROPHECY MANIFESTING IN DREAMS IN TWO DIFFERENT WAYS — FIRSTLY AS DREAMS IN WHICH WE FORESEE FUTURE EVENTS (OR FEEL THAT WE DO SO), AND SECONDLY AS DREAMS IN WHICH WE, OR OTHER CHARACTERS IN THE DREAM, ARE TRYING TO LOOK INTO THE FUTURE. WHETHER OR NOT YOU BELIEVE IT IS ACTUALLY POSSIBLE TO SEE INTO THE FUTURE, BOTH THESE KINDS OF DREAMS MIGHT SUGGEST THAT YOU FEEL A NEED TO DO SO; WHETHER IT IS THROUGH INSECURITY OR CURIOSITY IT IS WORTH ANALYSING WHY, OR WHAT IT IS YOU WANT TO FORESEE.

## PROPHETIC DREAMS

There have been countless reports of people having a dream that changed their life. They saw an elevator accident, so the next day they took the stairs and the elevator plunged to the ground, killing everybody in it. Or they saw a ship sinking and cancelled their cruise holiday, although hundreds of other passengers perished. Or perhaps they may have dreamt of a car crash and saved their lives by catching the train the next day.

Perhaps we should be a little sceptical of these many urban legends. Only the success stories survive – we do not get to hear of those who took a different course of action than planned and this subsequently turned out to be the wrong thing to do. Nor do we hear of people who change their plans because of a dream and find that it made no significant difference in their lives. Dreams of prophecy are actually very rare. And yet in those cases that actually do turn out to be prophetic we are dealing with something outside of the normal, something mysterious and inexplicable. It's only when we have had a dream that came true ourselves that we can judge whether such a thing is possible. Once it has happened to us we believe, we know, we don't doubt.

It may also be that we dream how we want the future to be, and having already created the desired scenario, we find we are more able to make it happen. In this way the dream may seem prophetic, but it might be more accurate to think of it as a prompt or suggestion.

## GAZING INTO THE FUTURE

Wanting to know what the future holds in store seems to be universal – no matter what society or what period in history you look at, you will find seers

---

### PROPHECY DREAM

"I'm a keen tarot reader, so I'm not surprised when I find myself doing this in my dreams. In this dream I was with a female friend of mine who is single. She and I were having a glass of wine together, sitting on purple cushions. We started playing with the tarot, and she turned up the card of the Lovers. I remember thinking that I must remember to tell her, that it looked like she would meet someone special very soon.

I actually had forgotten the dream until a couple of months later, when sure enough my friend started a new relationship! Then the memory of the dream came flooding back and I told her what had happened. I think I need more practice in recalling my dreams if they are to be any use!"

and prophets, in addition to numerous tools or methods employed, often by ordinary people, to foretell events that have yet to happen.

In your dream the kind of person who is foretelling the future may be significant – is it one of the great prophets (a biblical figure, perhaps, or Nostradamus) whose predictions may hold the authority of their fame and greatness, or is it a fairground "gypsy" in fancy dress, who gazes into a crystal ball and puts on something of a performance for you, and may just be pulling the wool over your eyes? How credible they are and whether you believe in prediction is critical to how much you believe what you hear.

Some kinds of prediction rely on a kind of sixth sense, while others make use of consistent and well-established methods, such as tarot reading, palmistry, astrology or numerology, and to some extent make their projections on the basis of existing trends or patterns. Either way there may still be a leap of

faith. Much of our desire to see into the future is an expression of our desire for certainty and clarity in a world that is so uncertain and so complex that clarity is hard to find.

We turn to prophecy to help us make decisions we are faced with, or to reassure us that we

are on the right path. Dreaming of prophecy could be showing you that you need to make some choices, or clarify what the issues are before you can do so. You may fear something is going to happen, and express your anxiety by trying to find out what you are going to be faced with.

**ABOVE** Our desire to know what the future has in store is universal. The symbolism of tarot cards can be interpreted in a similar way to dreams.
**ABOVE LEFT** Whether or not we can see into the future is open to debate. To dream of gazing into a crystal ball may mean you are looking for direction.

**LEFT** Traditionally, virgin priestesses were attributed with the power of "second sight". If such a figure appears in your dreams pay particular attention to what she is trying to communicate – it could be very important.

# MAGIC

In essence, magic is about two things – change and power. With magic, dramatic transformation can be brought about in our lives, whether we are the agents of change or whether some other magical figure is able to perform his or her art on us. Whoever has the ability to perform magic holds great power, especially over those ordinary mortals who do not. With magic we can do things that we are not normally able to do, and we feel both the joy and the danger of having this immense power. Magic can also mean trickery, however, and it might be this characteristic that we are dreaming of.

**ABOVE** Animals often take on supernatural characteristics. If you dream of an unearthly creature you need to explore your dream fully to find out what it means. In some cultures a black cat is said to symbolize good luck.

## TRANSFORMATION AND CHANGE

Dreams about magic may be a sign that we need to make changes, within ourselves or in our environment. They can be about movement or the lack of it, about being stuck and needing to make effort and expend energy in order to move on, to free ourselves from stagnation and from feeling stuck in a rut. Magic gives us an extra boost to get us to see things differently and get us moving again.

## MAGIC AND POWER

In our dreams we can perhaps move objects, conjure up demons, raise a storm or calm a sea. We can kill or heal from a distance, transform people into other creatures with the wave of a wand, and become invisible.

We have probably all wished occasionally that we could do these things in our waking lives. This would give us tremendous power and perhaps it is this that we are after when we dream about magic. Sometimes it would be wonderful to wave a magic wand and make everything better, to change things that are in reality beyond our control – even to subjugate those who normally hold us in their power. We may take great delight for instance, in being able to turn a bullying boss into a tiny mouse, or an unfriendly neighbour into a puff of smoke.

Conversely, having magic performed on us, particularly if it is done against our will, or if it is done by characters who have bad intentions or who in our waking lives have authority over us, can be immensely disempowering and could be drawing our attention to a lack of power or control in our lives. A dream of losing powers that we felt we previously had can also have a similar effect.

## HOPES AND FANTASIES

In a more general sense, though, dreaming of magic allows us to work out our fantasies – in our dreams nothing is impossible if we want it to come true, and we have the power to live out our hopes and desires. Dreams also prompt us to look at certain areas of our life that may be lacking in some way, and teach us what we need to do to make things happen. While in a literal way the tricks of magic in our dreams may only be possible in a dream world, their underlying truth can be carried into our daily lives and give us something to work with.

## PURVEYORS OF MAGIC

In our dreams it is important to look at the nature and intentions of those who hold the magical powers – whether they are our allies or are threatening and potentially harmful characters is vital to understanding why we are dreaming of magic.

Witches and wizards, as well as magicians and sorcerers, may be sources of good or evil alike. Magicians enthral us with their sleight-of-hand performances, but such trickery may also be more than entertainment, prompting us to look at people in our lives who deceive and trick us, who are trying to pull the wool over our eyes. We need to

**LEFT** Witches, devils and impish creatures have traditional associations with magic. Check to see if the figures are benign or menacing and what it is they are trying to bring about in your dream.

look at how we might be living a lie, lulled into a false sense of security by our own illusions or those put out by others. In Jungian thought the archetype of the Magician is also known as the Fool, whose surface folly disguises hidden depths of wisdom. Being outside the normal order of society he can say things that no one else would dare to, and thereby shows us things we might otherwise avoid looking at.

## THE TRICKS OF THE TRADE

Spells, potions and magic wands are the typical tools of witches and wizards and their presence is another indicator of magic dreams. Being "spellbound" in a dream is akin to being in the thrall of an influential person in waking life, and indeed the lesson to be learnt from such dreams could be to look at whether you are overly impressed by someone, being taken in or manipulated by them, or attracted to something in them which is not real.

If you think the dream character does seem to correspond to someone in your waking life, take note of your gut response to them, notice how trustworthy they are, and try to see beyond any surface appeal.

**ABOVE** A tall pointy hat and a broomstick are a witch's standard regalia. How often do you find yourself wishing you had the power to make radical changes in your life?

**ABOVE** The sorcerer's art lies in combining powders and potions to make spells. To dream of sorcery may mean that you need to take an inventive approach to a problem, or perhaps put things together in a unique, but powerful, way.
**RIGHT** A wizard is a powerful magic maker but make sure he is genuine. Is there someone in your life who has an unhealthy power over you?

# THE SUPERNATURAL

THE MYSTERIOUS WORLD OF THE SUPERNATURAL IS INHABITED BY GHOSTLY FIGURES, VAMPIRES, WEREWOLVES AND A HOST OF OTHER CREATURES. MANY OF US LIKE THE COMFORT OF FAMILIARITY, AND FIND THE IDEA OF THE SUPERNATURAL DISTURBING AND TERRIFYING. BY AND LARGE WE AVOID CONTACT WITH THIS WORLD, BUT SOME SEEK IT OUT AND LINK UP WITH IT IN SÉANCES OR BY EXTRA-SENSORY PERCEPTION (ESP). DREAMS OF THE SUPERNATURAL CAN IMPLY THAT OUR PSYCHE WANTS US TO SPEND MORE TIME AND EFFORT INVESTIGATING SUCH MATTERS AS ACKNOWLEDGING OUR SHADOW SELF. ALTERNATIVELY, WE MAY NEED TO MAKE A RADICAL CHANGE OF DIRECTION IN OUR LIVES.

## GHOSTS

When ghosts appear in our dreams they can represent unfinished business. Ghosts are the unsettled spirits of the dead who haven't yet found their place in the hereafter, perhaps because they still have some tie to earthly matters. As ghosts are neither fully present nor fully absent, they raise questions about uncertainty and lack of clarity, perhaps about who we are or what we are doing in our lives.

In ghostly figures we are confronted with our own mortality. They give us some sneak preview of the afterlife, without really offering any explanations. Perhaps they offer some hope as well that our existence does not terminate with our death. We can also see them as shadows of ourselves – personifications of our own dark nature, the shadowy side of our selves that we often dare not face.

How the ghosts behave in our dream and how we respond to them is important in discovering what they mean. Some are invisible, others may be shadowy translucent figures. They may be noisy poltergeists or silent figures that only betray their presence by moving things, pointing to our lack of control over our own environment. They may interact with us, but often don't do so directly. You may feel terrified or stressed, or be comforted by their presence. They may be recognizable as strangers, deceased friends or relatives, or famous people. Your relationship to them as such will also affect what they mean in your dream – for instance the ghost may be

**BELOW RIGHT** Ghosts and phantoms may haunt us in our dreams and this can feel very unnerving. Try to find out what the ghostly visitation is about.
**BELOW** Strange unearthly figures may appear in our dreams, but these are usually the products of our dreaming psyche.

### GHOSTLY DREAM

"I was sitting in a graveyard surrounded by pale, ghoulish figures. I knew they were out to devour me – it was as if I were destined to be a victim, to have my life drawn from me. There was nothing I could do as these ghastly, ghostly shapes crowded around me. But the horror that woke me wasn't them – it was the feeling of my own quiet acquiescence.

When I was thinking about this dream I realized this was exactly how I was behaving in my relationship, allowing my partner to make all the decisions, and it was burying my personality. On going back over the dream in my mind, I knew that I had to return to that graveyard and shout 'No!' and make them retreat, not just sit there and let them eat my soul."

your nagging mother-in-law who is very much alive but casts a shadow over you and is forever interfering with your life.

Ghosts may be all that remain to us of people who have already died, and seeing one may provide a welcome opportunity to have contact with a loved one who has died but whose death you may not yet have come to terms with.

## SUPERNATURAL PARASITES

Vampires are the infamous figures of the dead who leave the grave after dark and suck the blood of the living, drawing with it their life-force, or energy, which they need to survive, and often killing their victims in the process. These are the parasites of the supernatural world, and they share this dubious distinction with other ghostly figures such as ghouls, who prey on the dead, and the succubi and incubi, demons who take human form to suck the sexual energy out of sleeping people. In more superstitious times the Catholic Church blamed many a nocturnal

**RIGHT** A wolf baying at full moon is often associated with supernatural forces. Full moon is when the forces of nature are at their strongest, and traditionally has strong associations with lunacy.

sexual awakening on such apparitions, while in China ghosts are said to be "hungry".

Vampires are defeated by daylight or the simple but powerful icon of the wooden cross, showing us that even such basic forms of protection can give us an escape route from the horror. Indeed, dreams of parasitic ghosts and vampires are often about self-protection. If you dream of these creatures you should look at those aspects of your own life where you feel you are being devoured or having the life sucked out of you. Perhaps you are feeling either used or dominated by your partner, or you have an exploitative boss who makes you work long hours so that you don't have the life or energy to do the things you enjoy. More unusually you may be acting parasitically and have some kind of disturbance around

this. These dreams are our unconscious mind's way of working out such relationships, as well as making us aware that something is wrong.

## BATS AND WEREWOLVES

Like vampires, werewolves and bats are nocturnal creatures that suck their victim's blood. A vampire can "shape shift" into a bat, while a werewolf is a human who becomes a vicious beast at full moon. If these creatures appear in your dreams it may be to draw attention to something going on in your life that is frightening or tricky to deal with.

**BELOW LEFT** Be wary of bewitching figures, as vampires in particular often appear seductive. Who is trying to suck your blood?
**BELOW** The spirits of the dead come to life at night. A disused building can appear very spooky.

# ACKNOWLEDGEMENTS

Unless specified images used in the book belong to Anness Publishing Ltd. With thanks to the following agencies for additional images:

**Art Archive**: 12–13 *The Dream of Aescupalius*, Accademia Venice/Dagli Orti; 14t Musèe du Louvre/Dagli Orti; 15t Eileen Tweedy, 16l Egyptian Museum/Dagli Orti; 16r *Ruins of Thebes* by Carl Richard Lepsius, Musèe du Louvre/Dagli Orti; 19t National Archaeological Museum, Athens/Dagli Orti; 21 *The Death of Julius Caesar* by Vincenzo Camuccini, Galleria d'Arte Moderna, Rome/Dagli Orti; 22 V&A Museum, London/Eileen Tweedy; 25 British Library; 28 *The Dream of Tartini*, National Museum Budapest/Dagli Orti; 29b Bibliothèque Municipale Poitiers/Dagli Orti; 34r Turkish and Islamic Art Museum, Istanbul/Harper Collins Publishers; 35t *Joseph explaining the dreams of Pharoah* by Jean Adrien Guignet, Musèe des Beaux Arts, Rouen/Dagli Orti; 46 Ocean Memorabilia Collection; 57tr *The Guest of Stone* by Marco Marcola, Museo Civico Sartorio Trieste/ Dagli Orti; 68 *Dulle Griet*, detail, by Pieter Breughel the Elder, Mayer van den Bergh Museum; 72–73 *Ossian's Lament* by Karoly Kisfaludy, National Gallery, Budapest/Dagli Orti; 108l Ragab Papyrus Institute/Dagli Orti; 211tr Musèe Carnavalet, Paris/Dagli Orti; 238–239 *Queen of the Night*, Mozarteum, Salzburg/Dagli Orti; 240l *The Wild Swans* by Otto Svend, Dagli Orti; 241t *The Tower of Babel* by Pieter Breughel the Younger, Dagli Orti; 242 *The Depths of the Sea* by Sir Edward Burne Jones, Private Collection; 243c *Mount Helicon with Pegasus and centaur Chiron* by Giovanni Falconetto, Palazzo Arco, Mantua, Italy; 247b *Libuse* by Vitezlav Karl Masek, Musèe National d'Art Moderne, Paris/Dagli Orti.

**Corbis**: 2tl Markku Lahdesmaki; 2br William Whitehurst; 4b and 96–97 Julie Lemberger; 7t *Garden of Earthly Delights* by Bosch, Francis G Mayer; 11t Dianna Sarto; 11b Sygma; 14b Gianni Dagli Orti; 17r Marc Garanger; 18 *Calliope and Homer* by Antonio Canova, Archivio Iconografico, SA; 19b Ruggero Vanni; 20l Raphael, School of Athens, detail, Ted Spiegel; 20r Araldo de Luca; 24tl Richard A. Cooke; 24tr Dallas & John Heaton; 24b Craig Lovell; 26br Elio Ciol; 27t Greenhalf Photography; 27b Richard Hamilton Smith; 29t *The Witch* by David Ryckaert III, Ali Meyer; 30 Penny Tweedie; 31tl Ralph A. Clevenger; 31tr Otto Rogge; 32tl Tom Bean; 32tr Dave Bartruff; 32b Bob Rowan/Progressive Image; 33 Geoffrey Clements; 34l Chris Lisle; 35b *The Annunciation* by Edward Burne Jones, Christie's Images; 36–37 David Pu'u; 38 Charles Gupton; 39t Ron Lowery; 39bl Ryszard Horowitz, 39br Richard Cummins; 40 Sigmund Freud by Bettmann; 41t John Lund; 41bl Larry Williams; 42bl Carl Jung by Bettmann; 43tl Rick Gayle; 43tr Ron Lowery; 44l Benjamin Rondel; 44r David Pu'u; 45 Mark Cooper; 47t; 47b James Nazz; 48 Chris Lisle; 49l William Whitehurst; 49r David Aubrey; 50r Dale O'Dell; 51t Chris Hellier; 51br Chris Rainer; 52l Phil Banko; 52r Firefly Productions; 53 Shutter & Mouse; 54–55 *Destruction of Jerusalem* by Ercole de'Roberti, Historical Picture Archive; 57tl Stapleton Collection; 57b Roy McMahon; 58r Todd A. Gipstein; 60 *O Holy night* by Henry Raymond, Christie's Images; 61r *Maiden and Unicorn*, Araldo de Luca; 62 Art Becker Photo; 63t Ron Lowery; 64l Jim Zuckerman; 64r Jose Luis Peleaz, Inc.; 65t Douglas Kirkland; 67br Dale O'Dell; 70, Richard T. Nowitz; 71l Ron Lowery; 71r Norbert Schaefer; 74l George Shelley; 74r Denis Scott; 75 Dale O'Dell; 78l LWA-JDC; 79 Pete Saloutos; 81t Denis Anthony Valentine; 82 Ron Watts; 83t Danny Lehman; 83c Lindsay Hebberd; 88 Denis Scott; 89b Mendola/Jeff Mangiat; 92 Thomas Schweizer; 93t LWA/Stephen Welstead; 94r Mauro Panci; 99tl Ron Lowery; 99ct Ryszard Horowitz; 99cb Markku Lahdesmaki; 99bl Benjamin Rondel; 102b Art Becker Photo; 103b Digital Art; 105t Mug Shots; 105c Firefly Productions; 107tl Gianni Dagli Orti; 107 Adam Woolfitt; 107br *Charlemagne Receiving the Monk Alcuino* by Jean Victor Schnetz, Archivio Iconografico;

108r *Portrai of Ibn Rushd* by Andrea di Buonaioto, Archivo Iconografico; 109cl Mug Shots; 112 Michael Boys; 113tl Alfred Ko; 117bc B.S.P.I; 121t Bill Ross; 124 Julie Meech/Ecoscene; 125cl Ted Spiegel; 128r Galen Rowell; 138–139 Markku Lahdesmaki; 140 Dale O'Dell; 141t Al Francekevich; 141c Layne Kennedy; 142 David Woods; 143l Mendola/Doug Chezem; 143r Rick Gayle; 144tl Edward Holub; 144b Ted Horowitz; 145l Lawrence Manning; 145c Rick Gomez; 147t L. Clarke; 147c Joe Baraban; 148l LWA/Dann Tardif; 148r Paul Hardy; 149bl Jim Erickson; 149bc LWA/Dann Tardif; 149br Randy M. Ury; 150 Mark L. Stephenson; 151tl Markku Lahdesmaki; 151tr Benjamin Rondel; 151c John Heseltine; 151br Elizabeth Opalenik; 152–153 *Fairies Dancing* by Blake, Bettmann; 154l Myron Jay Dorf; 154c Michael Pole; 154r Jon Feingersh; 155tl Bo Zaunders; 155tc Anthony Redpath; 155tr Strauss/Curtis; 155bl Ariel Skelley; 155br Pete Saloutos; 156l Jose Luis Pelaez,Inc.; 156r James Noble; 157t Steve Prezant; 157c Ron Slenzak; 158 Roy Morsch; 159tl Mark Garten; 159tr John Acurso; 159c Terry W. Eggers; 159b Bill Binzen; 160l Norbert Schaefer; 160r Nancy Brown; 161bl Ronnie Kaufman; 161bc Westlight Stock; 161br Jose Luis Pelaez, Inc.; 162l Elena Segatini Bloom; 162c Jon Feingersh; 162r Douglas Kirkland; 163tl Trinette Reed; 163tc Gianfranco Benvenuto; 163tr Patrik Giardino; 163b Cheque; 166 Oddo & Sinibaldi; 167tr Lester Lefkowitz; 167c L. Clarke; 167bl Michael Barley; 167br LWA/Stephen Welstead; 168 LWA/Dann Tardif; 169t Mark Tuschman; 169c 2 Face; 169b David Woods; 172–173; 175tl Joe Bator; 175tr Roy Morsch; 175b C. Moore; 176r Markku Lahdesmaki; 177bl Don Mason; 177br Brian Bailey; 179t Bill Varie; 179c Jose Luis Pelaez, Inc.; 179b Paul Barton; 180 LWA/Dann Tardif; 181tl Alan Schein Photography; 181tr Anthony Redpath; 181c Jose Luis Pelaez; Inc.; 181br Mauro Panci; 182l Roy Morsch; 182r Robert Sememiuk; 183tl Shutter & Mouse; 183tr Tony Arruza; 183b Kevin Muggleton/Tim Bird; 184l Javier Pierini; 185t Steve Starr; 185b Rick Gayle; 186r Joel Sartore; 187 Andrea Pizzi; 188l Arthur Beck; 188r Julie Lemberger; 189l Robbie Jack; 189r Chuck Savage; 190l George Disario; 192 Franco Vogt; 193tr Roy McMahon; 193b Chris Carroll; 194 Chiselvision; 195t Robert Cassel; 195c Sandford/Agliolo; 196–197 Christie's

Images; 198l David Chmielewski; 199t Ron Lowery; 199c Steve Chenn; 201c Chuck Savage; 202l Markku Lahdesmaki; 203t Dale O'Dell; 204r Firefly Productions; 205t Jim Cummins; 208r Tim Davis; 209bl Myron Jay Dorf; 210r Philip Wallick; 211b *The Triumph of Death* by Pieter Brueghel the Elder, Archivo Iconografico, S.A.; 213tl Sanford/Agliolo; 213tr Al Francekevich; 213b Rob Lowery; 214l Bob Witkowski; 214r Roy Morsch; 215t Robert Bowen & Ryszard Horowitz; 215b Masahiro Sano; 216 Herrmann/ Starke; 217tl Bill Ross; 217tr Markku Lahdesmaki; 217b Grafton Marshall Smith; 218–219 Swim Ink/Griff Teller; 220l Bruno; 220r Ed Bock; 221t Sandford/Agliolo; 221bl Tom & Dee Ann McCarthy; 222t 2 Face; 222b Jeff Vanuga; 223t David H. Wells; 223b David Aubrey; 224l Denis Scott; 224r Firefly Productions; 225tl Roger Ressmeyer; 225tc Jim Erickson; 225tr Third Eye Images; 225b Galen Rowell; 226l Michael Setboun; 226r Philip Harvey; 227l David Raymer; 227r Lester Lefkowitz; 228 Derek Trask; 229tc Mark L. Stephenson; 229br Joe Bator; 230l Cynthia Diane Pringle; 230r Tom Young; 231t Marianne Haas; 231ct T. Kevin Smyth; 231cb Kelly-Mooney Photography; 233t Larry Lee Photography; 233bl John Lund; 233br Dale O'Dell; 234tl Lawrence Manning; 234b Firefly Productions; 235t Ed Bock; 235bl Ronnie Kaufman; 235br Jon Feingersh; 236r & 237t Firefly Productions; 237c Carl Schneider; 241br Chiselvision; 243l Chris Hellier; 243r Araldo de Luca; 244r Stocktrek; 245t Jim Zuckerman; 245b Dale O'Dell; 246r John Lund; 247tr Paul Barton; 248 Peter Steiner; 249tl KJ Historical; 249c *The Love Potion* by Evelyn De Morgan, Massimo Listri; 249b Strauss/Curtis; 250l Douglas Kirkland; 250r Mark Kessell; 251t Jeff Vanuga; 251bl Gerhard Steiner; 251br J Richardson.

**Fine Art Photographic Library**: 4t, 8–9 & 96–97 *Dolce Far Niente*, John William Godward; 23 *Bathing in the Ganges, India* by Valentine Cameron Princep; 56 *The Angel's Message* by George Hillyard Swinstead; 59 *The Rescue* by Arthur Hughes; 61l *Hermia and Lysander* by John Simmons; 63b *Spirit of the Night* by John Atkinson Grimshaw; 95b *Galahad and his Angel* by Payton; 151bl *A Bright and Happy Christmas*, Anon; 241bl *The Lily Fairy* by Falero.

ACKNOWLEDGEMENTS

# INDEX